DESIGNER KNITS

RUTH MARIA SWEPSON

DESIGNER KNITS

CHARTWELL
BOOKS, INC.

A Quarto Book

Published by Chartwell Books Inc.,
A Division of Book Sales Inc.,
110 Enterprise Avenue,
Secaucus, New Jersey 07094

ISBN 0-89009-942-1

This book was designed and produced by
Quarto Publishing Ltd
The Old Brewery, 6 Blundell Street
London N7 9BH

Senior Editor Tessa Rose
Editors Margaret Cawthorne, Sally Wood
Art Editor Nick Clark
Design James Culver
Photographers John Mason, John Heseltine, David Burch
Illustrators Gay Galsworthy, Steven Gardner

Art Director Alastair Campbell
Editorial Director Jim Miles

Typeset by Leaper and Gard Ltd, Bristol
Color origination by Universal Color Scanning Ltd, Hong
Kong
Printed by LeeFung Asco Printers Ltd, Hong Kong

• Special thanks to Hazel Edington and Mick Hill

Publishers Note The suggested yarns given with each pattern
are suggestions only and do not necessarily match the texture
of the yarns originally used for the garments shown in the
photographs. Readers are advised to take the patterns to their
local specialty yarn shop for advice and knit a test piece before
commencing.

CONTENTS

SECTION THREE
Designer Knits

FOREWORD

During the time I spent teaching handknitting and various other yarn crafts at local education establishments, I became increasingly frustrated by the fact that even highly competent knitters had been 'educated' by the system to believe that they should only ever knit to a pattern, always use the yarn stated and never deviate from it. Some of the most outstanding knitters had no idea about such basic principles as the way stitches are formed or how stitch patterns are created, which meant that they were unable to sort out any problems that arose. It also meant that they were unable to translate any of their ideas into finished garments for fear of failure.

Knitting is a very simple craft, based on the use of two main stitches worked in a variety of ways and combinations. I have tried in this book to expose some of the myths surrounding the craft, especially those to do with yarns, needles and gauge, and to explain some of the knitting processes in a way that will aid understanding of the subject rather than impose yet another set of rules to be followed blindly. I have set down very simply in the second section of the book some of the principles involved when writing patterns, to enable even complete beginners to create their own garments. And, finally, a word about the 'designer knits', which I hope will be not only very wearable, but inspiring and, above all, a joy to knit.

Ruth Musgrove

SECTION ONE
BACK TO BASICS

To start knitting all you need is a pair of
needles and some yarn. But before you cast
on the first stitch it would be as well to
know what you are going to make.

You can, of course, buy patterns. They can
be found in books like this one, magazines,
knit kits and the leaflets produced by the
yarn manufacturers. But you'll probably
come up with ways to adapt these patterns –
or even have ideas for new patterns of
your own.

The aim of this book is to encourage you
to use your own ideas. But to do that you
must first go back to basics. To translate
your ideas into finished garments, you must
have a full understanding of the techniques
and skills involved.

If you are a complete beginner, you will
need to spend some time on each section. It
is essential that you learn to envisage the
shape of stitches before you begin. And if
you are already an experienced knitter, it
would be as well to read through this
section to refresh your memory.

YARNS

THE YARNS AVAILABLE to the handknitter nowadays include many varieties of color, thickness and texture. When used imaginatively, these can create the kind of high fashion garments usually only seen in the pages of glossy magazines. However, this great choice can be confusing to the knitter. Some of this confusion arises from the great variety of terms used to describe the yarn thickness, the spinning process and the various fibers used to make knitting yarns.

2 ply

3 ply

Sports yarn

Quick knit

Knitting worsted

Aran thick

Mohair thick

Bulky

YARN THICKNESS All knitting patterns, whether commercially produced or 'home-made', are worked out on the basis of a gauge sample which alters according to the yarn thickness, the size of the needles and the stitch pattern. Gauge is dealt with in detail on page 25, but briefly, the gauge of a piece of knitting is the number of stitches and rows needed to knit a measured square. It is usually only necessary to have an accurate way of knowing the thickness of various types of yarn if you want to substitute one yarn for another, or use different yarns in the same garment; for

instance, when making stripes. The only sure way of doing this is to knit a gauge sample in the chosen yarn and check that it matches the gauge given for the original yarn.

There are several terms used by the yarn manufacturers to denote the thickness of a yarn, but these are very vague and differ from manufacturer to manufacturer. It is better to refer to a yarn as knitting to a certain gauge rather than being of a certain thickness. Yarn manufacturers often state the recommended gauge and needle size on the yarn label.

Listed below are the major weights or thicknesses of knitting yarn available in most knitting departments or stores, the sizes of needles appropriate for each, and a typical gauge for a mid-range needle size when used in stockinette stitch. Since gauge varies widely from one knitter to another, however, it is always necessary to check gauge before deciding which size needle to use.

Light: Fingering and baby yarn
    No 1-4
      7 st per inch on No 2
Medium : Sports yarn
    No 2-6
      6 st per inch on No 5
Heavy: Knitting worsted
    No 4-10
      5 st per inch on No 9
Very heavy: Rug or bulky
    No 7-15
      3 st per inch on No 11

Most novelty yarns such as mohair and bouclé fall into one or more of these categories. Very thin yarns, such as some cottons, may be used in double or triple strand to achieve these gauges.

Some yarns are even thicker than bulky but these are usually very individual and, unless an exact gauge match can be obtained, it is not a good idea to try using other yarns in their place, as variations in gauge over thick yarns cause a much greater difference in the finished size of a garment than differences in gauge in finer yarns.

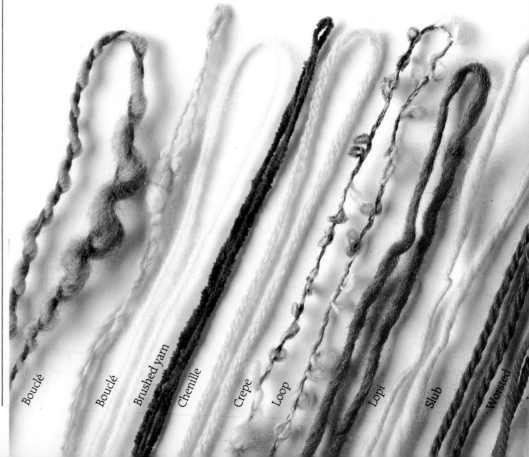

Bouclé   Bouclé   Brushed yarn   Chenille   Crepe   Loop   Lopi   Slub   Worsted

YARN SPINNING Yarns are made from natural and man-made fibers of various lengths. The two terms to describe these lengths are:

Filaments are very long fibers. Man-made filament fibers can be made to any length, but they are usually cut into shorter staple lengths before being spun to form handknitting yarns. The only natural filament fiber is silk.

Staples are comparatively short fibers. To form a yarn that is suitable for knitting they must be twisted together in one continuous strand of the required thickness. This continuous strand is called a single yarn. A single yarn is usually twisted together with others; this is called 'plying' or 'folding'. From this, the term 2 ply, 3 ply etc, originates, to denote the number of single yarns (of any thickness) plied together. The twisting process used to form yarns is called spinning. Here are some of the terms used for the various ways of spinning yarns together:

Bouclé is a knobbly yarn created by spinning one or more very fine taut yarns, together with a thicker, softer yarn, thus forming a random pattern of 'lumps' along the length of yarn.

Brushed Yarns are made from fibers with a long staple which can be brushed to produce a furry effect.

Chenille is the center of chenille and is made from fine, hard yarns, spun together, with other softer fibers anchored into this 'cord', and sticking out at an angle to it.

Crêpe is a very highly twisted yarn.

Gimp is a variation of bouclé yarn, with a more even appearance.

Loop is another variation of bouclé yarn. The 'lumps' formed are made of little loops of yarn.

Lopi is a thick, single yarn, not very strong.

Slub is an uneven-thickness yarn, made by spinning alternatively tight and loose.

Spiral is a core yarn, very taut and fine, wrapped around with a thicker yarn so that the core yarn is hidden.

Worsted is a smooth yarn, where all the fibers are fairly long and run parallel to each other. Most ordinary knitting yarns are worsted.

YARN FIBERS Yarns for handknitting are made from a variety of fibers, both natural and man-made, and sometimes, for reasons of strength or design, they are combined to form yarns made of mixed fibers. Each different fiber, whether man-made or natural, has a different set of advantages and disadvantages.

NATURAL FIBERS:

The wool family Wool is obtained from the fleece of a sheep. It comes in a variety of qualities, depending on the type of sheep, its condition, the climate in which it is reared, etc. High-quality wool has a short staple, but is not so strong or elastic as the poorer qualities. Lambswool, which is very soft and fine, is the wool from the first shearing of a lamb.

Advantages of wool It has good insulating properties, is very absorbent, holds its shape well and is very hardwearing.

Disadvantages of wool It has a tendency to shrink, it can be itchy and it takes a long time to dry.

Other yarns in the wool family that come from the fleece of animals are:

Alpaca comes from the alpaca and the llama, both found in South America. It is a fairly silky fiber, but the cheaper alpaca yarns can be very itchy.

Angora comes from the fleece of the Angora rabbit and is very soft and fluffy, but not very strong. It is usually mixed with wool when spinning to give extra strength.

Cashmere comes from goats found in the Kashmir region of the Himalayas. The yarn is very soft, warm and lightweight. However, it is very expensive and not very strong.

Mohair comes from a goat originally bred in Turkey. As they are very expensive, most mohair yarns are mixed with other fibers. The classic fluffy mohair look comes from brushing. It can be very itchy.

OTHER NATURAL FIBERS:

Silk is the only natural filament fiber and is taken from the cocoons of various types of silkworm. A very strong fiber with a smooth, shiny appearance, it is warm in winter and cool in summer. It mixes well with other fibers. The silkworm cocoons have to be unwound by hand to provide the silk filament, so it is very expensive. However, spun silk, made from broken lengths of this filament, is much cheaper. Tussah silk or wild silk, produced from an undomesticated silkworm, is resilient to dyeing and bleaching, so is often used in its natural brown color. It is a coarse, uneven yarn.

Cotton comes from the staple fibers of the seed of a cotton plant. High-quality cotton, made from the long staples, is very soft, strong and expensive. Although very strong, cotton has little elasticity. It is, however, useful for summer wear as it is a good conductor of heat. Cotton is sometimes blended with other fibers, such as wool, to good effect.

Linen is made from the long staple fibers obtained from the stalks of the flax plant. It is much stronger than cotton, especially when wet, but also has very little elasticity. Because of their naturally uneven fiber, linen knitting yarns are usually slubbed. Linen has a tendency to shrink.

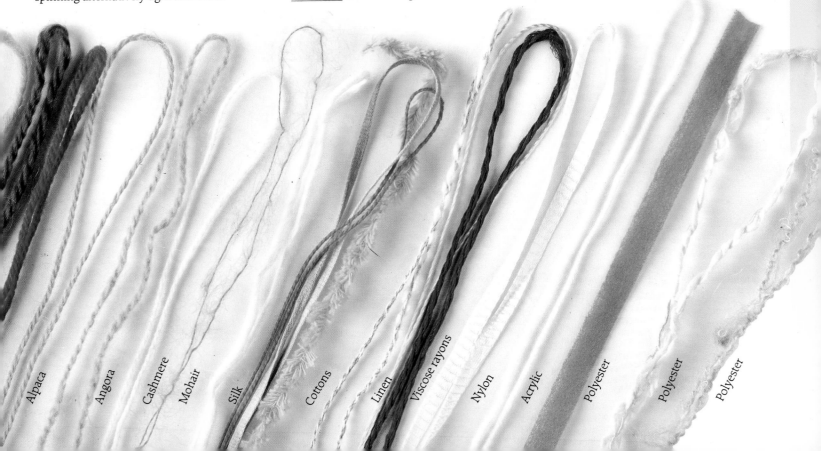

Alpaca   Angora   Cashmere   Mohair   Silk   Cottons   Linen   Viscose rayons   Nylon   Acrylic   Polyester   Polyester   Polyester

MAN-MADE FIBERS

Viscose Rayon This is produced from the cellulose extracted from wood pulp. Knitting yarns made from viscose rayon are often very shiny and for this reason it is often used as a substitute for silk. It is, however, a fairly weak fabric that needs careful washing and has only a little elasticity. On the plus side, viscose rayon is a fairly heavy yarn, and garments made from it drape well.

Nylon, also known as polyamide, is synthetic yarn made from petroleum-based chemicals. It is very strong and elastic but not very comfortable to wear in hot weather. Nylon can be used to great advantage when mixed with other fibers.

Acrylic is made from a type of plastic. It has various trade names that are in common use, the main ones being Acrilan®, Orlon® and Courtelle®. It is often used as a substitute for wool, but has a tendency to lose its shape and special care must be taken when washing, as acrylic garments crease easily.

Polyester is a synthetic fiber, similar to nylon but less shiny. It is fairly strong and elastic and does not crease easily.

UNUSUAL YARNS A knitting yarn can be any substance that has a length considerably longer than its width. It would in theory be possible to knit with metal wire, spaghetti, sewing thread, etc. but garments made from those substances would not be very useful.

The essence of creative design is the ability to 'break all the rules' and still produce a garment with all the required correct properties. For instance, it should be soft enough to fit round a body, it should hold its shape well, it may need to be washed, it should feel comfortable, etc. Here are a few ideas:
1. Cut lengths of 'fabric' knotted or sewn together, eg: chiffon, tweed, lurex, fur, leather, foam, aluminum foil, burlap, felt, etc.
2. Bias binding, ribbon, lace, fringing, and other bought 'tapes'.
3. Plastic tubing, garden string, lengths of chain and other items found in hardware shops.
4. Christmas wrapping tape, tinsel, etc.

It is also possible to create one's own yarns by knitting two or more different yarns together or by attaching 'objects' to the length of yarn and causing them to drop to the front of the work when knitting. This is often done with sequins and beads, but you could try paper clips, bottle tops, shells, home-made clay or acrylic shapes, buttons, curtain rings, etc. You can also create your own bouclé yarn by knotting it. When mixing yarns together, try using yarns not only of a different color, but also of a different texture, eg: mix cotton bouclé with mohair, bulky wool with rayon or silk, baby yarns with lurex, etc.

When using these more unusual yarns, any needle size can be used, provided that the resulting knitted 'fabric' is fairly firm so that the garment will hold its shape well. You will obviously have to write your own patterns in order to use your 'yarn'.

A rough guide to the gauges obtained by knitting various thicknesses of yarn together is shown on p. 157.

WASHING KNITTED GARMENTS Follow the instructions given on the label of the yarn that has been used. Where two or more yarns have been used, the washing instructions for the yarn with the lowest temperature wash and iron should be used.

If you have created your own yarn, or are unsure of the properties of a garment, try washing the gauge sample to see how it reacts. Some garments specifically require dry cleaning, but most can be washed in cool water. Do not press a garment that you are unsure about.

After washing, knitted fabrics should be dried flat, to preserve their shape. If necessary, they should be pulled back into the correct shape when laying them out for drying.

1 wool swatch card
2 row counter
3 tape measure
4 sewing needles
5 double-pointed needles
6 stitch holder
7 cable needles
8 needles
9 graph paper
10 crochet hook
11 needle gauge
12 circular needles

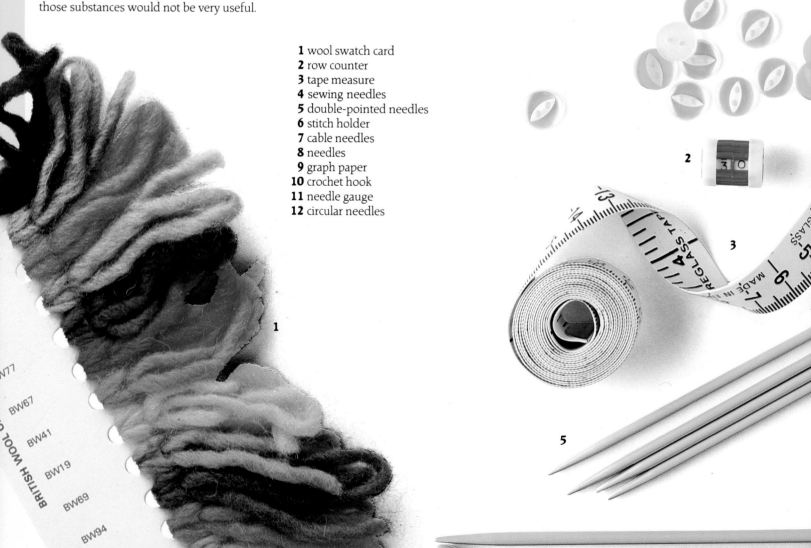

EQUIPMENT

PAIRS OF NEEDLES come in a variety of lengths and sizes, and are used to produce flat knitting. The size of the needle is determined by the yarn thickness and required gauge.

Sets of Double Pointed Needles produce seamless knitting for socks or stockings. They come in the same range of sizes as pairs of needles and are usually sold and used in sets of four.

Circular Needles used either in place of pairs of needles or in place of sets of needles. A circular needle is a pair of short needles attached to each other by a length of nylon cord. They come in the full range of sizes and also in different lengths.

It is important to use the correct length when working seamless knitting.

Cable Needles short, double-pointed needles used for working cables. Normally they are available in a medium and a large size. The size nearest to the main needle size should be used.

Needle Gauge used to determine the size of needles. Whereas pairs of needles are usually marked with the size, sets of needles or circular needles are often unmarked.

Stitch Holders used to hold stitches when they are removed from the needle but not bound off. Alternatively, a piece of contrasting colored yarn can be threaded through stitches on a stitch-holder. To hold small numbers of stitches, a safety pin can be used.

Yarn Needle used for sewing up finished knitted items. A yarn needle should have a large eye and a blunted point.

Crochet Hook for picking up dropped stitches or attaching decorations such as tassels

Tape Measure or Ruler to measure the work in progress.

Row Counter to keep count of the rows while knitting. It is especially useful for working shapings. However, a paper and pencil can be used just as effectively.

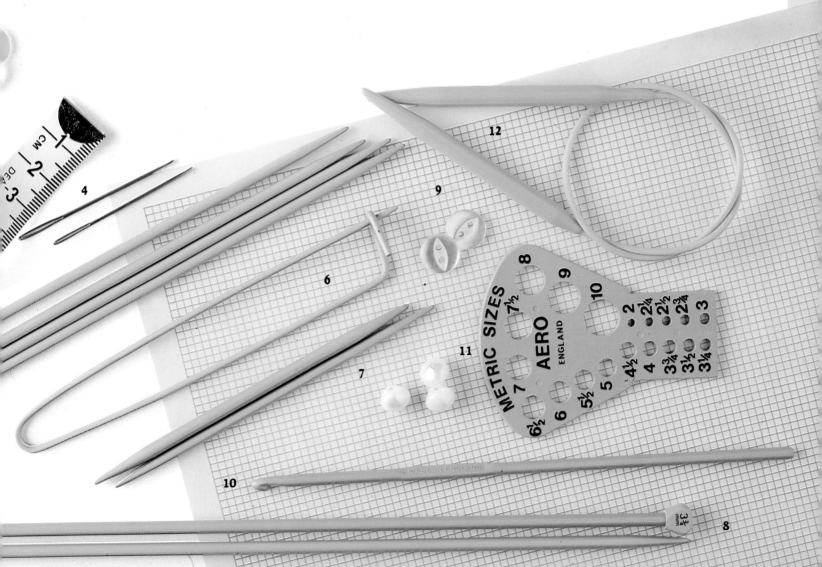

BASIC TECHNIQUES

BEFORE BEGINNING to knit, the first row of loops must be placed onto one needle. The number of loops to be placed onto the needle, depends on how wide the work is to be.

Obtaining this first row of loops is known as casting on. There are many different ways to do this and each way gives a different type of edge. Here are the two ways that are most commonly used.

SLIP LOOP This is the first loop that is formed before beginning most methods of casting on.

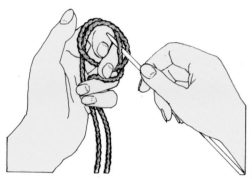

① Wind the yarn twice around the fingers, as shown.

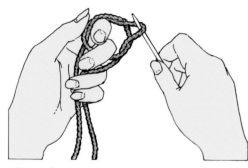

② Use the knitting needle to pull a loop through the yarn wound round the fingers.

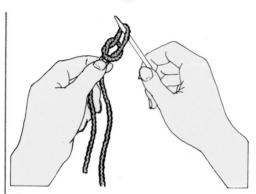

③ Remove fingers from the twist of yarn and pull both loose ends to tighten up the loop formed.

LOOSE KNIT STITCH CAST ON This method uses two needles and creates a very loose edge, suitable only for lacy garments or where the edge is to be hidden, eg, in a hem.

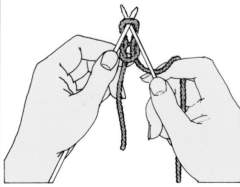

① Place the needle with the slip loop in the left hand. Insert the right-hand needle through the loop from front to back.

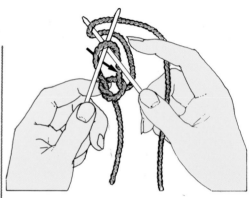

② Pass the end of yarn attached to the ball under and over the tip of the right-hand needle.

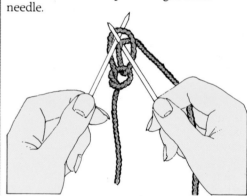

③ Bring the right-hand needle, with yarn wound round it, back through the loop and place on left-hand needle. Repeat these three steps, each time working into the last loop formed, until the required number of stitches (or loops) has been cast on.

FIRM KNIT STITCH CAST ON This produces a very firm but elastic edge, suitable for most cast-on edges.

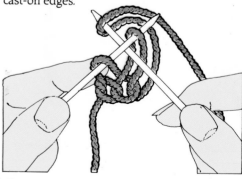

① Form the first two loops as shown for the loose knit stitch cast on, then insert the right-hand needle between the first two loops and wind the yarn under and over the tip of the right-hand needle.

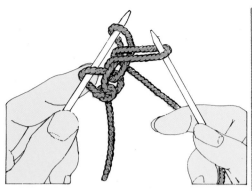

② Bring the right-hand needle, with yarn around it, back between the two loops.

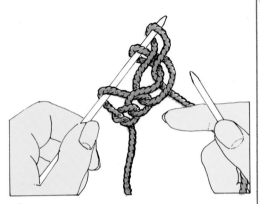

③ Place this new loop on the left-hand needle. Continue working in this manner until the required number of stitches (or loops) has been cast on.

Having cast on the required number of loops, you now need to know how to make the work grow in depth. This is done by working in rows (or rounds if the work is tubular).

A row is worked by forming new loops in each of the loops already on the needle. Each of these separate loops is called a stitch. There are two main ways of creating these new stitches. One is called the knit stitch, the other is called the purl stitch.

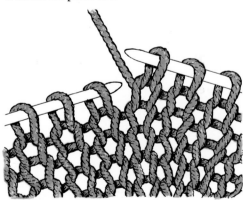

The knit stitch looks like a 'chain' on the right side of the work (the side facing you as you knit).

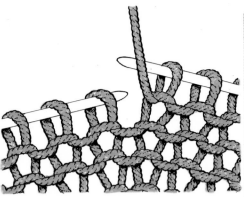

The purl stitch looks like a small knot or 'bump' on the side of the work facing you as you work it.

You will notice, if you turn the knit stitch around and look at it from the back, that it looks like the purl stitch and vice versa. The knit stitch creates a stitch like a chain at the front with a 'bump' at the back, and the purl stitch creates a stitch with a 'bump' at the front and a chain at the back. Using these two stitches, you can create either 'chains' or 'bumps' on a piece of knitting to create a variety of patterns. All stitch patterns use these two stitches in a variety of ways and combinations. It is very important that you master the working of both these stitches, and that you learn to identify them.

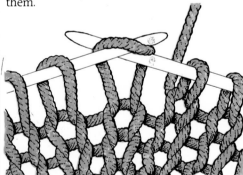

The Knit Stitch
① Holding the yarn at the back, insert the right-hand needle through the front of the first stitch from left to right.

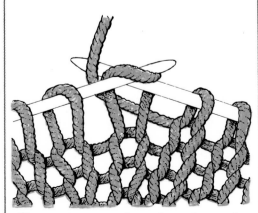

② Bring the yarn under and over the tip of the right-hand needle.

Page 15

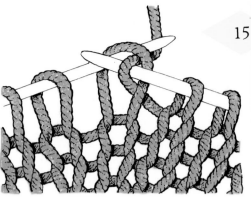

③ Draw the right-hand needle back through the stitch with the yarn still around it forming a new loop, and let the old stitch slip off the left-hand needle.

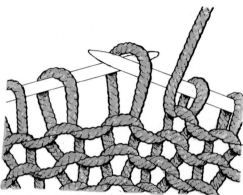

The Purl Stitch
① Holding the yarn at the front of the work, insert the needle through the front of the first stitch from right to left.

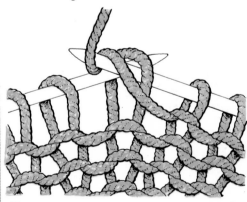

② Bring the yarn over and around the tip of the right-hand needle.

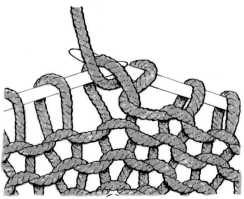

③ Draw the right-hand needle back through the stitch, forming a new stitch. Let the old stitch slip off the left-hand needle.

Stockinette stitch

Garter stitch

Examples of edge stitches: **1.** slip stitch; **2.** garter stitch; **3.** stockinette stitch.

GARTER STITCH When you have worked across all the stitches of the first row, working each of them as a knit stitch, you will then have all the stitches on the right-hand needle and the chain side of each stitch facing you. The back of the work will be a row of 'bumps'. In order to work the next row you must change hands, placing the needle with the stitches on it into the left hand and the empty needle into the right hand. You will notice that you now have the wrong or 'bumpy' side of the work facing you. When working garter stitch, all the stitches of each row are knit, so for the second row, work each stitch as a knit stitch. You will now have two rows of knitting on the right-hand needle, and as the work faces you, the first row is a row of 'bumps' and the second row is a row of 'chains'. The back of the work will have a first row of 'chains' and a second row of 'bumps'. If you continue working in this way, you will have a fabric where both sides consist of alternate rows of 'chain' and 'bump' stitches. Garter stitch fabric is quite thick and bulky because of the 'bumps' on both sides of the fabric. The same effect can be obtained by working all the stitches of each row as purl stitches.

STOCKINETTE STITCH You may wish to form a fabric with all the right-side, knit stitches (or chains) on one side, and all the wrong-side knit stitches (or bumps) on the other side, so that the back and front of the fabric are quite different. To do this you must work the knitting so that you always work 'chains' into 'chain' stitches and 'bumps' into 'bump' stitches. In other words, you will always work the right side of the fabric using knit (or chain) stitches and the wrong side of the fabric using purl (or bump) stitches. Thus, the stitch pattern required to work stockinette stitch is: 1 row knit, 1 row purl, and these two rows are repeated in the same order to the depth of work required. The chain side of the work is usually taken to be the right side, but when the 'bump' side of the fabric is to be used as the right side, the stitch is then called reverse stockinette stitch.

EDGE STITCHES The first and last stitches of each row are the edge stitches, which can be worked according to the pattern. That is knit them on knit rows and purl them on purl rows. As the edge sometimes becomes a little untidy and loose when this is done, it is a good idea always to work the first and last stitches of every row as knit stitches. Because garter stitch needs more rows than stockinette stitch for every inch worked, the edge is tightened up and looks much neater. The edge can also be tightened by not working the first stitch of every row. The stitch is merely transferred from the left-hand needle to the right-hand needle.

These different ways of working the edge stitches are sometimes, but not always, included in the directions in a commercial pattern, but where the edge is to be enclosed in a seam, the kind of edge stitch used is entirely a question of personal preference. Where the edge is to be seen with no other added edging, the pattern should state what to do with the edge stitches.

HOLDING NEEDLES AND YARN
The needles are held, with the stitches to be worked, in the left hand, and the needle doing the work, together with the yarn, in the right hand. The yarn should be threaded through the fingers of the right hand as shown, in order to control the gauge. The yarn is moved around the working needle by moving the right index finger. As you become practiced at knitting, you will find that you develop a method of holding the needles and yarn that is comfortable for you.

Left-hand knitters should hold the needle with stitches on it in the right hand, and the needle doing the work in the left hand. Diagrams in this book can be used by looking at them in a mirror.

PICKING UP DROPPED STITCHES

Occasionally, stitches come off the needle and must be replaced on the needle, so that a run is not formed. If the stitch has run down only one row or so, the stitch can be reformed using the needles. But, when the stitch has run down several rows, it is easier to pick up the stitch using a crochet hook.

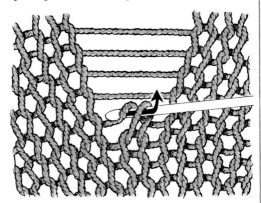

Picking up a knit stitch From the front, insert the crochet hook into the fallen stitch. Catch the first of the horizontal strands with the hook and pull it through the stitch, thus forming a new stitch. Repeat this process for the length of the run, placing the last stitch back on the needle.

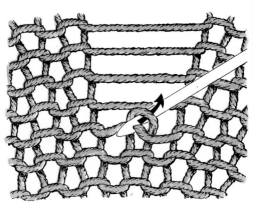

Picking up a purl stitch Purl stitches are most easily picked up from the back of the work, following the procedure for the knit stitches. If you need to pick up from the purl side, insert the crochet hook through the fabric and into the stitch from the front of the stitch, or the back of the work. Catch the horizontal strand lying at the front of the work and pull it through the stitch. The stitch will now be twisted so the hook must be removed from the stitch and re-inserted in order to repeat the process up the length of the run.

When a section of work is completed, it is necessary to remove the stitches from the needle in a way that will prevent the last row of stitches from 'running', and the work unraveling. This is known as casting or binding off. In most places, the bound-off edge should be firm, but occasionally it needs to be loose. To obtain a loose bind off, the stitches can be worked very loosely, or a larger needle can be used. When working with yarns that have a very fine core thread such as mohair, it is important not to bind off too tightly as this can ruin the shape of the garment. Usually the bound-off edge should have the same 'tension' as the rest of the garment.

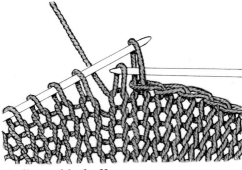

Ordinary bind off
① Knit the first two stitches. Insert the left-hand needle through the first of these two stitches and lift it up.

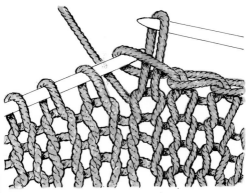

② Pass this first stitch over the second stitch and drop it off the needle. Continue in this manner to the last stitch. Break the yarn and pass it through the last stitch drawing it up tightly.

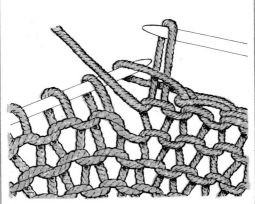

③ The same bound-off edge can be worked across a purl row.

When the stitches are bound off working the stitches as knit stitches, it is called binding off knitwise. If the stitches are purled, it is called binding off purlwise. When binding off on a ribbed fabric, the stitches should be bound off ribwise, which means that each stitch should be worked either as a knit stitch or a purl stitch, following the pattern. When you bind off knitwise, a row of horizontal chain stitches is formed on the work facing you, and a row of 'bumps' at the back. If you bind off purlwise this is reversed.

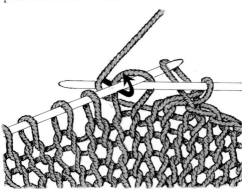

Loose bind off
Work the first two stitches. Lift the first stitch over the second stitch, leaving the first stitch on the left needle. Now work the third stitch and drop the second stitch from the left needle, when the third stitch is knitted onto the right needle.

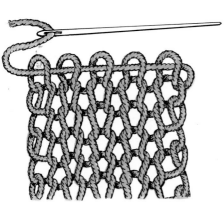

Invisible bind off
Pass a thread through each of the removed stitches. Take care not to draw this thread too tight or you risk altering the gauge of the knitting at this edge. If you are using this method merely to hold the stitches temporarily, you can draw the thread as tight as you wish.

INCREASING

AT VARIOUS TIMES in the making of a garment, you may need to add stitches to the work, either at the edge or at some point across the row. If you intend to design your own garments, you will need to understand the various methods of increasing, so that you can use the correct form of increasing in the correct place.

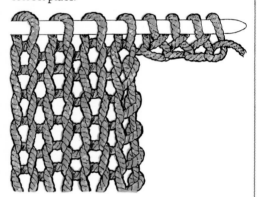

Cast on increase
This is used to add several stitches at the edge or in the middle of a row, eg, over the bound-off stitches of a buttonhole. It is not possible to place cast-on stitches at the end of a row, unless a separate length of yarn is used.
① The new stitches are cast on to the left-hand needle using one of the methods shown on page 14.

WORKING TWO STITCHES FROM ONE

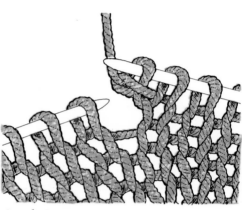

On a knit row
① This method of increase causes a knot to form to the left of the worked stitch.

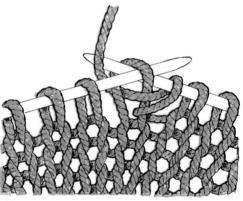

② Knit the stitch as usual, but do not drop the stitch from the left-hand needle; knit into the back of the same stitch, then remove it from the left-hand needle.

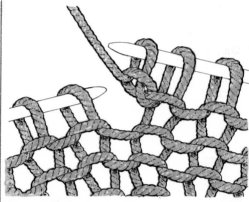

On a purl row
① A knot is formed to the left of the worked stitch.

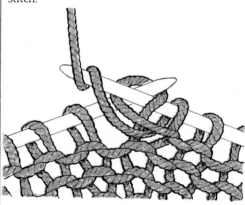

② Purl into the stitch as usual, but do not remove stitch from left-hand needle. Purl into the back of the same stitch, then remove it from the left-hand needle.
Because a knot is formed to the left of the worked stitch when working these increases at the edge of the work, the right-hand edge will be smooth and the left-hand edge will be 'bumpy'. In order to make both edges the same, work the increase at the left side one stitch in from the edge.

18

RAISED INCREASE The loop lying between two stitches is raised, twisted and placed on the needle. (It must be twisted in order to prevent a hole forming.)

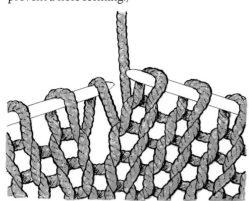

On a knit row

① Insert tip of left-hand needle under thread running between the stitches, from front to back.

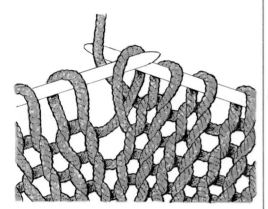

② Work a knit stitch into the back of this raised stitch.

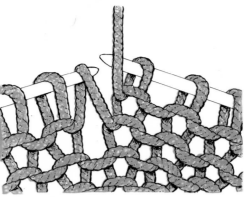

On a purl row

① Insert tip of left-handle needle under thread running between the stitches, from front to back.

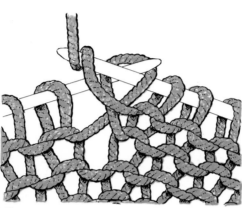

② Work a purl stitch into the back of this raised stitch.

DECORATIVE INCREASE When this increase is worked it forms a hole that can be used in a decorative manner.

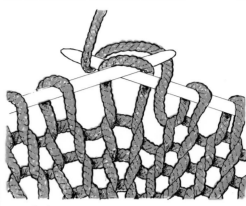

On a knit row

Bring yarn to front of work, then knit the next stitch as usual, forming a loop over the needle. On the following row this loop is purled as usual and a hole is formed.

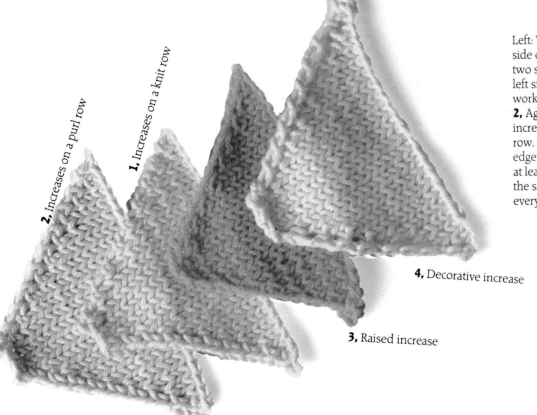

2, Increases on a purl row

1, Increases on a knit row

3, Raised increase

4, Decorative increase

Left: Various styles of increasing. **1,** The right side of this example (which has been worked two stitches from one) has a smooth edge. The left side is 'bumpy' when the increases are worked on the first and last stitches of the row. **2,** Again working two stitches from one, the increases are worked in the first stitch of the row, then the last but one stitch, so that both edges are smooth. **3-4.** Both are made at least one stitch in from either edge and look the same at both edges. They are worked on every alternate (or knit) row.

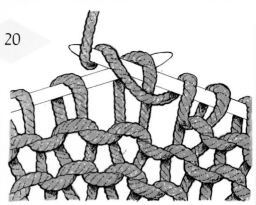

On a purl row

Take yarn to back of work, then purl the next stitch as usual, forming a loop over the needle. On the following row this stitch is knitted as usual and a hole is formed.

FULLY FASHIONED INCREASE These are formed by working any of the increases several stitches in from the edge, causing the edge stitches to slant in the direction of the shaping.

Ⓐ Working two stitches from one, work in the third stitch from the beginning of the row and the fourth stitch from the end of the row, worked here on every alternate (or knit) row.
Ⓑ Raised increases are worked here on every alternate (or knit) row, four stitches in from each edge.
Ⓒ Decorative increases are worked here on every alternate (or knit) row three stitches from the edge.

DOUBLE INCREASE Increases can also be made more than one at a time. To increase more than one stitch, the extra stitches should be alternatively knit into the front and back loops of the stitch from which they are being worked. They can also be worked by alternately knitting and purling into the front loop of the stitch, or by working [knit 1, yarn over needle] several times into the front loop of the stitch. Double decorative increases can be worked by winding the yarn twice over the needle instead of once. On the following row, the 'yarn over twice' stitches should be knitted and then purled.

A

B

C

Fully fashioned increases

DECREASING

DECREASES, LIKE increases, have to be worked at various times during the making of a garment in order to achieve the correct shaping.

BIND-OFF DECREASE This is used where several stitches are to be bound off either at the edge or in the middle of a row. Stitches are not usually bound off at the end of a row, but if this is necessary, the yarn has to be cut and rejoined at the beginning of the next row.

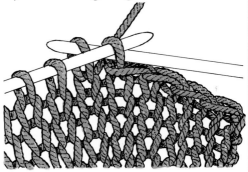

Bind off in the usual manner for the required number of stitches. The last stitch left on the right-hand needle must not be counted as a bound-off stitch.

SIMPLE DECREASE When the decrease is to be worked at the edge of a piece of work, and where that edge is to be enclosed within a seam, the easiest way to work this decrease is to work the two edge stitches together, either knitwise or purlwise.

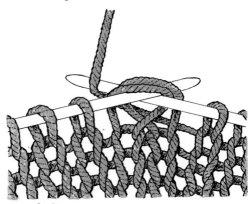

On a knit row
From the front, insert right-hand needle through the next two stitches. Work them together as a single knit stitch.

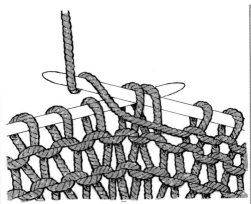

On a purl row
From the front, insert the right-hand needle through the next two stitches. Work them together as a single purl stitch.

VISIBLE OR FULLY FASHIONED DECREASE When decreases are worked they form a slant, either to the right or to the left. There are two main ways of decreasing: a) where two stitches are worked together, and b) when one stitch is passed over another stitch, as in binding off. This is called the slip-stitch decrease. Each of these methods can be worked either on the knit or on the purl side of stockinette stitch fabric, and each can be worked to produce a slant to the right or the left. When designing knitted garments it is important to know each of these variations so that slants to the right or left can be used as part of the design feature. When forming fully fashioned decreases, these visible decreases are used several stitches in from the edge.

KNIT TWO STITCHES TOGETHER

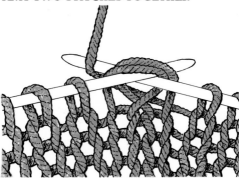

With slant to right on right side of work
Work two stitches together knitwise as for the simple decrease.

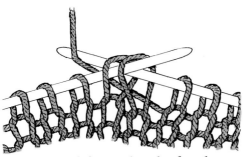

With slant to left on right side of work
Slip first two stitches from left needle to right needle separately, knitwise. Replace them both on left needle, then knit them together through back of loops.

PURL TWO STITCHES TOGETHER

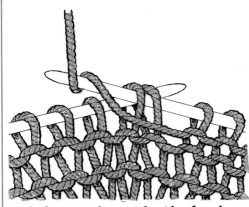

With slant to right on right side of work
Work two stitches together purlwise, as for the simple decrease.

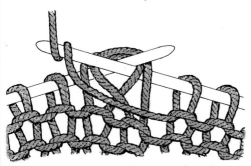

With slant to left on right side of work
Slip first two stitches from left needle to right needle separately, knitwise. Replace them both on the left needle and purl both stitches

together through back of loops (insert needle from back of second stitch, through both stitches).

SLIP STITCH DECREASE WORKED KNITWISE

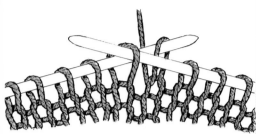

With slant to right on right side of work

Knit one stitch, replace this stitch on left needle, pass next stitch over this stitch, return the first stitch to right needle.

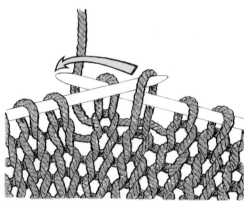

With slant to left on right side of work

Slip next stitch onto right needle, knit next stitch, pass the first stitch over this new stitch as in binding off.

SLIP STITCH DECREASE WORKED PURLWISE

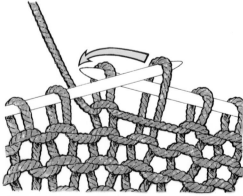

With slant to right on right side of work

Slip next stitch onto right needle, purlwise. Purl next stitch, pass slip stitch over this stitch as in binding off.

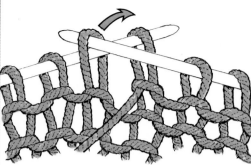

With slant to left on right side of work.

Purl one stitch, slip next stitch knitwise then return it to left needle, return the purled stitch to left needle also, pass the slip stitch over this stitch, return the stitch to right needle.

Visible or fully fashioned decrease

Ⓐ These decreases are worked on the knit side of the fabric (2 sts in from edge) by knitting two stitches together with slant to left at right edge and slant to right at left edge.

Ⓑ These decreases are worked on the purl side of the fabric (2 sts in from edge) by purling two stitches together with slant to left at right edge and slant to right at left edge.

Ⓒ The slip-stitch decrease is worked on the knit side of the fabric (2 sts in from edge) with slant to left at right edge and slant to right at left edge.

Ⓓ The slip-stitch decrease is worked on the purl side of the fabric (2 sts in from edge) with slant to left at right edge, and slant to right at left edge.

DOUBLE DECREASE

DOUBLE DECREASE Decreases can be worked more than one at a time, slanting either to the right or the left, or they can have a central vertical stitch. Some methods of working these are:

With slant to right, on right side of fabric

① Knit 2 together, return stitch to left needle, pass next stitch over it and then return the stitch to right needle.
② Knit 3 (or more) together.
③ Purl 3 (or more) together.

With slant to left on right side of fabric

① Slip 1, knit 2 together, pass slip stitch over.
② Purl 3 together through back loop (or more stitches).
③ Knit 3 together through back loop (or more stitches).

With central vertical stitch

Slip 2 stitches knitwise (as though knitting 2 together). Knit 1, then pass the 2 slip stitches over this stitch.

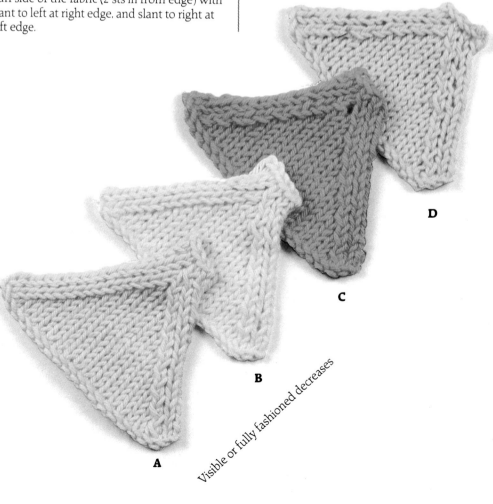

Visible or fully fashioned decreases

PICKING UP STITCHES

THE EDGES OF a finished garment are usually finished by the addition of a band of knitting. This band of knitting also holds the edge firm and keeps the garment in shape. Picking up stitches is not difficult, but it is possible to spoil a well knitted garment by inattention to detail at this point.

Most bands to be added need to be slightly tighter than the rest of the work in order to keep the garment in shape. This is achieved by any one of the following: using smaller size needles; using a stitch pattern that pulls the work in, eg, ribbing; using finer yarn and needles; picking up fewer stitches. Commercial patterns will state how many stitches should be picked up along the edge. Don't be afraid to change the number of stitches if you are not happy with the result.

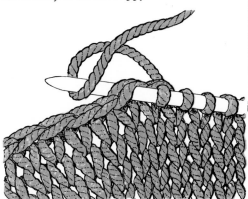

How to pick up a stitch

① With one needle in the right hand, insert tip through edge of work from the right side, pass end of yarn around needle and, taking care not to lose this 'stitch', pull it through to the front. The stitches shown here are being picked up from a horizontal section of work.

② The stitches shown here are picked up along a vertical section of work.

CURVES AND CORNERS Although the band must be shaped if it is to have a corner, the stitches are picked up evenly as given for a straight edge. Curves must be treated differently.

① Where the work is convex, slightly more stitches should be picked up. When binding off a band on a convex curve, it is a good idea to bind off slightly looser than for the rest of the work.

② Where the work is concave, slightly fewer stitches should be picked up. When binding off a band on a concave curve, bind off slightly tighter than for the rest of the work.

PICKING UP STITCHES FROM THE MIDDLE OF A PIECE OF WORK

Sometimes it is necessary to pick up stitches across the center of the fabric. First baste a line where the stitches are to be picked up, then pick up stitches as for the edge, but insert the needle through the fabric. Make sure that the stitches are always picked up from the same line or row of stitches, and from the same section of each stitch.

Points to remember

● Pick up stitches at least one stitch in from the edge (or the approximate width of one stitch). Never pick up stitches right on the edge.

● When working along a straight horizontal or vertical edge, pick up all the stitches along the same line or row of stitches.

● Avoid picking up stitches into loose or baggy stitches.

● When working along a vertical edge, pick up one stitch for every row except every third or fourth row.

● The stitches should be picked up evenly along the edge. To achieve this, divide the work into sections, marking each section with a pin. Divide the total number of stitches into the same number of sections, then pick up the correct number of stitches within each section.

BUTTONHOLES

KNITTING FORMS a very elastic fabric so, if worked incorrectly, buttonholes can look unsightly.

Buy the buttons before working the buttonholes so that the correct size of buttonhole can be worked. Because of the elasticity of the knitted fabric, the buttonhole needs to be smaller than the diameter of the button to keep the buttons fastened. However, if the buttonhole is too large, it can be partially sewn up without looking too unsightly whereas if the buttonhole is too small there is very little that can be done about it, other than changing the buttons or reknitting the buttonhole.

SIMPLE EYELET BUTTONHOLE
This forms a very small buttonhole, although the size of a hole does vary with the gauge of the knitting.

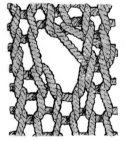

The buttonhole is worked over two stitches by bringing yarn to the front of work, then knitting two stitches together. On the following row, the 'yarn over' stitch should be worked as a normal stitch.

HORIZONTAL BUTTONHOLE

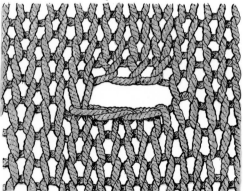

Worked over two rows Work in pattern to the position of the buttonhole, bind off the required number of stitches, then continue in pattern to the end of the row. On the next row, work in pattern to the bound-off stitches, cast on the same number of stitches as bound off, then continue in pattern to the end of the row.

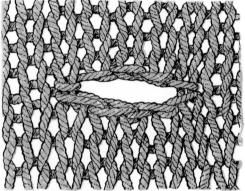

Worked over one row Work in pattern to the position of the buttonhole, bring yarn forward, slip the next stitch, take yarn back, slip the next stitch, pass the first slip stitch over the second, slip the next stitch, pass the second slip stitch over the third slip stitch, continue to bind off for the required number of stitches. Slip the last stitch back onto the left needle, turn the work and take the yarn to the back. Then cast on the same number of stitches as those bound off, using the firm knit stitch. Cast on one extra stitch and, before placing it on the left needle, bring the yarn forward, then place it on the left needle. Turn work, slip the next stitch and pass the last cast-on stitch over this slip stitch. Now continue in pattern across the row.

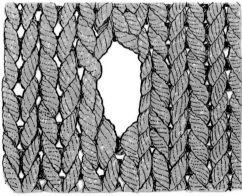

VERTICAL BUTTONHOLE Work to the required position, turn the work and work the required number of rows on the first group of stitches only. Break yarn and rejoin to second set of stitches. Work the same number of rows on these stitches. Break yarn and continue to work in pattern across all the stitches.

REINFORCING BUTTONHOLES
In order to prevent the buttonhole from pulling out of shape during wear, it is sometimes necessary to reinforce the buttonhole area. This can be done in two ways: work in buttonhole stitch around the edge of the buttonhole or sew a piece of ribbon or knit fabric behind the buttonhole, with a hole that corresponds with the buttonhole. Sew the two layers together around the buttonhole edge using buttonhole stitch.

SEWING ON BUTTONS
To reinforce the button area, sew a piece of ribbon or knitting to the back of the button area. When sewing the button into place, simultaneously sew a second smaller button to the back of the work.

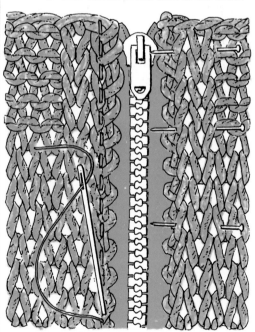

ZIPPERS Unless used as an obvious decorative feature, zippers are best avoided as they can look very unsightly. To insert a zipper, prepare the edge by using one of the edge stitch treatments described on page 16 while knitting the garment. Pin the zipper into place, without stretching the knitting. Place the edge stitches as close to the teeth of the zipper as possible. Using backstitch and self color sewing thread, sew the zipper into place.

GAUGE

IT CANNOT BE overstated that a garment may be drastically altered in shape and size if you do not check that you have the correct gauge.

Knitting patterns are written by means of mathematical calculations based on two sets of figures, the first being the size of the piece of work required in inches; the second being the number of stitches and rows required to knit each inch. This is called the gauge. Gauge is affected by: thickness of yarn, size of needles, the flow of yarn which is controlled by the knitter and the stitch pattern.

In theory it would be possible to knit any thickness of yarn using any size of needle. However, a bulky yarn knitted on very small needles would both look and feel like cardboard, while a fine yarn knitted on very large needles would produce a fabric that was too loose to be of any use. There is obviously a happy medium, where the fabric both looks and feels good and is also elastic and firm. Each yarn has a gauge recommended by the manufacturer, some of whom display this information on the yarn label, as shown.

Individual knitters vary so sometimes, to achieve the correct gauge, it is necessary to change to larger or smaller needles than those recommended. Recommended needle sizes are often given on the yarn label, as shown.

Having obtained the correct gauge over stockinette stitch, the remaining factor that influences gauge is the stitch pattern. Textured or fairisle stitch patterns often pull the work in so that more stitches are needed, whereas lace patterns often need fewer stitches as they are very open. Unless otherwise stated, the gauge sample should always be worked in the stitch pattern used for the main part of the garment. Once you have worked a fairly large area of the garment, check the gauge in part of the knitting, as gauge sometimes changes during the knitting, either because the knitter relaxes or because a larger number of stitches affects the way the yarn and needles are held.

WORKING A GAUGE SAMPLE Gauge is usually measured over an area of 2in or 4in square. It is more accurate when measured over a larger area. It can be checked in one of the following ways:
● Cast on the exact number of stitches given for the gauge and knit the exact number of rows given. Measure the work and if it is too small, change to larger needles; if it is too large, change to smaller needles.

● Knit an area larger than the gauge sample, count the required number of stitches and rows for the gauge, within the sample, then measure the area formed by them and change to different needles (as given for the previous method) if necessary. Often you will find that the number of stitches matches the gauge requirement, but the number of rows does not or vice versa. In this case it is usually better to match the number of stitches rather than the number of rows, as the length of a piece of knitting is often given as a measurement, rather than in numbers of rows. Some patterns, however, require that the number of rows should be exact. Examples are garments where there is a stitch or color pattern on the yoke, some raglan garments, and garments where the sleeves have stripes that must match with stripes on the yoke, where they are sewn in. In this case only experience can tell you whether it is better to lose or gain width or lose or gain length.

On the whole, a minor difference in gauge over a fine yarn will not change the size of the finished garment as drastically as a minor difference in gauge over a very bulky yarn.

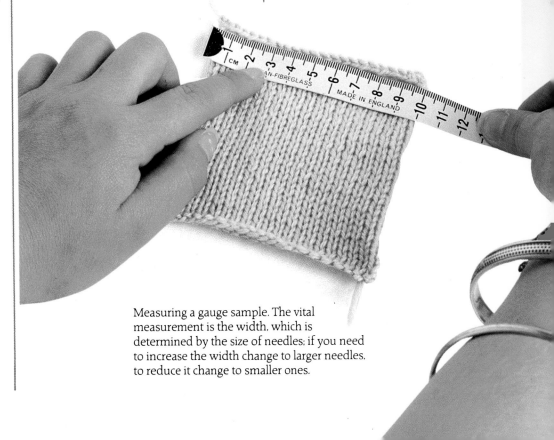

Measuring a gauge sample. The vital measurement is the width, which is determined by the size of needles; if you need to increase the width change to larger needles, to reduce it change to smaller ones.

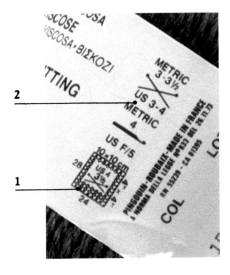

A yarn label showing recommended gauge ① and needle size ②

HOW TO READ A PATTERN

IN ORDER TO save space and convey instructions simply, patterns make use of abbreviations. Because of this, a pattern may at first look very complicated, but once you have started working you will find that this is not so. Abbreviations used in this book can be found on page 156.

SIZES Patterns are usually designed for several sizes and the instructions for each consecutive size are written in parentheses. For example, cast on 12(14;16;18;20) sts, and knit for 1(1¼;1¼;1½) in.

In this example there are five different sizes given in the pattern, the smallest size being outside the parentheses and each consecutive size being given within the parentheses in the same order throughout the pattern.

To prevent confusion, after choosing your size, circle each of the relevant instructions before starting to knit.

ASTERISKS These are used to show where a series of stitches is to be repeated. Groups of asterisks may be used to repeat different series of stitches. For example, k2(3;3;4;5) sts,** k4, *p2, k2, rep from * once more, k2, rep from ** 4 more times. In this example, all the work from the double asterisks has to be repeated four more times and the single asterisks once, within each of the repeats. Parentheses are used sometimes in place of asterisks.

REVERSING SHAPINGS AND PATTERN
Sometimes the instructions for one side of a garment are given and for the other side the instructions will state that you should work

the same as the first side "reversing shapings" (and sometimes the stitch or color pattern). This usually only happens in simple patterns. Where the pattern is more complex, it may be easier to work out and write down specific instructions, using the first side as a guide.

MATERIALS All patterns state the amount of yarn required but as this can only ever be an approximation, it is a good idea to buy an extra ball or make sure that you will be able to get extra yarn in the same color and dye lot if necessary.

CHARTS & GRAPHS These sometimes appear instead of written instructions for a stitch or color pattern.

Box feature giving details of each knit; for example, materials, sizes, abbreviations and needle size

All the garments are graded, according to the following scale.

★
Very simple, suitable for a beginner.

★★
Simple stitches and simple shapings for a knitter of average ability.

★★★
Simple stitch pattern with more complex shapings.

★★★★
Complex stitch pattern with simple shapings.

Graph showing the composition of the pattern

Line drawings of the components of the garment

Alternative swatches are shown when necessary

RIBBING AND HEMMING

WHEN THE KNIT and purl stitches are alternated not only in rows but also across the stitches of each row forming vertical lines of alternate knit and purl stitches, it is called ribbing. Alternating the stitches in this way gives the fabric a great deal of elasticity. Because of this, ribbing is usually used at the hem or wrist of a garment or wherever it needs to fit well. Ribbing can be worked in a variety of combinations of groups of knit and purl stitches.

When working a purl stitch after a knit stitch, the yarn should be brought to the front of the work, prior to working the purl stitch, and when working a knit stitch after a purl stitch, the yarn should be taken to the back of the work, before working the knit stitch.

Double rib (also called 2×2 rib)
Cast on a number of stitches divisible by 4, with 2 extra stitches at the end.
1st row: * k2, p2, rep from * to last 2 sts, k2.
2nd row: * p2, k2, rep from * to last 2 sts, p2.
Repeat these 2 rows to the required depth.

The two extra stitches are added in order to centralize the pattern so that it is the same at both edges.

Ribbings can also be worked in a variety of other combinations, such as 3×4, 2×1 and 5×3.

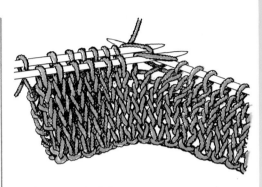

Double rib

Single rib

HEMS The lower edges of a knitted garment are usually worked ribwise, but sometimes they are 'turned up' as in dress-making. When this kind of hem is worked, care should be taken that it does not curl up. To prevent this it should be partly or wholly worked using smaller needles, or fewer stitches. It is also important that the depth of the hem on the wrong side should be fractionally shorter than the depth of the hem on the right side. This helps to prevent the edge from curling. The fold line of the hem is usually marked in one of two ways:
● Using a row of purl stitches on the right side of the work.
● Knitting the fold row using a needle 2 or 3 sizes larger than for the rest of the hem.

Hems can either be sewn up or knitted up to finish them.

Stockinette stitch hem
Cast on the required number of stitches using the loose knit stitch method. Knit to the required depth of the hem, ending with a purl row. Mark the fold of the hem by working the next row as a purl row, then work the same number of rows as for the first side of the hem, plus an extra row so that the work ends with a purl row. With a spare needle of the same size, pick up each of the stitches of the cast-on edge. Hold this needle next to and behind the needle with the stitches on it, both of them being in the left hand, knit together one stitch from each needle all across the row.

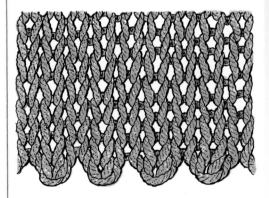

Picot edge hem
The number of stitches cast on must be an odd number. The hem is worked as for the stockinette stitch hem but on the foldline row a row of holes is worked, as follows: k1, * yo, k2 tog, rep from * to end of row. When this hem is folded, it will form a row of picots.

Single rib (also called 1×1 rib)
Cast on an odd number of stitches.
1st row: * k1, p1, rep from * to the last st, k1.
2nd row: * p1, k1, rep from * to the last st, p1.
These 2 rows should be repeated in the same sequence until the work measures the correct depth.

As you knit you will find that the fabric pulls in so that only the knit stitches are visible and the purl stitches are hidden.

USING SETS OF NEEDLES

THIS IS THE MOST common method of producing tubular fabric for socks, stockings, sleeves, etc.

The needles are double-pointed so that the work can be knitted from either end. They are usually sold in sets of four needles and are available in several lengths. They can be used in more or less quantity, although knitting with six is usually the maximum. The number of stitches required is divided between the needles, leaving one needle free to knit with.

Knitting with four needles.

Cast the required number of stitches onto each needle. Draw the first of these cast-on stitches close to the last cast-on stitch. Using the spare needle, knit the first cast-on stitch, thus closing the 'circle'. Then continue to knit to the last of the stitches on the first needle. All the stitches are now transferred to the 'spare needle' and the first needle is now the 'spare needle'. Continue to knit from the next needle, using this 'spare needle'. Continue working in this manner to the end of the row (or round). Mark the first or the last stitch of the round with a colored thread and move it up every time a row is completed as it is very easy to get lost and not know the beginning from the end.

When knitting a tubular fabric, it is not necessary to work any purl rows in order to obtain stockinette stitch as all the rows are worked from the front, or knit side, of the fabric. To obtain garter stitch, knit and purl rows must be alternated (as for stockinette stitch worked on two needles). Obviously, stitch patterns for tubular fabric must be written differently and some patterns cannot be adapted from two needles to tubular fabric, or

vice versa.

If you have trouble keeping the stitches on the needles, a cork or something similar can be stuck onto the ends of the needles.

USING CIRCULAR KNITTING NEEDLES

These usually come in the following lengths: 16in, 24in, 29in and 36in. They can be used instead of pairs or sets of needles. Some advantages of using a circular needle are: they can accommodate more stitches; there is no possibility of losing one of the needles; the stitches cannot fall off the ends; and they are less cumbersome to carry around.

When working in place of two needles any length of circular needle can be used. With one end of the needle in each hand, cast on the required number of stitches. Now commence knitting, starting by working into the last cast-on stitch and then continuing to transfer all the stitches from the left-hand needle to the right-hand needle in the usual manner. When the last stitch has been worked, change hands so that the last stitch worked is now at the end of the 'needle' in your left hand. Knit

this last stitch using the right hand 'needle', and continue in this manner changing hands every time a row is completed.

The length of needle to be used in place of sets of needles depends on the number of stitches to be cast on, or worked on. They must be able to be evenly spaced from end to end without being stretched. It is sometimes necessary to change to a different length of needle during the working of a garment if the shaping causes the number of stitches to decrease.

The required number of stitches should be cast on, then the circle is closed by changing hands and working into the first of the cast-on stitches. Continue knitting in rounds without changing hands. As with sets of four needles, mark the first or the last stitch with a colored thread.

Knitting with circular needles.

PARTIAL KNITTING

GARMENTS CAN BE given shaping not only by means of increases and decreases but also by means of partial knitting. Areas of garments can be partially knitted so that one edge of the work is longer than the other edge, and by this means shaping can be created to form darts, shoulder seams, yoke shapings, collars, etc. In order to prevent the formation of holes when turning the work, wrap the yarn around the first of the stitches to be left unworked before continuing to knit on the remaining stitches.

Example 1: Partial knitting
The sample shown here was worked over 21 stitches and the outside edge became twice as long as the inside edge.
1st row: knit.
2nd row: purl.
3rd row: knit to last 7 sts, yf, sl1, yb, return sl st to LN, turn work.
4th row: purl these 14 sts.
5th row: knit all the sts.
6th row: purl all the sts.
7th row: knit to last 14 sts, yf, sl1, yb, return sl st to LN, turn work.
8th row: purl these 7 sts.
Rep from row 1 as necessary.

Partial knitting

WORKING INTO THE BACK OF A STITCH
The knit and purl stitches are normally formed by working into the front loops of the stitches on the left needle, but they can also be worked by knitting into the back loops. When this is done, the resulting dropped stitch is twisted. If all the stitches of stockinette stitch fabric are worked into the back of the loop (on both the knit and the purl rows) the result will be a very twisted fabric with little elasticity. However, if the stitches are knitted into the back of the loop on either the knit or the purl row but not on both, the resulting fabric will have a slightly twisted stitch effect called Continental stockinette stitch.

Working into the back of a knit stitch
Insert the needle into the back loop of the next stitch on the left needle, from right to left, and knit in the usual way.

Working into the back of a purl stitch
Insert the needle into the back loop of the next stitch on the left needle, from left to right, and purl in the usual way.

Continental stockinette stitch

FINISHING

THE PIECES OF A garment should be pressed before they are sewn up. Follow the pressing instructions on the yarn label, as different fibers need different treatment. All loose ends should be sewn in before pressing.

Place a folded blanket covered with a sheet on the floor or on a table. Lay the garment pieces on this.

Pin the pieces of the garment with right sides down, to the cloth. Make sure that each piece of the garment is the correct shape and size, and that all rows and lines of stitches are straight.

Adjust the iron to the correct setting and, with a cloth between the work and the iron, lightly press each piece (a damp cloth may be used for wool). Do not use a rubbing motion with the iron as this distorts the stitches. Lay the iron on the work, lift it and lay it down again until you have worked over all the pieces.

Leave the pieces pinned down until they are cool and dry, except where there is ribbing. Remove the pins around the ribbing so that is can spring back to its natural shape.

Non iron yarns and embossed stitches
Pin the pieces of the garment as above. Cover them with a cold damp cloth for a few hours, then remove the cloth and allow the work to dry naturally overnight.

SEWING UP This should be done using a yarn needle and the same yarn as the garment has been knitted in, unless the yarn is very bulky or a bouclé yarn, in which case a finer yarn in the same color should be used. The edges to be sewn should first be pinned, then sewn in one of the following ways.

Edge to edge seam
Use this seam when it is necessary for the work to lie flat. The edges are worked in stockinette stitch rather than any of the alternative edge stitches.

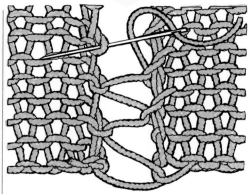

① Place the edges next to each other, rows matching each other, row for row. Sew in a zig-zag fashion through the knot of each row, alternating from edge to edge, pull the work together so that it is firmly held but not too tight.

② The finished edge to edge seam.

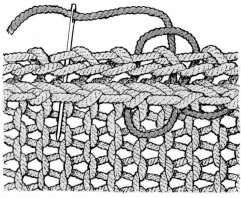

Backstitch seam
① This is the most commonly used form of seam. Strong and firm, it looks neat on the right side of the work. The edges should be

placed next to each other, with right sides facing. Ordinary backstitch is worked along the seam, at least ¼in in from the edge. Work through the center of each stitch to match with the same stitch on the other edge. Work in straight lines through the center of the same line or row of stitches, throughout.

② The finished backstitch seam, from back.

Grafting
The stitches to be grafted should be held on a spare needle or a piece of yarn. Remove them a few at a time and sew the edges together using matching yarn as shown.

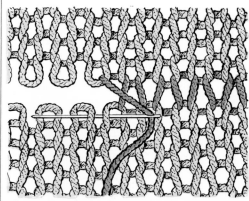

① Grafting on the knit side of the fabric.

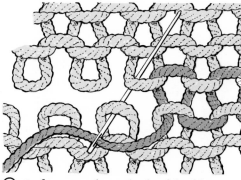

② Grafting over the purl side of the fabric.

TEXTURED STITCH PATTERNS

LIKE THE VARIOUS ribbings, textured stitch patterns are based on the use of knit and purl stitches in different combinations, repeated across the row and usually worked over two or more rows. More complex stitch patterns can be created by working into these knit and purl stitches in a variety of different ways.

As explained previously, unless otherwise stated in the pattern, you have to take the yarn from the back of the work to the front in order to make a purl stitch straight after a knit stitch and vice versa to make a knit stitch after a purl stitch.

The textured stitch patterns shown here are for flat knitting worked with pairs of needles. The instructions for all stitch patterns can be shown by means of written instructions or in graph form. The abbreviations used are shown on page 157. When following a graph, the right side rows should be read from right to left and the wrong side rows from left to right.

SIMPLE TEXTURED PATTERNS

These are worked using the simple knit or purl stitch in various combinations.

Garter stitch stripes

1st, 2nd & 3rd rows: knit
4th row: purl
Rep rows 1-4 as necessary.

Moss stitch

Cast on a number of stitches divisible by 2 with 1 extra stitch at the end.
1st row: k1, * p1, k1, rep from * to end of row.
Repeat this row as necessary.

Basket weave

Cast on a number of stitches divisible by 8, plus 5 extra stitches.
1st row: knit
2nd row: k5, * p3, k5, rep from * to end.
3rd row: p5, * k3, p5, rep from * to end.
Repeat row 1 and then row 2.
6th row: k1, * p3, k5, rep from * to last 4 sts, p3, k1.
7th row: p1, * k3, p5, rep from * to last 4 sts, k3, p1.
8th row: as row 6.
Rep rows 1-8 as necessary.

Raised triangles

Cast on a number of stitches divisible by 6.
1st row: knit.
2nd row: * k1, p5, rep from * to end.
3rd row: * k4, p2, rep from * to end.
4th row: * k3, p3, rep from * to end.
5th row: * k2, p4, rep from * to end.
6th row: * k5, p1, rep from * to end.
Rep rows 1-6 as necessary.

TEXTURED PATTERNS WORKED USING SLIPPED STITCHES

A stitch is 'slipped' when it is passed from the left needle to the right needle without being worked. A slipped stitch can be worked knitwise or purlwise. However, when working slipped stitch patterns, unless otherwise stated, the stitches should be slipped purlwise; i.e., the needle is inserted from right to left, through the front loop of the stitch, as this prevents the stitch from twisting. The yarn should be left where it is before working the slip stitch, unless the instructions state otherwise. Slipped stitch patterns can be used to create a woven effect.

Small honeycomb stitch

Cast on a number of stitches divisible by 2.
1st row: and all alt rows, knit.
3rd row: * k1, sl1, rep from * ending k2.
4th row: k2, * sl1, k1, rep from * to end.
Rep rows 1-4 as necessary.

Horizontal slip stitch

Cast on a number of stitches divisible by 3, plus 1 extra stitch.
1st row: knit.
2nd row: * k1, sl2, rep from * to last st, k1.
Rep these 2 rows as necessary.

Garter stitch stripes — Moss stitch — Basket weave — Raised triangles — Small honeycomb stitch — Horizontal slip stitch

Woven herringbone

Cast on a number of stitches divisible by 4, plus 2 extra stitches.

1st row: k2, * yf, sl2, yb, k2, rep from * to end.
2nd row: p1, * yb, sl2, yf, p2, rep from * to last st, p1.
3rd row: yf, sl2, yb, * k2, yf, sl2, yb, rep from * to end.
4th row: p1, * p2, yb, sl2, yf, rep from * to last st, p1.
Rep rows 1-4 once more.
9th row: as row 3.
10th row: as row 2.
11th row: as row 1.
12th row: as row 4.
13th-**16**th rows: as rows 9-12.
Rep rows 9-12 once more.
Rep rows 1-16 as neccessary.

Lattice stitch

Cast on a number of stitches divisible by 6 plus 3 extra stitches.

1st row: and all alt rows, purl.
2nd row: k2, * yf, sl5, yb, k1, rep from * to last st, k1.
4th row: k4, * k next stitch, passing right-hand needle under loose strand in row 2 and drawing it out under this strand when the stitch is knitted, k5, rep from * to last 5 sts, k1, under strand as before, k4.
6th row: k1, yf, sl3, yb, * k1, yf, sl5, yb, rep from

* to last 5 sts, k1, yf, sl3, yb, k1.
8th row: k1, * k1, under strand in row 6 (as shown in row 4), k5, rep from * to last 2 sts, k1 under strand in row 6, k1.
Rep rows 1-8 as necessary.

TEXTURED STITCH PATTERNS WORKED USING INCREASES & DECREASES

When several stitches are increased in one stitch and then decreased, either in the same row or in a following row, an embossed shape or bobble is formed. These can be scattered over a garment in regular patterns or at random. Care must be taken not to include these increased numbers of stitches, into instructions for shaping.

Small bobble

For a regular pattern, cast on a number of stitches divisible by 6 plus 5 extra stitches.

1st to **6**th rows: work in st st, starting with a knit row.
7th row: k5, * make bobble (k1, p1, k1, p1, all into next st, then pass the 1st, 2nd and 3rd stitches over the 4th st.) k5, rep from * to end.
8th to **12**th row: work in st st.
13th row: k 2, make bobble, * k5, make bobble, rep from * to last 2 sts, k2.
Rep rows 2-13 as necessary.

Large bobble

For a regular pattern, cast on a number of stitches divisible by 6 plus 5 extra stitches.

1st to **6**th row: work in st st.
7th row: k5, * make bobble (k1, p1, k1, p1, k1, all into next st, turn work, p5, turn work, k5, turn work, p2tog, p1, p2tog, turn work, sl1, k2tog, psso) k5, rep from * to end.
8th to **12**th rows: work in st st.
13th row: k2, make bobble, * k5, make bobble, rep from * to last 2 sts, k2.
Rep rows 2-13 as necessary.

Nut stitch

Cast on a number of stitches divisible by 4 plus 3 extra stitches.

1st row: * p3 (k1, yo, k1) into next st, rep from * to last 3 sts, p3.
2nd row: * k3, p3, rep from * to last 3 sts, k3.
3rd row: * p3, k3, rep from * to last 3 sts, p3.
4th row: * k3, p3tog, rep from * to last 3 sts, p3.
5th row: purl.
6th row: knit.
7th row: * p1 (k1, yo, k1) into next st, p2 rep from * to last 3 sts, p1 (k1, yo, k1) into next st, p1.
8th row: k1, *p3, k3, rep from * to last 4 sts, p3, k1.
9th row: p1, *k3, p3, rep from * to last 4 sts, k3, p1.
10th row: k1, *p3tog, k3, rep from * to last 4sts, p3tog, k1.
11th row: purl.
12th row: knit.
Rep rows 1-12 as necessary.

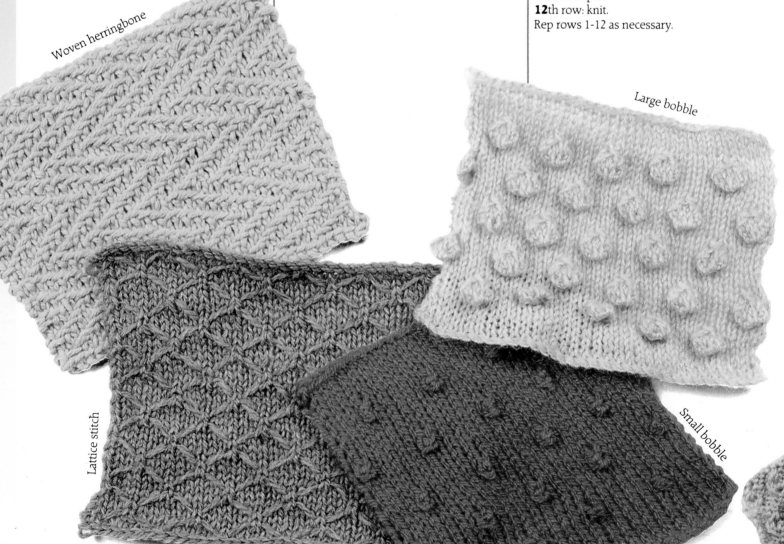

Woven herringbone

Lattice stitch

Large bobble

Small bobble

Blackberry stitch

Cast on a number of stitches divisible by 4.
1st row: * k1, yo, k1, into 1st st, p3, rep from * to end.
2nd row: *p3tog, k3, rep from * to end.
3rd row: *p3, k1, yo, k1, into next st, rep from * to end.
4th row: *k3, p3tog, rep from * to end.
Rep rows 1-4 as necessary.

Ripple stitch

Cast on any number of stitches and use both thick and thin needles.
1st-**6**th rows: knit, using thin needles.
7th row: using thick needles, * inc in next st knitwise, rep from * to end.
8th-**11**th rows: work in st st, starting with a purl row, using thick needles.
12th row: using thick needles, *p2tog, rep from * to end.
Rep rows 1-12 as necessary, ending by working rows 1-6.

Leaf motif

For a single motif, cast on an odd number of stitches. The sample here is worked over 13 sts.
1st row: p6, yo, k1, yo, p6.
2nd row: k6, p3, k6.
3rd row: p6, k1, yo, k1, yo, k1, p6.
4th row: k6, p5, k6.
5th row: p6, k2, yo, k1, yo, k2, p6.
6th row: k6, p7, k6.
7th row: p6, k3, yo, k1, yo, k3, p6.
8th row: k6, p9, k6.
9th row: p6, sl1, k1, psso, k5, k2tog, p6.
10th row: k6, p7, k6.
11th row: p6, sl1, k1, psso, k3, k2tog, p6.
12th row: k6, p5, k6.
13th row: p6, sl1, k1, psso, k1, k2tog, p6.
14th row: k6, p3, k6.
15th row: p6, sl1, k2tog, psso, p6.
16th row: knit.

Bow motif

For a single motif, cast on an even number of stitches; the sample here is worked over 24 sts.
1st-**6**th rows: work in st st.
7th row: k12, turn work and cast on 20 sts, turn work, k rem 12 sts.
8th-**14**th rows: work in st st.
15th row: k12, bind off 20 sts, k12.
16th-**22**nd rows: work in st st.
When work is completed, arrange the increased section into a bow shape, and overcast the center firmly together.

TEXTURED PATTERNS WORKED USING ELONGATED STITCHES

Elongated stitches are formed when the yarn forming a stitch is wrapped several times around the needle.

Drop stitch

Cast on any number of stitches.
1st-**4**th rows: knit.
5th row: knit across row, each time wrapping the yarn 3 times around the needle.
6th row: knit across row, dropping the extra loops.
Rep rows 2-6 as necessary, ending with rows 6-4.

Floral motif

Cast on an odd number of stitches; the sample here is worked over 13 stitches. [This pattern makes use of cable techniques shown on page 34.]
1st-**4**th rows: work in reverse st st.
5th row: p6 (k1, p1, k1, all into next st, each time winding the yarn 3 times round the needle) p6.
6th row: k6, yf, sl3, dropping extra loops, yb, k6.
7th row: p6, yb, sl3, yf, p6.
8th row: k6, yf, sl3, yb, k6.
9th row: p3, C3B, sl next st onto front end of CN, k2tog tbl, p2 all from CN, yb, sl1, yf, C1F (Cable 1 Front), p2, sl1 st from CN onto LN, 2ktog tbl, p3.
10th row: k6, yf, sl1, yb, k6.
11th row: p13.
12th row: k13.
13th row: p6, make bobble (k1, p1, k1, all into next st, turn work, p3, turn work, sl1, k2tog, psso.) p6.
14th row: k13.
Rep rows 1-14 as necessary, ending with rows 1-4 once more.

Bow motif

Ripple stitch

Leaf motif

Drop stitch

Floral motif

Nut stitch

Blackberry stitch

TEXTURED PATTERNS WORKED USING CABLES

A cable is formed when the stitches on a needle are worked out of sequence, thereby crossing one group of stitches over another. To do this, the first group of stitches is slipped onto a cable needle and held either at the back or at the front of the work, while the second group of stitches is worked. The first group of stitches is then worked from the cable needle.

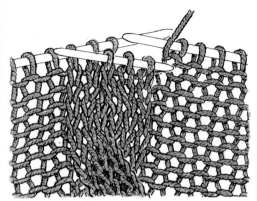

① Purl into the second stitch on the left needle, but do not remove from left needle. Purl into first stitch and remove both stitches together from left needle.

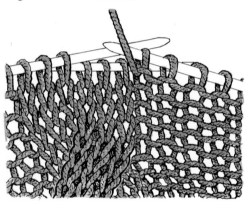

② Method of cabling one stitch with slant to the right on right side of work.

TWO-STITCH CABLES

When only two stitches are to be cabled, this can be done without the use of a cable needle. These 'two-stitch cables' can be worked either with a twist to the left or with a twist to the right, on the knit (or right) side of the fabric. They can be worked from either the knit (or right) side, or the purl (or wrong) side of the fabric.

CABLING TWO STITCHES WITH A TWIST TO THE RIGHT ON THE RIGHT SIDE OF THE FABRIC

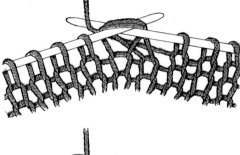

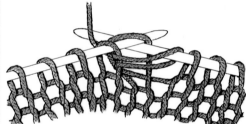

On a right side row

Knit 2 together but do not remove from left needle. Knit into the first of the 2 stitches, then remove both stitches from left needle together.

On a wrong side row

Purl into the second stitch on left needle, but do not remove from left needle. Purl into first stitch and remove both these stitches from left needle together.

CABLING TWO STITCHES WITH A TWIST TO THE LEFT ON THE RIGHT SIDE OF THE FABRIC

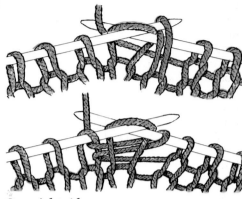

On a right side row

Knit into the front of the second stitch on left needle from behind the first stitch. Do not remove from left needle. Knit into the front of the first stitch and remove both stitches from left needle together.

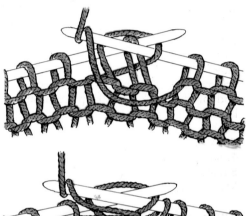

On a wrong side row

Purl into the back of the second stitch on left needle but do not remove it from left needle. Purl into the back of the first stitch and remove both stitches from left needle together.

Fisherman's rib

Fur stitch

Four-stitch cable

TRADITIONAL ARAN PATTERNS

Aran patterned sweaters were originally worn by the fishermen on the islands of Aran, just off the West coast of Ireland. Each locality or family had its own particular design and, since many of the designs were reputed to have symbolic meanings, they also told a story.

The traditional Aran sweater was worked from the collar downwards in a tubular fashion. The only sections worked on two needles as flat knitting were the shoulder panel and the front and back sections from the collar to the underarm seam. However, Aran patterns can be knitted either in a tubular fashion or as flat knitting with two needles. The instructions given here are all for the two-needle versions.

Four-stitch cable

The sample shown here is worked over 16 sts.
1st & **3**rd rows: k6, p4, k6.
2nd row: p6, k4, p6.
4th row: p6, C2B, k2, K2CN, p6.
Rep rows 1-4 as necessary.

Twist stitch rib

Cast on a number of stitches divisible by 7, plus 2 extra stitches.
1st row: p2, *LTK, k3, p2, rep from * to end.
2nd row: and all alt rows, *k2, p5, rep from * to last 2 sts, k2.
3rd row: p2, *k1, LTK, k2, p2, rep from * to end.
5th row: p2, *k2, LTK, k1, p2.
7th row: p2, *k3, LTK, p2, rep from * to end.
8th row: as row 2.
Rep rows 1-8 as necessary.

Lattice cable

Cast on a number of stitches divisible by 6 plus 2 extra stitches.
1st row: *RTK, k4, rep from * to last 2 sts, RTK.
2nd row: and all alt rows, purl.
3rd row: k1, *LTK, k2, RTK, rep from * to last st, k1.
5th row: k2, *LTK, RTK, k2, rep from * to end.
7th row: k2, *k1, RTK, k3, rep from * to end.
9th row: k2, *RTK, LTK, k2, rep from * to end.
11th row: k1, * RTK, k2, LTK, rep from * to last st, k1.
12th row: purl.
Rep rows 1-12 as necessary.

Ring cable

The sample shown here is worked over a panel of 12 sts.
1st row: and all alt rows, k2, p8, k2.
2nd row: p2, C2B, k2, K2CN, C2F, k2, K2CN, p2.
4th row: p2, k8, p2.
6th row: p2, C2F, k2, K2CN, C2B, k2, K2CN, p2.
8th row: p2, k8, p2.
Rep rows 1-8 as necessary.

Framed cable

The sample shown here is worked over a panel of 20 sts.
1st row: k6, p8, k6.
2nd row: p5, C1B, k1, P1CN, k6, C1F, p1, K1CN, p5
3rd row: and all alt rows, knit all the purl sts of previous row and purl all the knit sts.
4th row: p4, C1B, k1, P1CN, p1, k6, p1, C1F, p1, K1CN, p4.
6th row: p3, C1B, k1, P1CN, p2, C3F, k3, K3CN, p2, C1F, p1, K1CN, p3.
8th row: p2, C1B, k1, P1CN, p3, mk6, p3, C1F, p1, K1CN, p2.
10th row: p2, C1F, p1, K1CN, p3, k6, p3, C1B, k1, P1CN, p2.
12th row: p3, C1F, p1, K1CN, p2, C3F, k3, K3CN, p2, C1B, k1, P1CN, p3.
14th row: p4, C1F, p1, K1CN, p1, k6, p1, C1B, k1, P1CN, p4.
16th row: p5, C1F, p1, K1CN, k6, C1B, k1, P1CN, p5.
Rep rows 1-16 as necessary.

OTHER TECHNIQUES FOR TEXTURED PATTERNS

Fur stitch

Cast on an odd number of stitches.
1st row: knit.
2nd row: k1, *k1, but do not remove st from LN, yf, pass yarn around left thumb, and then to back of work, k into the same st again and remove from needle, wind yarn round needle once and then pass the 2 sts just worked over this made st, k1, rep from * to end.
3rd row: knit.
4th row: * work loop as given in 2nd row, k1, rep from * to last st, work loop.
Rep rows 1-4 as necessary.

Fisherman's rib

Cast on an odd number of sts.
1st row: purl.
2nd row: * p1, k into the stitch on the row below, thus dropping the stitch on LN, rep from * to last st, p1.
3rd row: k1, * p1, k into stitch on row below, rep from * to last 2 sts, p1, k1.
Rep rows 2-3 as necessary.

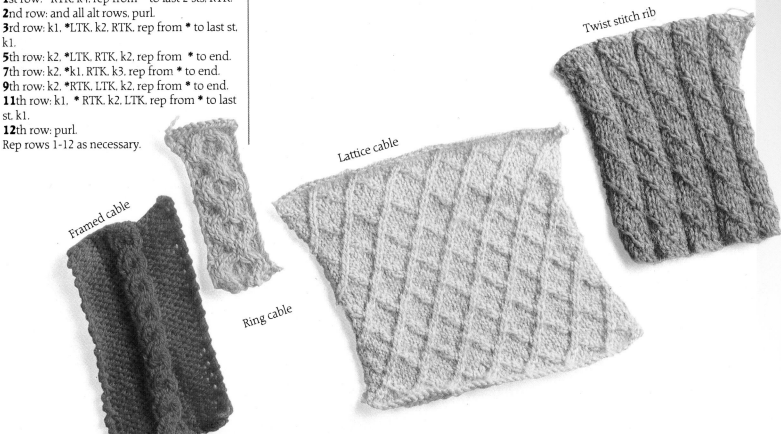

Framed cable

Ring cable

Lattice cable

Twist stitch rib

LACE PATTERNS

THE BASIS FOR ALL lace stitches is the eyelet, a small hole formed by working a decorative increase paired with a decrease, either next to the increase, somewhere in the same row or on a following row.

THE EYELET

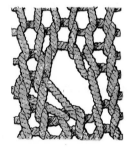

Formed by knitting two stitches together

The eyelet is formed thus: yo, k2tog. On the following rows, the 'yarn over' loop is worked in the usual way (usually as a purl stitch).

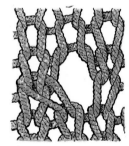

Formed by working a slipped stitch decrease

The eyelet is formed thus: yo, sl1, k1, psso. On the following row the 'yarn over' loop is worked in the usual way (usually as a purl stitch).

As can be seen, the decreases form either a slant to the right or a slant to the left, and these slanting stitches are used as part of the design of any lace stitch pattern. Where the corresponding decrease is several stitches away from the increase, several stitches can be made to slant in a given direction.

Because lace patterns are worked using increases and decreases, make sure, when working shapings, that the correct number of increases or decreases are worked for the shaping in addition to the increase and decreases required for the stitch pattern.

SIMPLE EYELET LACE PATTERNS

Horizontal lace stripe

Cast on a number of stitches divisible by 2 plus 1 extra stitch.
1st-**5**th rows: work in st st, starting with a knit row.
6th row: knit.
7th row: k1, * yo, k2tog, rep from * to end.
8th row: knit.
9th-**12**th rows: work in st st, starting with a knit row.
Rep rows 1-12 as necessary.

Vertical lace zig zag

Cast on a multiple of 7 stitches.
1st row: *k1, yo, k2tog, k4, rep from * to end.
2nd row: and alt rows, purl.
3rd row: *k2, yo, k2tog, k3, rep from * to end.
5th row: *k3, yo, k2tog, k2, rep from * to end.
7th row: *k4, yo, k2tog, k1, rep from *to end.
9th row: *k3, sl1, k1; psso, yo, k2, rep from * to end.
11th row: *k2, sl1, k1, psso, yo, k2, rep from * to end.
13th row: *k1, sl1, k1, psso, yo, k4, rep from * to end.
14th row: purl.
Rep rows 1-14 as necessary.

Mesh stitch

Cast on an odd number of stitches.
1st row: k1, * yo, k2tog, rep from * to end.
2nd row: purl.
3rd row: *sl1, k1, psso, yo, rep from * to last st, k1.
4th row: purl.
Rep rows 1-4 as necessary.

SIMPLE LACE PATTERNS MAKING USE OF THE SLANT OF THE DECREASES

Horizontal zig zag

Cast on a number of stitches divisible by 10 plus 1 extra stitch.
1st row: and all alt rows, purl.
2nd row: *k5, yo, sl1, k1, psso, k3, rep from * to last st, k1.
4th row: *k3, k2tog, yo, k1, yo, sl1, k1, psso, k2, rep from * to last st, k1.
6th row: *k2, k2tog, yo, k3, yo, sl1, k1, psso, k1, rep from * to last st, k1.
8th row: *k1, k2tog, yo, k5, yo, sl1, k1, psso, rep from * to last st, k1.
10th row: k2tog, yo, k7, *yo, sl1, k2tog, psso, yo, k7, rep from * to last 2 sts, yo, sl1, k1, psso.
Rep rows 1-10 as necessary.

Lace rib

Vertical lace zig zag

Horizontal zig zag

Horizonta[l]

Lace diagonals

Cast on a number of stitches divisible by 5 plus 2 extra stitches.

1st row: k1, *yo, sl1, k1, psso, k3, rep from * to last st, k1.
2nd row: and all alt rows, purl.
3rd row: k1, * k1, yo, sl1, k1, psso, k2, rep from * to last st k1.
5th row: k1, *k2, yo, sl1, k1, psso, k1, rep from * to last st, k1.
7th row: k1, *k3, yo sl1, k1, psso, rep from * to last st, k1.
9th row: k2, *k3, yo, sl1, k1, psso, rep from * to end.
10th row: purl.
Rep rows 1-10 as necessary.

Horseshoe lace

Cast on a number of stitches divisible by 8.
1st row: p3, k1, p1, *p1, k1, p4, k1, p1, rep from * to last 4 sts, p1, k1, p2.
2nd row: k2, p1, k1, *k1, p1, k4, p1, k1, rep from * to last 4 sts, k1, p1, k2.
3rd row: as row 1.
4th row: as row 2.
5th row: p1, k2 tog, yo, p1, *p1, yo, sl1, k1, psso, p2, k2 tog, yo, p1, rep from * to last 4 sts, p1, yo, sl1, k1, psso, p1.
6th row: k1, p2, k1, *k1, p2, k2 p2, k1, rep from * to last 4 sts, k1, p2, k1.

7th row: k2tog, yo, p2, *p2, yo, sl1, k1, psso, k2tog, yo, p2, rep from * to last 4 sts, p2, yo, sl1, k1, psso.
8th row: p2, k2, *k2, p4, k2, rep from * to last 4 sts, k2, p2.
Rep rows 1-8 as necessary.

LACE STITCH PATTERNS IN WHICH THE DECREASE IS WORKED SEVERAL STITCHES AWAY FROM ITS CORRESPONDING INCREASE

Broken horseshoes

Cast on a number of stitches divisible by 12 plus 2 extra stitches.
1st row: k1, *k2tog, yo, k5, yo, k3, sl1, k1, psso, rep from * to end, k1.
2nd row: and all alt rows, purl.
3rd row: k1, *k2tog, k5, yo, k1, yo, k2, sl1, k1, psso, rep from * to end, k1.
5th row: k1, *k2tog, k4, yo, k3, yo, k1, sl1, k1, psso, rep from * to end, k1.
7th row: k1, *k2tog, k3, yo, k5, yo, sl1, k1, psso, rep from * to end, k1.
9th row: k1, *k2tog, k2, yo, k1, yo, k5, sl1, k1, psso, rep from * to end, k1.
11th row: k1, *k2tog, k1, yo, k3, yo, k4, sl1, k1, psso, rep from * to end, k1.
12th row: purl to end.
Rep rows 1-12 as necessary.

Lace entrelacs

Cast on a number of stitches divisible by 13 plus 2 extra stitches.
1st row: k1, *k2, sl1, k1, psso, k4, k2tog, k2, yo, k1, yo, rep from * to last st, k1.
2nd row: and all alt rows, purl.
3rd row: k1, *yo, k2, sl1, k1, psso, k2, k2tog, k2, yo, k3, rep from * to last st, k1.
5th row: k1, *k1, yo, k2, sl1, k1, psso, k2tog, k2, yo, k4, rep from * to last st, k1.
7th row: k1, *yo, k1, yo, k2, sl1, k1, psso, k4, k2tog, k2, rep from * to last st, k1.
9th row: k1, *k3, yo, k2, sl1, k1, psso, k2, k2tog, k2, yo, rep from * to last st, k1.
11th row: k1, *k4, yo, k2, sl1, k1, psso, k2tog, k2, yo, k1, rep from * to end, k1.
12th row: purl.
Rep rows 1-12 as necessary.

LACE PATTERNS WHICH USE DOUBLE DECREASES

These patterns often give a scalloped edge which can be used effectively for the hem of lacy garments. If the scalloped edge is to be used as a hem, the loose knit stitch cast on should be used.

Lace rib

Cast on a number of stitches divisible by 10 plus 1 extra stitch.
1st row: k1, *yo, k3, sl1, k2tog, psso, k2, yo, k1, rep from * to end.
2nd row: purl.
Rep these 2 rows as necessary.

Snowdrops

Cast on a number of stitches divisible by 8 plus 5 extra stitches.
1st row: k1, *yo, dec 2 (k2tog tbl, place new st back on LN, pass the next st over this st, then return it to RN), yo, k5, rep from * to last 4 sts, yo, dec 2, yo, k1.
2nd row: and all alt rows, purl.
3rd row: as 1st row.
5th row: k1, *k3, yo, sl1, k1, psso, k1, k2tog, yo, rep from * to last 4 sts, k4.
7th row: k1, *yo, dec 2, yo, k1, rep from * to last 4 sts, yo, dec 2, yo, k1.
8th row: purl.
Rep rows 1-8 as necessary.

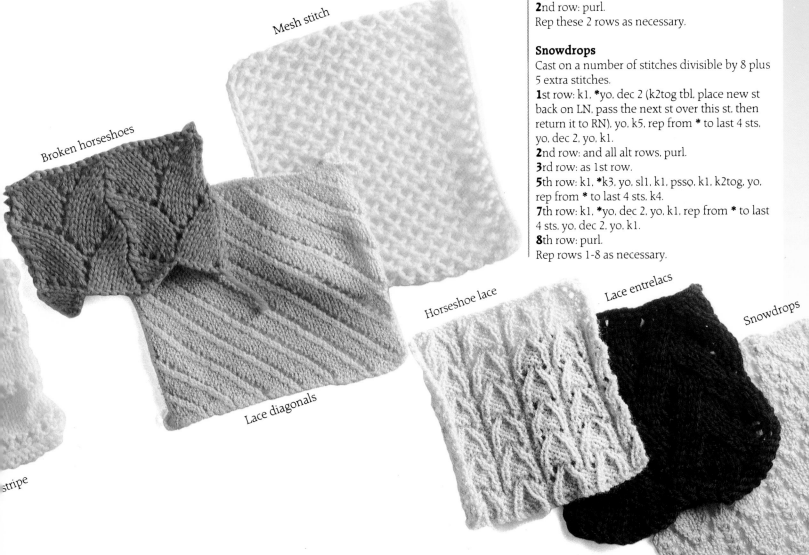

Mesh stitch

Broken horseshoes

stripe

Lace diagonals

Horseshoe lace

Lace entrelacs

Snowdrops

Falling leaves

Cast on a number of stitches divisible by 8 plus 1 extra stitch.

1st row: k1, *yo, k2, sl1, k2tog, psso, k2, yo, k1, rep from * to end.
2nd row: and all alt rows, purl.
3rd row: k1, *k1, yo, k1, sl1, k2tog, psso, k1, yo, k2, rep from * to end.
5th row: k1, *k2, yo, sl1, k2tog, psso, yo, k3, rep from * to end.
7th row: k2tog, *k2, yo, k1, yo, sl1, k2tog, psso, rep from * to last 7 sts, k2, yo, k1, yo, k2, sl1, k1, psso.
9th row: k2tog, *k1, yo, k3, yo, k1, sl1, k2tog, psso, rep from * to last 7 sts, k1, yo, k3, yo, k1, sl1, k1, psso.
11th row: k2tog, *yo, k5, yo, sl1, k2tog, psso, rep from * to last 7 sts, yo, k5, yo, sl1, k1, psso.
12th row: purl.
Rep rows 1-12 as necessary.

LACE PATTERNS WORKED TOGETHER WITH TEXTURED STITCHES

Lace columns

Cast on multiple of 9 stitches plus an extra 2 stitches.

1st row: *p2, sl1, k1, psso, yo, k3, yo, k2tog, rep from * to last 2 sts, p2.

2nd row: and all alt rows, k2, *p7, k2, rep from * to end.
3rd row: *p2, k2, yo, sl1, k2tog, psso, yo, k2, rep from * to last 2 sts, p2.
4th row: as 2nd row.
Rep rows 1-4 as necessary.

Lace scallops

Cast on a number of stitches divisible by 18.
1st row: knit.
2nd row: purl.
3rd row: *(k2tog) × 3 (yo,k1) × 6(k2tog) × 3, rep from * to end.
4th row: knit.
Rep rows 1-4 as necessary.

Arrowheads

Cast on a number of stitches divisible by 8 plus 1 extra stitch.
1st row: *k2, yo, sl1, k1, psso, k1, k2tog, yo, k1, rep from * to last st, k1.
2nd row: and all alt rows, purl.
3rd row: *p1, k2, yo, sl1, k2tog, psso, yo, k2, rep from * to last st, p1.
5th, **7**th, **9**th & **11**th rows: *p1, sl1, k1, psso, k1, yo, k1, yo, k1, k2tog, rep from * to last st, p1.
13th row: *k1, yo, sl1, k1, psso, k3, k2tog, yo, rep from * to last st, k1.
14th row: purl.
Rep rows 1-14 as necessary.

LACE STITCH PATTERNS IN WHICH INCREASES HAVE THEIR CORRESPONDING DECREASES ON DIFFERENT ROWS

Lace pillars

Cast on a number of stitches divisible by 3 plus 2 extra stitches.
1st row: *p2, yo, k1, yo, rep from * to last 2 sts, p2.
2nd row: k2, *p3, k2 rep from * to end.
3rd row: *p2, k3, rep from * to last 2 sts, p2.
4th row: k2, *p3tog, k2, rep from * to end.
Rep rows 1-4 as necessary.

Vine stitch

Cast on a number of stitches divisible by 8 plus 4 extra stitches.
1st row: k2, *yo, k1, tbl, yo, sl1, k1, psso, k5, rep from * to last 2 sts, k2.
2nd row: p6, *p2tog tbl, p7, rep from * to last 7 sts, p2tog tbl, p5.
3rd row: k2, *yo, k1, tbl, yo, k2, sl1, k1, psso, k3, rep from * to last 2 sts k2.
4th row: p4, *p2tog tbl, p7, rep from * to end.
5th row: k2, *k1, tbl, yo, k4, sl1, k1, psso, k1, yo, rep from * to last 2 sts, k2.
6th row: p3, *p2tog tbl, p7, rep from * to last st.
7th row: k2, *k5, k2tog, yo, k1, tbl, yo, rep from * to last 2 sts, k2.
8th row: p5, *p2tog, p7, rep from * to last 8 sts, p2tog p6.
9th row: k2, *k3, k2tog, k2, yo, k1, tbl, yo, rep from * to last 2 sts, k2.
10th row: *p7, p2tog, rep from * to last 4 sts, p4.
11th row: k2, *yo, k1, k2tog, k4, yo, k1, tbl, rep from * to last 2 sts, k2.
12th row: p1, *p7, p2tog, rep from * to last 3 sts, p3.
Rep rows 1-12 as necessary.

Falling leaves

Lace pillars

Lace scallops

Vine stitch

Arrowheads

Lace columns

MULTI-COLORED KNITTING

A WIDE VARIETY of stitch patterns can be created by the use of different colors which can be worked into plain stockinette stitch or any of the textured or lace patterns. Colors may be introduced into the work in three main ways: by changing the color at the beginning of a row; by working two or more colors across every row, as in Fairisle knitting; or by introducing a new color over a small area of each row ('motif knitting').

KNITTING WITH SEVERAL COLORS WHERE ONLY ONE COLOR IS WORKED ACROSS EACH ROW

All stripe patterns are worked in this way, but a variety of more complex stitch patterns can be worked using the slip-stitch method, where the stitches are slipped purlwise or knitted, according to the pattern.

Simple stripes
Using col A, cast on any number of stripes.
1st-**4**th rows: work in st st, using col A.
5th & **6**th rows: work in st st, using col B.
Rep rows 1-6 as necessary.

Simple stripes worked in reverse stockinette stitch (see inset below)
The stripe pattern is used as shown for the simple stripes, but the reverse side of the fabric becomes the right side.

Garter stitch stripes
Cast on any number of stitches.
1st-**4**th rows: work in st st, using col A.
5th & **6**th rows: work in g st, using col B.
Rep rows 1-6 as necessary.

Two-color moss stitch
Using col B, cast on a number of stitches divisible by 2.
1st row: using A, k1, *k1, sl1, rep from * to last st, k1.
2nd row: using A, k1, *yf, sl1, yb, k1, rep from * to last st, k1.
3rd row: using B, k1, *sl1, k1, rep from * to last st, k1.
4th row: using B, k1, *k1, yf, sl1, yb, rep from * to last st, k1.
Rep rows 1-4 as necessay.

Three-color check
Using col A, cast on a number of stitches divisible by 4 plus 3 extra stitches.
1st row: using A, knit.
2nd row: using A, k1, *k1, winding yarn twice round needle, k3, rep from * to last 2 sts, k1, winding yarn twice round needle, k1.
3rd row: using B, k1, *sl1 (dropping extra loop), k3, rep from * to last 2 sts, sl1, (dropping extra loop), k1.
4th row: using B, k1, *yf, sl1, yb, k3, rep from * to last 2 sts, yf, sl1, yb k1.
5th row: using C, k1, *sl 2, k2, rep from * to last 2 sts, sl1, k1.
6th row: using C, k1, yf, sl1, * p2, sl 3, rep from * to last st, k1.
Rep rows 1-6 as necessary.

Box pattern
Using col A, cast on a number of stitches divisible by 8 plus 3 extra stitches.
1st row: using A, knit.
2nd row: using A, knit.
3rd row: using B, k3, *(sl1, k1) × 2, sl1, k3, rep from * to end.
4th row: using B, p3, *(yf, sl1, yb, k1) × 2, yf, sl1, p3, rep from * to end.
5th row: using A, k1, sl2, *k5, sl3, rep from * to last 8 sts, k5, sl2, k1.
6th row: using A, k1, yf, sl2, yb, *k5, yf, sl3, yb, rep from * to last 8 sts, k5, yf, sl 2, yb, k1.
7th row: as row 3.
8th row: as row 4.
9th row: as row 1.
10th row: as row 2.
11th row: using B (k1, sl1) × 2, *k3 (sl1, k1) × 2, sl1, rep from * to last 7 sts, k3 (sl1, k1) × 2.
12th row: using B (k1, yf, sl1, yb) × 2, *p3 (yf, sl1, yb, k1) × 2, yf, sl1, yb, rep from * to last 7 sts, p3 (sl1, k1) × 2.
13th row: using A, k4, *sl3, k5, rep from * to last 7 sts, sl3, k4.
14th row: using A, k4, *yf, sl3, yb, k5 rep from * to last 7 sts, yf, sl3, yb, k4.
15th row: as row 11.
16th row: as row 12.
Rep rows 1-16 as necessary.

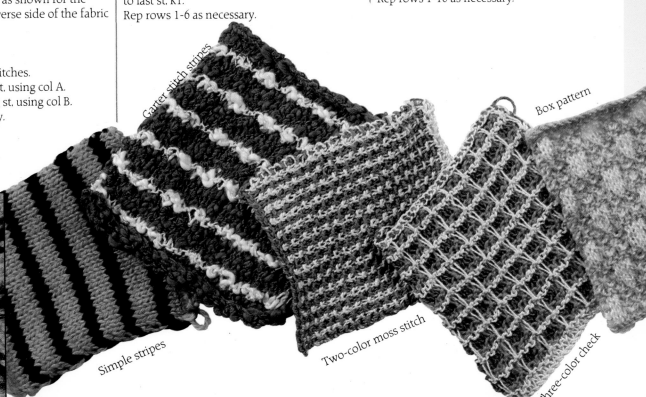

Garter stitch stripes

Box pattern

Simple stripes

Two-color moss stitch

Three-color check

FAIRISLE

'Fairisle' refers to the working of several colors in one garment forming an allover multi-color pattern. Nowadays, the term 'fairisle' is used to describe more-or-less any kind of knitting where several colors are worked in a pattern sequence across each row. Originally, fairisle garments were worked by the knitters on the Fairisle in Scotland. They were knitted on sets of needles in a tubular fashion, where every row is worked as a knit row, and the colors are carried continuously around the garment. It is not easy to adapt true fairisle patterns for working as flat knitting on pairs of needles. Whereas they were able to use both odd and even numbers of rows for each color, only even numbers of rows can be used in flat knitting unless the yarn is cut at the end of every row. This would involve the knitter in sewing in all the ends and would also produce a weaker fabric and bulky seams. When working with two or more colors in one row, the color not being used must be left to lie very loosely at the back of the work, so that the gauge is not altered. Because of these loose strands lying at the back of the work, the garment will feel thicker, so a knitting worsted sweater will feel like a bulky knit garment, and a sports yarn sweater like a knitting worsted one.

True fairisle patterns

The pattern shown here is suitable for use only when knitting tubular fabric on a circular needle or sets of needles as it involves the use of colors for odd and even numbers of rows. As shown here, most fairisle patterns are worked from charts but they can also be shown in written form.

This is worked over a repeat of 8 stitches plus 1 extra stitch at the beginning to centralize the pattern, which is worked over a repeat of 10 rows.

Fairisle patterns adapted for knitting with two needles

The pattern shown here has colors worked in even numbers of rows so that the yarns can be held at the side edge of the garment while not in use, and do not need to be cut when each color row is completed.

This is worked over a repeat of 8 stitches plus 1 extra stitch at the end to centralize the pattern, which is worked over a repeat of 14 rows.

WORKING WITH SEVERAL COLORS ACROSS A ROW

When working color patterns where the colors are knitted evenly across the row with no large 'one color' areas, all the yarns being worked in that row are taken across the row, and the yarns not in use must be stranded (or held) at the back of the work. It is every easy to pull these strands too tight, causing the fabric to have a bubbled or quilted effect which is very unsightly. So before knitting the next stitch in a new color, space out all the stitches widely across the right needle, so that an adequate amount of yarn is left to lie loosely at the back of the work. It is much better to make these strands too loose, as they can be tacked to the back of the garment later if necessary. There is nothing that can be done when they have been worked too tightly.

If a yarn has to be stranded across the back of several stitches, causing a long loop, this long stranded yarn can be 'woven in' while knitting.

WEAVING IN

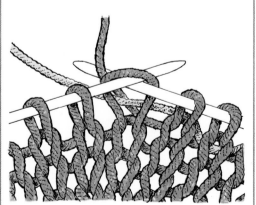

On a knit row

Insert the needle knitwise into the next stitch, place the stranded yarn between this stitch and the yarn in use and knit the stitch as usual. The stranded yarn is then 'caught' into this stitch on the wrong side, but does not show on the right side.

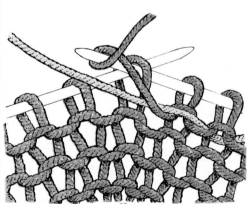

On a purl row

Insert the needle purlwise into the next stitch, place the stranded yarn between this stitch and the yarn in use and purl this stitch in the normal way.

Strands should be woven in on every third or fourth stitch. Again it is very important that the yarn is not pulled too tightly across the back of the work. In general, weaving in should be avoided as very few knitters are able to do this without causing some distortion on the right side of the fabric.

MOTIF KNITTING

When a color pattern consists of large areas of color, use a separate ball of yarn for each color area. The back of the work will be neater if this is done; the garment will be less bulky; and less yarn will be used. Where there are several color areas, several balls of yarn will be in use, so wind the yarn onto small bobbins that can hang loosely at the back of the work. Bobbins can be bought or very simply made out of cardboard as shown.

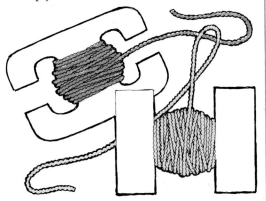

Bobbins can be cut in either of these shapes.

Twisting yarns together

When using separate balls of yarn for each color area, it is important to twist the yarns together when changing colors or there will be vertical gaps between each color area.

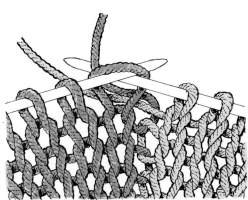

① Insert the needle in the next stitch, place the 'old' yarn between this stitch and the 'new' yarn, work the stitch knitwise or purlwise in the usual way.

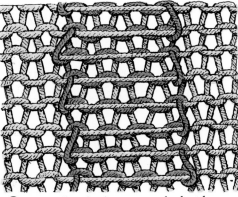

② A completed color area worked with yarns twisted at each end, shown from the wrong side.

The yarns should also be twisted together when working fairisle color patterns, especially where there are vertical lines of color.

TRANSLATING A PICTURE INTO KNITTING

Any picture or diagram can be worked as a piece of knitting; it merely has to be translated into graph or chart form. Because of the nature of knitting, it is better to use very simple designs or diagrams, especially if the yarn to be used is fairly thick. Once you have found a picture to use, the chart can be made as follows:

● Drawing on the picture in pencil, divide the picture into 4in squares. If you want the finished knitted motif to be smaller than the actual picture, use squares larger than 4in, but if you want it to be larger, use squares smaller than 4in.

● Divide each of these large squares into smaller squares according to the gauge in 4in of the yarn being used. For example, for a gauge of 24 sts and 32 rows to 4in, divide each square into 24 vertical sections and 32 horizontal sections.

● The work can be knitted directly from this chart, working each square in the color shown predominantly in that square. Alternatively, the chart can be drawn onto conventional graph paper. When this is done, the picture looks elongated, because there are always more rows than stitches to every inch.

If you do not want to draw onto the original picture, the gauge graph can be drawn onto tracing paper or acetate, and then placed over the drawing.

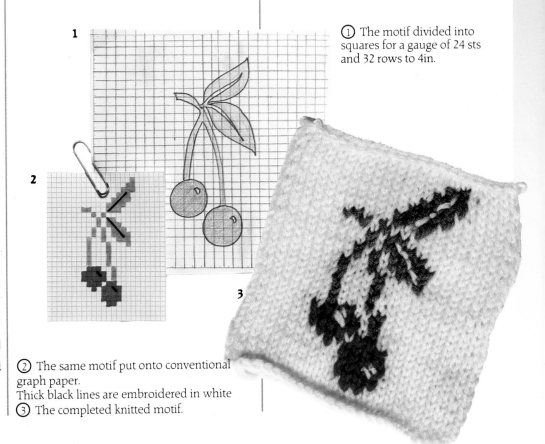

② The same motif put onto conventional graph paper.
Thick black lines are embroidered in white
③ The completed knitted motif.

OTHER MULTI-COLOR TECHNIQUES

Color can be introduced into texture or lace patterns in a variety of ways.

Cable in contrasting colors

Here only the cable is worked in two contrasting colors.

Lace worked in contrasting stripes

Here part of each pattern repeat is worked in contrasting colors.

① The motif divided into squares for a gauge of 24 sts and 32 rows to 4in.

DECORATIVE ACCESSORIES

KNITTED FABRICS can be decorated in the same way and using the same techniques as woven fabrics. However, because knitted fabric is so elastic, care should be taken to ensure that the fabric is not stretched out of shape or weighed down with too many heavy objects such as beads.

CORDS

Cords, made in a variety of ways, can be purely decorative or used as ties.

Crochet cord

Using a crochet hook and several strands of yarn, work a length of chain to the required length.

Twisted cord

Cut several lengths of yarn, each three times the required length of the cord. Place all these lengths together and knot each end. Attach one end to a fixed object, such as a hook in the wall, place a pencil or knitting needle through the other end, and begin to twist it, holding it taut. When the length is tightly twisted, carefully fold the cord in half. The cord will now twist back on itself, thus forming a firm double twisted cord. Knot both ends together and cut the folded ends to make a fringe.

Cotton reel cord

A cord made by this method is a narrow piece of tubular knitting. The width of the work will be related to the width of the hole through which it is formed and the number of stitches with which it is formed. For wider cords, other 'frames' must be found or made, but any cylindrical shape, into which nails can be fixed, is suitable. Shown here is the method of working a 5 stitch cord on a cotton reel.

① Fix 5 nails evenly around the center hole.
② Pass the end of yarn through the hole and hold on to it while 'casting on'.
③ Wind the yarn from left to right, around each nail in turn, pulling each 'loop' fairly taut.
④ When the 5 stitches have been cast on, wind yarn around the 1st nail again. Using a blunt needle, lift the first loop over the 2nd loop just formed and repeat this process continuously around the nails.
⑤ Pull the cord down as it emerges through the cotton reel, and continue working until the cord is the required length.
⑥ Bind off by placing the next loop to be worked onto the following nail, lift the 1st loop on this nail over the 2nd loop and repeat this process until one stitch is left. Break yarn and pass it through this last stitch.

Braided cords

Single strands of yarn can be braided together to form a braided cord.

BOBBLES

Bobbles are usually knitted into the garments as part of a stitch pattern. They can be added later if required.

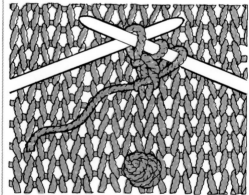

Insert a crochet hook through a stitch in the chosen position, pull through a loop of yarn, place this loop onto the left-hand needle, and proceed as follows: k1, p1, k1, all into the loop. Turn, p3, turn, sl1, k2tog, psso, break yarn and pass through last loop. Sew both ends of yarn firmly to wrong side of garment. Any size of bobble can be made in this manner.

POM POMS

These can also be used either as separate decorations or attached to the end of cords. Cut out two cardboard circles whose diameter is the same as that required for the pom pom. Cut a smaller circle in the center of each of these. Place the two circles together, and wind the yarn continuously around this 'frame', until the center hole is completed closed up ① . Cut around the outside edge of this shape, between the two layers of cardboard and separate the two cardboard circles a little ② . Tie a length of double yarn lightly round the middle of the pom pom and remove the cardboard ③

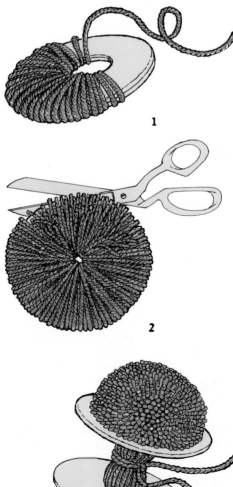

1

2

3

TASSELS

These can be used as separate decorations or attached to the end of cords. Cut a piece of cardboard the width of the length of the required tassel. Wind the yarn around this card. Thread the end of the yarn through a yarn needle and pass this under the threads at one end of the card①. Pull it up and tie tightly. Cut the threads at the other end. Wind the yarn tightly round the tassel near the folded end ② . Attach the tassel by sewing the folded end in the required position.

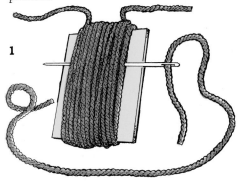

1

2

FRINGES

Fringes can be added to the edge of a garment using a crochet hook.

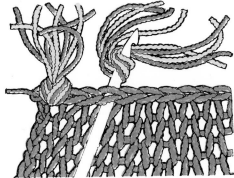

① Cut 2 or more lengths of yarn twice the required depth of the fringe. Insert the crochet hook through the edge of the fabric from the right side, fold the yarns in half and pull this folded end through the fabric, using the crochet hook. Pass the cut ends of the yarns through the loop.
② The fringe can also be worked by inserting the hook from the wrong side of the fabric.

EDGINGS

The edges of knitted garments are usually finished with ribbings, but occasionally it is necessary to finish the edge of a garment in a way that does not 'pull in'. Such alternative edgings can be either decorative or unobtrusive. Crochet is a popular method of finishing edges as there are many more suitable crochet edgings, than knitted ones. Edges can be finished with knitted hems (see page 43); with a very unobtrusive 'cast-on, bind-off' edge; or they can be piped, which looks decorative, especially when worked in a contrast color; or finished with a knitted lace edge.

Cast-on/bind-off edge

① Pick up stitches from right side of work, bind off on the next row knitwise.
② Pick up stitches from right side of work, bind off on the next row purlwise.

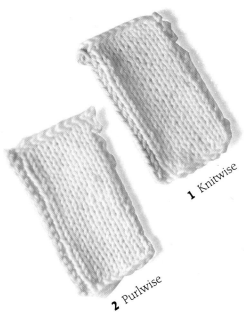

1 Knitwise

2 Purlwise

Piped edge

Pick up stitches from wrong side of work, starting with a knit row. Work in st st for 6 rows, bind off knitwise. Do not press, but let the edge roll up naturally.

There are a variety of knitted lace edgings that can be worked, one is shown here:

Knitted lace edging

Cast on 12 stitches
1st row: sl1, k1 tbl, yo, k1 (yo, sl1, k1, psso) × 3, k3.
2nd row: and all alt rows, purl.
3rd row: sl1; k1 tbl, yo, k3, (yo, sl1, k1, psso) × 3, k2.
5th row: sl1, k1 tbl, yo, k5, (yo, sl1, k1, psso) × 2, k3.
7th row: sl1, k1 tbl, yo, k7, (yo, sl1, k1, psso) × 2, k2.
9th row: sl1, k1, psso, k1, yo, sl1, k1, psso, k3, (k2tog, yo) × 2, k4.
11th row: sl1, k1, psso, k1, yo, sl1, k1, psso, k1, (k2tog, yo) × 3, k3.
13th row: sl1, k1, psso, k1, yo, sl1, k2tog, psso (yo, k2tog) × 2, yo, k4.
15th row: sl1, k1, psso, k2, (k2tog, yo), × 3, k3.
16th row: purl.
Rep rows 1-16 as necessary. Sew the straight edge of the lace to the edge of the garment.

Edges can also be finished with bought trims. These should be sewn on with sewing thread taking care not to stretch the knitted edge.

① Lace edging
② Woven braid edging
③ Piping
④ Edges laced with thonging

Objects attached to knitting should be sewn on with sewing thread, or the same yarn as that used for the main garment

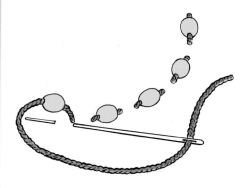

Beads

Knot the yarn and insert from wrong side of fabric to right side. Thread the bead onto the yarn, insert needle back through same hole, make a stitch slightly longer than the bead, then secure the bead by pulling the yarn firmly. Repeat the process for the correct number of beads.

Sequins

Knot the yarn and insert from wrong side of fabric to right side and through the middle of the sequin. Insert needle back through fabric to right of sequin, and bring it out to left of sequin. Insert needle back through center of sequin, and bring it out approximately the distance of half the diameter away to the left, passing it through a new sequin.

EMBROIDERY STITCHES

Embroidery can be worked onto knitted fabric in the same way as onto woven fabric. It is also possible to embroider a motif imitating the knitted stitches onto a knitted garment, making it look as though it has been knitted in. This process is known as duplicate stitching.

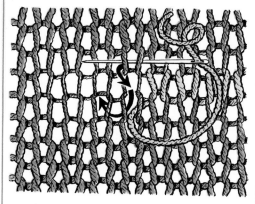

Duplicate stitch

Knot the yarn and pass through the fabric from back to front, emerging in the center of a stitch. Follow the direction of the stitch as shown in the diagram. Repeat this process over the required area.

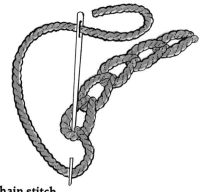

Chain stitch

Knot the yarn and pass from back to front of fabric. Make a loop of yarn, insert needle back into same hole, and make a small stitch emerging inside loop of yarn. Repeat from * for required amount.

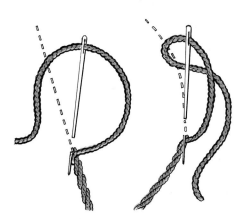

Stem stitch

Make a series of stitches at a slight angle, always keeping yarn to same side of needle when working.

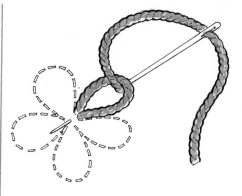

Lazy daisy

Work 1 chain stitch, insert needle back into fabric just outside chain and bring it back through the first hole. Make a new chain at an angle to the previous one. Repeat this process for the required number of 'petals'.

French knots

Knot the yarn and pass from back to front of the fabric.* Twist the yarn round the needle several times, then insert needle back into same hole. Fasten off or pass needle across back of work to next position prior to working another knot in the same manner.

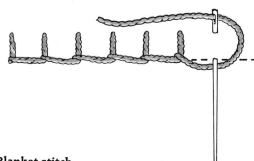

Blanket stitch

This is usually worked along an edge or around the edge of buttonholes. Knot the yarn and pass from back to front of fabric, about ¼in from edge. Take yarn around edge and re-insert through same hole from back to front. Pass needle under loop of yarn just made around edge. Insert needle from back to front through fabric, about ¼in away from first stitch and ¼in away from edge. Pass the needle under the stitch and repeat from * for length of edge.

APPLIQUE

Appliqué can be worked onto knitted fabric but should not be used to cover large areas of the work as it will then lose its elasticity. The appliqué shape should be cut out of contrasting knitted or woven fabric and attached in the required position on the garment by means of basting stitches. The edges should be sewn down, either by machine or hand embroidery stitches. Care must be taken not to stretch the fabric, thereby causing it to bubble, as this would be very unsightly.

An exuberant example of appliqué worked onto knitted fabric, by Kansai Yamamoto.

SMOCKING

Knitted fabric can be smocked in the same way as woven fabric. It has the added advantage that the gathering lines can be kept straight and in line by following the lines and rows of stitches. The knitting should be worked two or three times the width of the finished piece. When the work is gathered it should be pulled up to the required finished width. A variety of embroidered smocking stitches can now be worked onto the fabric. Knitted fabric made from thicker yarns is not suitable for smocking as the resulting work would be very thick and bulky.

Smocking worked on a sports yarn stockinette stitch fabric.

SECTION TWO
PATTERN WRITING

Knitting pattern instructions are usually given in written form, and are sometimes accompanied by a small chart showing the arrangement of colors. Alternatively, they can appear entirely in chart form if an overall color pattern is being worked into the knitting. Before you can create your own garments you need to know how to translate measured shapes into knitting. This section will show you how to do this and how to work garments to the design you desire. Almost any flat or three-dimensional shape can be worked in knitting. The more usual method is to work garments as flat pieces which are sewn together. Flat shapes can be translated into a written pattern by a simple mathematical process. All that is required is commonsense, a calculator and a gauge sample using the correct yarn, needles and stitch pattern.

SQUARES AND RECTANGLES

SQUARES AND RECTANGLES are the simplest shapes to translate into knitting patterns, as there is no need for any shaping.

THE SQUARE: Example 1

1. The gauge must be obtained. For this example the square is to be worked in a standard sports yarn with a plain stockinette stitch pattern. The gauge for this is 28 sts and 36 rows to 4in on No 3 needles.

The gauge over 1in square is required when working out the pattern and this is very easily obtained by dividing the figures given for the 4in square by 4. The gauge for this example now becomes: 2.8 sts and 3.6 rows to the inch.

2. The number of stitches to be cast on equals the measurement A-B in inches, multiplied by the number of stitches needed to work 1in. Thus: $2\frac{3}{4}$in × 7 sts = $19\frac{1}{4}$. Since it is not possible to cast on $\frac{1}{4}$ of a stitch, the number must be rounded up or down to the nearest whole number. In this case, it is rounded up to 20.

3. The number of rows to be knitted in order to obtain the correct depth of knitting is the measurement B-C in inches multiplied by the number of rows needed to work 1in. Thus: $2\frac{3}{4}$ × 9in = $24\frac{3}{4}$ rows. Again, the number of rows must be rounded up or down to the nearest whole number. In this case, it is rounded up to 25. Since the cast on and bind off rows each count as 1 row in depth, the number of rows actually worked is 23.

This pattern, when written down will be:

Using No 3 needles, cast on 20 sts and work in st st for 23 rows. Bind off on next row.

When noted down as a chart, this pattern will be as shown.

① Diagram of a $2\frac{3}{4}$in square which is to be interpreted as a knitting pattern.
② Each square represents 1 stitch and 1 row.

As more rows than stitches are required to form the same length of knitting, any color design or charted pattern will look very elongated when drawn on squared graph paper.
③ The completed knitted square.

Example 2 (not illustrated)

The written pattern for a square of 14in, when worked on No 6 needles in a yarn that has a gauge over stockinette stitch of 18 sts and 24 rows to 4in, will be:

Using No 6 needles, cast on 63 sts (that is: 14in × $14\frac{1}{2}$ sts) and work in st st for 82 rows (that is: 14in × 6 rows, less 2 rows for the cast on and bind off rows), bind off on next row.

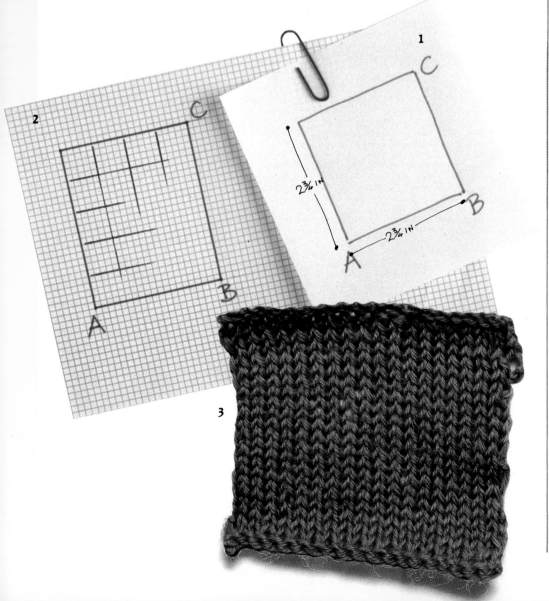

THE RECTANGLE

This is worked out in the same way as the square, but the width and height are different.

Example 1

① Diagram of a rectangle with a width of 2½in and a depth of 3¼in which is to be interpreted as a knitting pattern.

The written pattern for this rectangle, when worked on No 3 needles in a yarn that has a gauge over stockinette stitch of 28 sts and 36 rows to 4in, will be:

Using No 3 needles, cast on 17 sts (that is: 2½in × 7 sts rounded down to nearest whole number) and work in st st for 27 rows (that is: 3¼in × 9 rows, rounded down to nearest whole number, less 2 rows for the cast on and bind off rows), bind off on the next row.

When noted down as a chart, this pattern will be as shown below.

② Each square represents 1 stitch and 1 row.

③ The completed knitted rectangle.

USING STITCH PATTERNS

So far, all the examples have been given on the basis of working all the shapes in stockinette stitch. The basic pattern-writing techniques remain the same if a stitch pattern is to be used but there are one or two points to remember. A 4in gauge sample must be worked in the correct yarn and stitch pattern before starting to write the pattern, as different gauges are obtained for different types of stitch pattern. These differences can be generalized as follows:

(a) any stitch pattern that contains garter stitch or slipped stitches will have an increased number of rows for every inch of depth worked.

(b) any stitch pattern involving quite extensive use of vertical lines of knit and purl stitches (that is, ribbings), will pull in and thus require an increased number of stitches for every inch of width worked. Rib-style stitch patterns always pull in more over a larger area, so either work a large gauge sample or allow for this extra pulling in when measuring the gauge sample. These stitch patterns should be measured without stretching unless the garment is to fit very tightly.

(c) any stitch pattern containing eyelets will have fewer stitches for every inch of width worked.

Most stitch patterns are worked over a repeated number of stitches and rows. When working out the number of stitches to be cast on and the number of rows to be worked, these 'multiples' have to be taken into account. It is often impossible to obtain an exact measurement as the number of stitches and rows have to be rounded up or down to the nearest multiple required for that stitch pattern.

Stitch patterns need to be centralized so that the center of the stitch pattern falls at the center of the work. This is usually done by adding a few stitches at the end or the beginning of the row and working them to match the same number of stitches at the other edge. The number of rows worked may also need to be centralized in the same manner.

Example 1

A square of approximately 2¾in worked in three-color check, as shown on page 39.

Writing the pattern The gauge must be obtained. For this example, a standard knitting worsted yarn has been used. The gauge, when worked over the stitch pattern on No 5 needles, is 23 sts and 45 rows to 4in.

● It is necessary to know the number of stitches and rows (that is, the multiple) required to work one centralized pattern. For this example, the pattern has a multiple of 4 sts plus 3 extra sts, and 6 rows plus 2 extra rows.

● The number of stitches to be cast on is: 2¾in × 5.8 sts = 15.9 sts. This figure must be rounded up to the nearest multiple of 4, plus 3 extra stitches. So the number of stitches to be cast on is 15.

● The number of rows to be worked is: 2¾in × 11¼ rows = 31 rows. This figure must be rounded down to the nearest multiple of 6 plus 2 extra rows. So the number of rows to be worked is 32 rows, plus the cast on and bind off rows, that is, 34 rows.

When noted down in written form, this pattern will be:

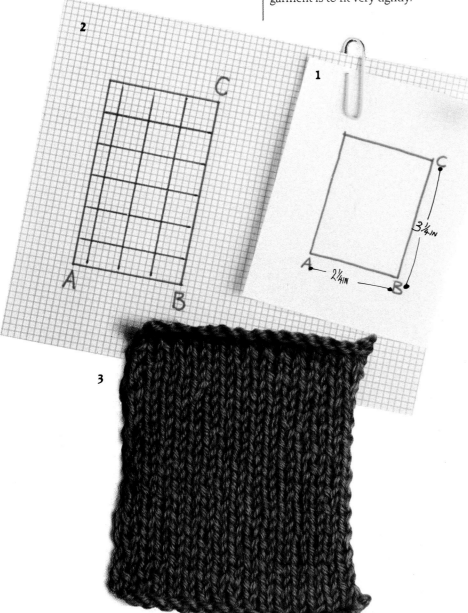

Using No 5 needles and col A, cast on 15 sts and work in three-color check pattern (see page 39) for 32 rows. Bind off on next row using col A.

When noted down as a chart, the pattern is worked out in a similar way to the previous squares. It is possible to indicate the working of a stitch pattern by means of symbols on this chart, but since it is an all-over repeat, this is not necessary, as the pattern can be attached to the chart in written form.

Example 2

① The completed knitted rectangle worked in raised triangles.

Writing the pattern

The written pattern for a rectangle of approximately 1½in wide by 5¼in deep when worked in raised triangles with a multiple of 6 sts and 6 rows, using standard sports yarn, on No 3 needles, which has a gauge over the pattern of 24 sts and 42 rows to 4in, will be:

Using No 3 needles, cast on 12 sts (that is: 1½in × 8½ sts, rounded down to the nearest multiple of 6 sts), and work in raised triangle pattern for 54 rows (that is: 5¼in × 10½ rows, rounded down to the nearest multiple of 6 rows), bind off on next row.

When noted down as a chart, the pattern will be worked out in the same way as the previous examples. Again, it is possible to indicate the stitch pattern by means of symbols on the chart.

CREATING SQUARE & RECTANGULAR HOLES IN A PIECE OF KNITTING

So far, instructions have been given for the creation of measured squares or rectangles in knitting, but it is also possible to create a measured square or rectangular hole in a piece of knitting.

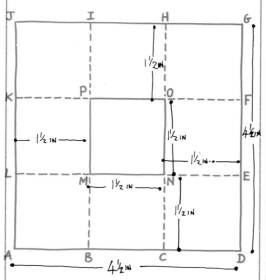

Example 1

Diagram of a 4¾in square with a centrally placed 1½in square hole, which is to be interpreted as a knitting pattern.

Writing the pattern

● Write the pattern as though the piece of work were made up of several rectangles.
● Firstly, write the pattern for the rectangle ADEL, with the last row as a partially bound off row as follows.

Last row: (divide the number of stitches into three sections, taking into account the size of each section). Work across the first section of stitches, bind off the central section of stitches; work across the last section of stitches.
● Work on the last section of stitches, the required number of rows to obtain the depth EF. Break the yarn and rejoin to the first section of stitches; work the same number of rows on this section of stitches.
● Break the yarn and rejoin to edge of work. Work across first section of stitches, cast on the same number of stitches as were originally cast off, then work across the last section of stitches. Continue working on all the stitches until the number of rows required to obtain the depth FG (counting the row with cast-on stitches as one row) has been worked.
● If this shape is to be worked in a stitch pattern, it is very important that the same number of rows are worked on each side of the hole. So that the pattern remains continuous when the next complete row is worked.

Obviously the hole can be worked into any shape piece of knitting and can be of any size. This sort of hole is sometimes used to form a neckline in poncho-type garments.

A selection of building blocks, worked in different colors, stitch patterns and yarn thickness.

BUILDING BLOCK PROJECT: CUBES

Method 1

These blocks are made from 6 separate squares of the same size. They can be worked in any yarn, any stitch pattern and any color. Work them as follows:

● Choose the yarn, stitch pattern and needle size, and work a gauge sample.

● Work out the written pattern for the square (see page 48).

● Knit the square according to the pattern you have written.

● For the remaining squares, either use this same pattern and yarn, or repeat the pattern-writing process for each square. Sew the squares together leaving last part of last seam open, insert washable stuffing, then close seam.

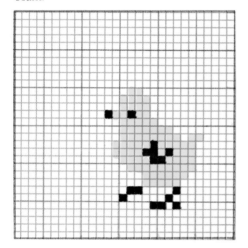

The square can be noted down in chart form. Here it is a shown for a standard knitting worsted yarn with a motif design worked into it.

Method 2

The same block can be worked using only one piece of knitting.

Below is a diagram showing the shape required for a 3¼ square block. Dotted lines are fold lines.

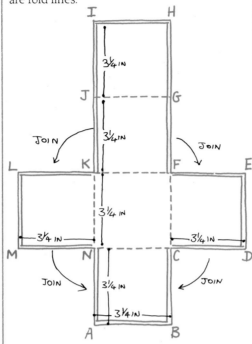

To finish join seams as indicated by arrows then join IJ to LM, HG to ED, and IH to AB.

Working out the pattern

● Seam allowances of 1 stitch or 1 row must be allowed around all the edges to be seamed together, as shown in the diagram.

● Starting at AB, cast on the number of stitches and work the number of rows required to form the square ABCN.

● At the beginning of the next 2 rows, cast on the number of stitches required to obtain the widths CD and MN. Continue on these stitches for the depth DE.

● Bind off the number of stitches previously cast on over the next 2 rows.

● Continue on these stitches for the depth FH. Bind off.

● Sew up as shown in the diagram, but leave one seam partially open. Insert washable stuffing, then close the seam.

The same design can be worked using various stitch patterns or color designs but, to avoid difficulties when writing the pattern, each of the stitch patterns should have a very similar gauge. It is possible to adjust the number of stitches between each section by working increases or decreases across the first and last rows of each section. So stitch patterns with different stitch gauges can be used. But it is not so easy to adjust stitch patterns that have different numbers of rows if they are to be worked next to each other in the same row (for example: the three squares that form the rectangle MDEL should all have the same row gauge).

SIMPLE SHAPES

IN ORDER TO WORK the shapings for an angled slope, the required number of increases or decreases must be spaced in an even manner so that the slope has a smooth edge. The method of working these shapings is best demonstrated by means of examples based on various types of triangles.

THE BASIC TRIANGLE: Example 1
This triangle has an angled slope that decreases by 5in over a height of 10in.

Writing the pattern 1. The gauge must be obtained. For this example, the triangle is to be worked in a standard knitting worsted yarn with a plain stockinette stitch pattern. The gauge for this is 24 sts and 30 rows to 4in on No 5 needles.
2. Knitting is to start at the line AB (although it could be started at any of the points of the triangle or any of the straight lines of the triangle). So the number of stitches to be cast on is 30 sts (that is 5in × 6 sts).
3. The depth of the knitting is the depth of the line AC, so the total number of rows to be worked is 75 rows (that is: 10in × 7½ rows).
4. It can be seen from the diagram that all the stitches cast on at AB have to be decreased over the depth AC. Therefore, 30 sts have to be decreased over 70 rows. (In this example the cast-on row forms an extra row.) To find out how many rows have to be worked between each decrease, divide the number of rows to be worked by the number of stitches to be decreased, as follows: 75 rows ÷ 30 sts = 2.5 rows. So 2.5 rows have to be worked between each decrease, but since this figure is not a whole number, it has to be multiplied up to the nearest whole number, and the number by which it was multiplied is the number of stitches to be decreased over the resulting number of rows. Thus: 2.5 rows × 2 = 5 rows. Therefore 2 stitches have to be decreased over every 5 rows, so let us say that the decreases should be worked at the shaped edge of every 3rd and 5th row.
     When noted down in written form, this pattern will be:

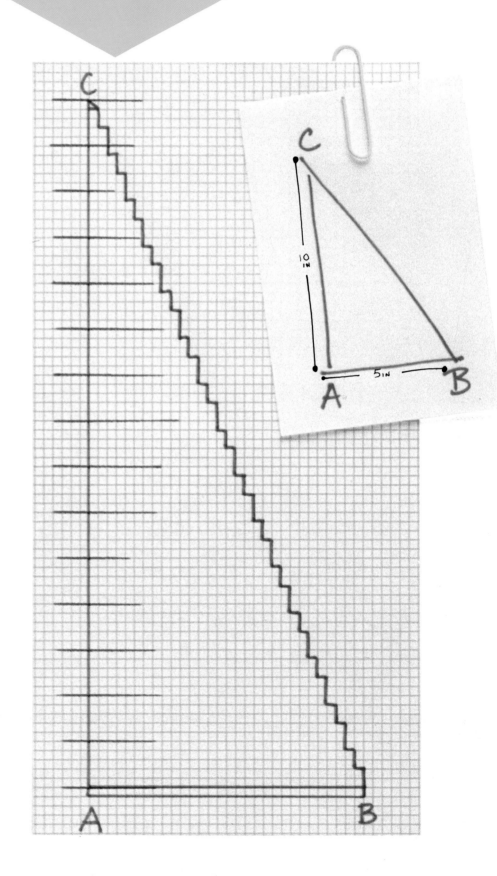

● Using No 5 needles, cast on 30 sts and work in st st, decreasing 1 st at the right-hand edge only of every foll 3rd and 5th row, until all the stitches have been decreased. Fasten off.

Below left and right: In these charts each square represents 1 stitch and 1 row. It can be seen clearly from them that it is necessary to have the same number of rows between each decrease so that the slope remains as smooth as possible.

Example 2
This is the same triangle with the same dimensions as Example 1 but worked from point C (see below).

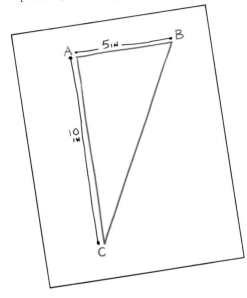

Writing the pattern The pattern for this triangle is written following the same method as for example 1, but the shapings are worked as increases rather than decreases.

When noted down in written form, this pattern will be:
● Using No 5 needles, cast on 1 st and work in st st, increasing 1 st at right-hand edge only of every foll 3rd and 5th rows, until there are 30 sts. Bind off on next row.

Example 3
The triangle with 2 angled slopes, each decreasing by 5in over a height of 10in.

Writing the pattern The 2 angled slopes of this triangle each decrease at the same rate, so shapings can be worked identically at both edges.
1. Calculate the instructions for the triangle BCD, following the methods shown for example 1; here the instructions and gauge given for example 1 are used.
2. Since AB is the same measurement as BC, the number of cast-on stitches is doubled and the decreases calculated for the triangle BCD are worked at both edges, thus decreasing double the number of stitches.
When noted down in written form, the pattern will be:

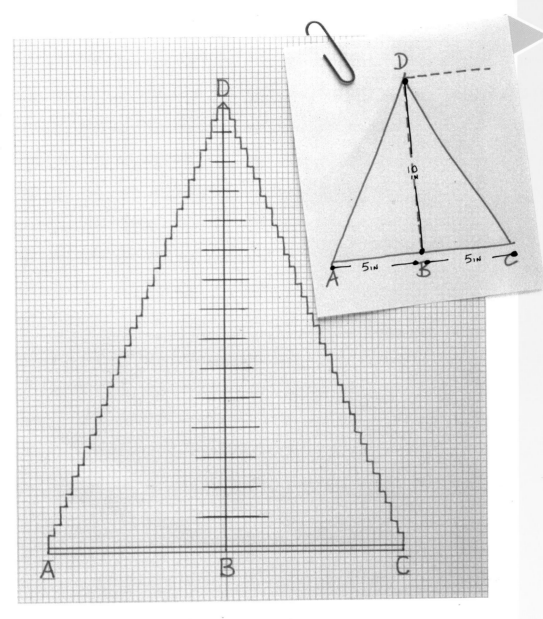

● Using No 5 needles, cast on 60 sts and work in st st, decreasing 1 st at both edges of every foll 3rd and 5th row, until all the stitches have been decreased (working the last 2 decreases as k2tog, then fasten off).

When noted down in chart form, the pattern will be as shown overleaf.

If the triangle is turned upside down so that the knitting starts at the point, it should be started by casting on 2 stitches and then the increases are worked at both edges as in example 2. When writing patterns for triangles that begin or end with a point, it is better to adjust the number of stitches to an odd number, so that the work can be started or finished with one stitch.

ACUTE TRIANGLES For angled slopes that increase or decrease very rapidly, casting on or binding off must be used. It is possible to work cast-on and bind-off stitches at the end of a row by using a separate length of yarn (and with bulky yarns, this is necessary). But it is more usual to work these cast-on or bind-off shapings at the beginning of a row, adjusting the pattern accordingly.

WHOLE NUMBERS To calculate the number of rows between increases or decreases for an angled slope, the number of rows for the depth must be divided by the number of stitches to be increased or decreased. However, all too often you will be left wondering what to do about the imposing array of numbers after the decimal point, making it difficult to multiply it up to the nearest whole number. It is not necessary to be totally mathematically accurate about this, and indeed it is not possible to be. The number should be rounded down to the nearest half and then treated as shown in example 1. Any extra rows needed to make up the required depth can be added at the beginning of the work, before starting the shapings, at the end, or at any point in between, but for the purposes of noting patterns in written form, it is easier to add these extra rows before or after shaping.

Example 4

In this example, the triangle has an angled slope that decreases by 10in over a height of 5in.

Writing the pattern 1. The gauge must be obtained. For this example, the triangle is worked in a standard knitting worsted yarn with a plain stockinette stitch pattern. The gauge for this is 24 sts and 30 rows to 4in on No 5 needles.
2. Knitting is to start at the line AB, so the number of stitches to be cast on is 60 (that is: 10in × 6 sts).
3. The depth of the knitting is the depth of the line AC, so the total number of rows to be worked is 38 (that is: 5in × 7½ rows, rounded up to the nearest whole number).
4. Therefore, 60 stitches have to be decreased over 38 rows (counting the cast-on and bind-off rows as an extra row). When 38 rows are divided by 60 stitches, the answer is less than one, from which it can be deduced that the stitches must be decreased at a faster rate than one decrease for every row. To find out how many stitches must be decreased on every row, divide the number of stitches by the number of rows as follows: 60 sts ÷ 38 rows = 1.57 sts (forget all the extra numbers after 1.5, as the number of rows can be adjusted later). So 1.5 sts have to be bound off at the left edge only of every row. But, since stitches are only bound off at the beginning of a row, the shapings can only be worked on every alternate row, so 3 stitches will be bound off on every alternate row. When this is done 19 times so that 38 rows have been worked, you will still have 3 extra stitches to bind off, which can be worked over the next 2 rows, which means that you will then have worked 40 rows plus the cast-on row. If it is important that no more than 38 rows are worked, the 3 extra stitches can be decreased one by one at three equal points over the depth of the work, either by binding off 4 instead of 3 stitches at the beginning of a row, or by decreasing 1 stitch at the end of an unshaped row.

The pattern (over 40 rows) when noted down in written form will be:
● Using No 5 needles, cast on 60 sts and work in st st, starting with a purl row (so that the beginning of the next alt row from the cast-on row is at the right-hand edge of the st st fabric), and bind off 3 sts at beg of every foll alt row, 20 times in all. Fasten off.

Example 5

It can be seen when looking at the chart that this slope will be made up of several small steps so that the edge is not smooth. An edge like this will usually be enclosed within a seam and the unevenness will not be problem. It is, however, possible to write the pattern making use of the technique of partial knitting as shown on page 29, so that the edge remains smooth. (In this method, instead of binding off the edge stitches they are simply not worked.) The pattern for this method of working the triangle, in example 1, will be as follows:

Using No 5 needles, cast on 60 sts and work as follows:
1st row: purl to last 3 sts, yf, sl1, yb, return sl st to LN, turn work.
2nd row: knit to end.
3rd row: purl to last 6 sts, yf, sl1, yb, return sl st to LN, turn work.
4th row: knit to end.

Cont working in this manner, each time leaving 3 more unworked sts at the end of every purl row, until only 3 stitches have been worked. Bind of all 60 stitches on next purl row.

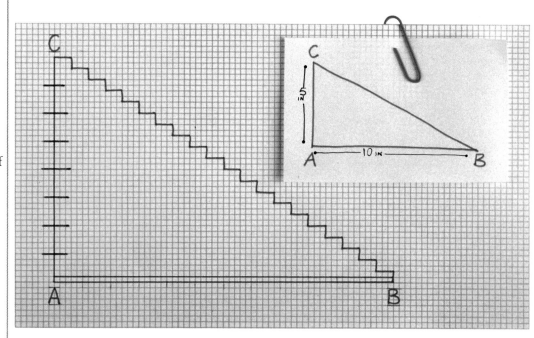

Example 4

The triangle worked by binding off on every alternate row (top) and by means of partial knitting.

USING STITCH PATTERNS The basic principles for using stitch patterns when writing knitting patterns are shown in the section on squares and rectangles (see page 48). These principles remain the same when working increased and decreased sections of work, but it is usually left to the knitter to adjust the stitch pattern while working shapings and not written down in the pattern. Always remember that the stitch pattern should remain continuous over the main part of the garment. Any stitches that are increased should be worked in pattern as far as possible and any decreases should affect only the pattern repeat nearest the shaped edge of the work. It is especially important when working stitch patterns that make use of increases and decreases not to confuse the increases or decreases necessary for the stitch pattern, with the increases or decreases necessary for the shapings. For this reason, every knitter should understand the formation of the stitch pattern being worked before embarking on any shaped sections of the work.

Other odd shapes

① ② ③ A variety of shapes that can all be translated into knitting patterns by converting them into separate rectangles and right-angle triangles. The measurements needed are those shown by the letters A-Z. The different colors show the separate sections.

④ Any shape can be worked as a 'hole' following the principles already given. The 'hole' here is marked with a broken line.

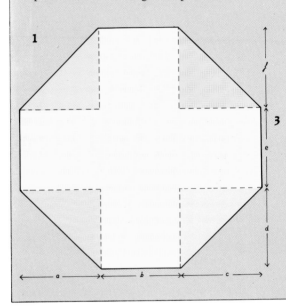

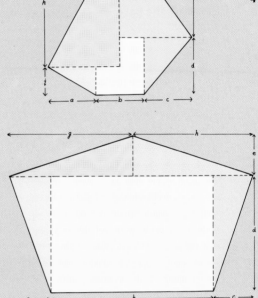

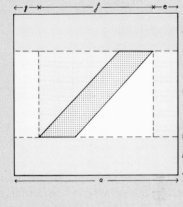

Example 6

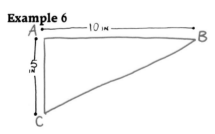

This is the same triangle worked from the point C.

Writing the pattern You should by now be able to write this pattern using the previous example as reference as it is the same, but worked using cast-on increases rather than bound-off decreases. It is also possible to work this edge by means of partial knitting, in which case all 60 stitches would be cast on, the first 2 rows would only be worked over the first 3 stitches, the second 2 rows would be worked over the first 6 stitches, and so on. When all 60 stitches have been worked, bind off.

If a triangle is to be worked so that both sides of the work have a sharply shaped edge (with both edges sloping at the same rate, as in example 3 on page 53), then the cast-on or bound-off stitches will be worked at the beginning of every row so that the shaping is the same at both edges.

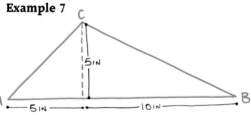

The triangle worked by casting on the extra stitches on every alternate row (top) and by partial knitting (below).

ODD TRIANGLES Triangles come in all shapes and sizes as do garments, and they do not always have similar shaping at both edges.

Example 7

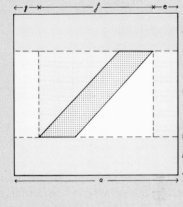

This triangle has a right-hand slope that decreases by 10in over a height of 5in while the left edge only decreases by 5in over the same height.

Writing the pattern The pattern for this triangle is written as though it were 2 right-angled triangles, following the instructions for each triangle as in the examples on the previous pages. When the pattern is noted down in written form, these 2 sets of instructions must be combined to form one set of instructions as follows:

Using No 5 needles and standard knitting worsted yarn, cast on 90 sts and work in st st, decreasing 1 st at left edge of every row, except every 4th row, and at the same time bind off 3 sts at beg of every alt row (at right-hand edge). Continue in this manner until all the sts have been decreased. Fasten off.

Any triangular shape or angled slope can be worked out in this manner; by treating it as a separated right-angled triangle. To create a right-angled triangle, draw a straight horizontal line at the lowest point of the slope and a vertical line down through this horizontal line from the highest point of the slope, thus forming a triangle which can then easily be translated into a knitting pattern, and incorporated into the main pattern.

Sometimes two identical angled slopes are found on either side of a larger shape, e.g. the raglan seams of a sweater. In this case, when translating the shape into a knitting pattern, the shape is divided into segments with triangles at the edges and a rectangle in the center and each section is then calculated separately and brought together in the final written or charted instruction.

Example 8

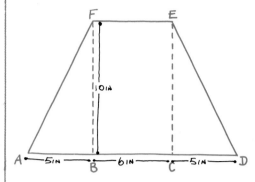

This shape is made up of a central rectangle BCEF and two triangles, ABF and CDE.

Writing the pattern 1. The gauge must be obtained. In this example, the same gauge is used as in the examples on the previous pages. 2. The instructions for the triangle CDE are calculated, as shown in example 1 on page 51. 3. Since the triangle ABF is a mirror image of the triangle CDE, the same instructions can be used, but working the decreases at the left edge instead of the right edge. 4. The pattern for the rectangle BCEF is calculated as shown on pages 48-49.

When noted down in written form, the pattern will be:

Using No 5 needles, cast on 96 sts (that is the total number of stitches for all 3 sections), and work in st st, decreasing 1 st at both edges of every foll 3rd and 5th row until 36 sts remain. Bind off. (In this example the cast-on and bound-off rows count as 2 extra rows.)

BUILDING BLOCK PROJECT: PYRAMIDS

Building blocks can be made, based on the triangle shape. To make them, work out a pattern for a triangle with three sides of equal length. You will need four of these triangles to form a single triangular block or four triangles and one square, where the sides are both the same. Try working out the same pattern using a variety of stitch patterns or color patterns. The triangle can also be worked in one piece, as shown here.

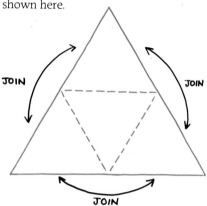

Each of the dotted lines is a fold line. All of the sides of each small triangle measure the same.

Below: A selection of triangular building bricks. **1-4,** Four triangles and a square sewn together; **5-6,** Triangle worked in one piece.

CURVED SHAPES

MOST GARMENT SHAPES consist not only of rectangles and angled slopes but also of curved shapes. There are no simple-to-follow rules for writing patterns for curved shapes as the increases or decreases must vary in rate for each section of the curve.

THE SEMI-CIRCLE:

Writing the pattern The pattern for any curved shape is easier if it is treated in triangular segments, although the resulting knitted shape will, of course, be slightly angular. On the whole, the more segments the curve is divided into, the more circular will be the end result. For this example, the two halves of the semi-circle are each divided into three segments, and from each of the dividing points on the circular line, a horizontal and a vertical line must be drawn. You will then have three triangular segments in each half of the semi-circle (assuming that the curved line is treated as though it were straight). The segments do not have to be drawn very precisely or accurately, provided that the sum total of all the depths of each segment is not more or less than the total depth, and the sum total of all the widths of each segment is not more or less than the total width.

1. The gauge must be obtained. For this example, the semi-circle is to be worked in a standard knitting worsted yarn with a plain stockinette stitch pattern. The gauge for this is 24 sts and 30 rows to 4in on No 5 needles.

2. Knitting starts at B, the total number of cast-on stitches is 14 (that is, the line AC, which is 2¼in × 2.4 sts), the total number of rows for the depth AB is 18 (that is: 2¼in × 3.0 rows).

3. The number of stitches to be cast on and the number of rows to be worked in each segment are:

   a)   The segment BIE has 6 sts cast on over 4 rows.

   b)   The segment IJM has 5 sts cast on over 6 rows.

   c)   The segment JCN has 3 sts cast on over 8 rows.

Therefore, the total number of stitches cast on over these 3 sections is 14, and the total number of rows over which they are cast on is 18. Decreases are made over the remaining segments as follows:

   d)   The segment NCK has 3 sts bound off over 8 rows.

   e)   The segment OKL has 5 sts bound off over 6 rows.

   f)   The segment HLD has 6 sts bound off over 4 rows.

Therefore, the total number of stitches bound off over these 3 sections is 14; the total number of rows over which they are bound off is 18.

When noted down in written form, this pattern will be:

Using No 5 needles, cast on 3 sts and work in st st as follows:

Work 1 row, then cast on 3 sts at beg of next row, work 1 row, then work 5 rows, increasing 1 st at shaped edge of every row, work 1 row, then inc 1 st at shaped edge of next and every foll 3rd row until there are

14 sts. Work 4 rows, then dec 1 st at shaped edge of next and every foll 3rd row until there are 11 sts, work 1 row, then dec 1 st at shaped edge of next 5 rows, bind off 3 sts at beg of next and foll alt row.

It is far easier and more accurate to write the pattern for any curved section of a garment using the charted method because you can see what you are doing and amend the shape so that it is properly curved. It is a good idea to draw out these curved sections on graph paper, even when expressing the pattern in written form, and then translate them back into written form.

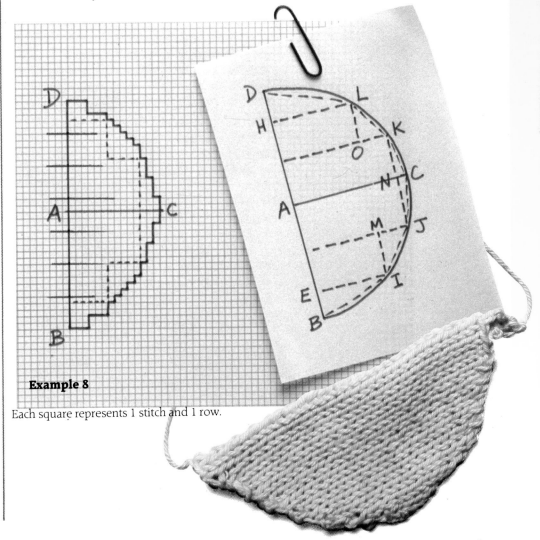

Example 8

Each square represents 1 stitch and 1 row.

The completed knitted semi-circle.

THE COMPLETE CIRCLE This is worked as the semi-circle, but all the shapings given are worked at both edges.

THE ARC There are times when a piece of shaped knitting is required to be worked in such a way that the lines of stitches follow the curve of the work. This can be done by means of partial knitting (see page 29).

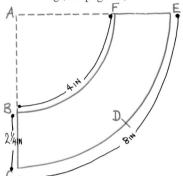

The ARC. Ordinarily this would be worked either by starting at the line BC or at the point D, and increasing or decreasing at each edge to form the shaping.

Writing the pattern 1. The gauge must be obtained. For this example, a standard knitting worsted yarn is used, with a plain stockinette stitch pattern. This has a gauge of 24 sts and 30 rows to 4in, on No 5 needles.
2. Knitting starts at the line BC which is 2¼in long, so the number of stitches to be cast on is 14.
3. The required length of the knitting at both edges must be worked out as a number of rows. So the number of rows required to work the length CE is 60 (that is: 8in × 3.0 rows).
4. This means that twice the number of rows have to be worked at the right-hand edge than at the left-hand edge. Partial knitting can only be worked over a multiple of 4 rows (that is: 2 rows of partial knitting and 2 rows across all the sts). If you divide the 60 rows by this multiple of 4, you will find out how many of these groups of 4 rows will be worked. This is 15.
5. The shape will be very uneven if you always partially knit the same number of stitches so, since 15 is easily divisible by 3, it is a good idea to work the partial knitting over 3 different amounts of stitches. Divide the number of cast-on stitches into 4 nearly equal groups and then work the partial knitting, first over the first group of stitches only, then over the first and second groups, then over the first, second and third groups, each time working across all the stitches on the needle for the 2 rows in between.

When noted down in written form, this pattern will be:

Using No 5 needles, cast on 14 sts and work in st st as follows:
1st row: knit across all sts.
2nd row: purl across all sts.
3rd row: knit 4 sts, sl next st, yb, return sl st to LN, turn work.

4th row: purl to end.
5th & **6**th rows: as 1st and 2nd rows.
7th row: knit 7 sts, yf, sl next st, yb, return sl st to LN, turn work.
8th row: purl to end.
9th & **10**th rows: as 1st and 2nd rows.
11th row: knit 10 sts, yf, sl next st, yb, return sl st to LN, turn work.
12th row: purl to end.
Rep rows 1-12, four more times, then bind off on next row across all stitches.
This type of pattern is not suited to the charted form of pattern writing.

The completed knitted arc.

BUILDING BLOCK PROJECT: SPHERES
Building blocks can be made using curved shapes as part of their construction.

The semi-circle Work 2 identical semi-circles, measure all round the edge, work a piece of straight knitting the length of this measurement and to any width required, eg, the width could be the same as the width of the other building blocks. Sew together, leaving one seam partially open, insert washable wadding, then close the seam.

The column Work 2 identical circular shapes and one straight length, long enough to fit around the circumference. Sew the cast-on and bound-off edges of the strip together, then sew a circle into the opening at each end. Sew together, leaving one seam partially open, insert washable wadding, then close the seam.

The ball A knitted ball can be made from a number of shaped pieces (all identical) as shown below:

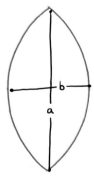

a = half the circumference
b = the circumference divided by the number of segments

THREE-DIMENSIONAL SHAPES
So far, all the instructions given have been based on working flat pieces of knitting. It is also possible to knit three-dimensional shapes by working increases or decreases in the middle of a row. Round yokes and various types of hats are usually worked in this way.

The triangular building block This can be worked either from the point or from the base.

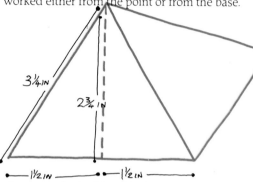

The triangular building block. Each side has the same measurement.

Writing the pattern 1. Calculate the instructions for 1 triangle (see page 52). The base triangle is knitted separately from this pattern.
Don't forget that the height, and therefore the calculation for the number of rows, is different from the length of a side. You may need to draw a 'template' in order to obtain a triangle with three sides of equal length.
2. The three 'walls' of the shape are knitted in one piece on a set of 4 needles and the shapings are worked, 2 together, at 3 regular intervals around the work, each time placing the double increase or decrease in a direct line with the previous one.

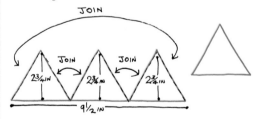

The decreases for this shape are worked in the position of the dotted lines, one decrease in the position of each dotted line across the round. Because the dotted lines are next to each other, two decreases (or a double decrease) are worked at each of three points across the row.

Right: A variety of curved shapes. **1,** Ball made from either segments; **2-3,** Three-dimensional ball; **4,** Three-dimensional circle; **5,** Column; **6,** Semi-circle.

When noted down in written form, this pattern will be:

Using knitting worsted yarn and No 5 needles, cast on 60 sts (place 20 sts on each of 3 needles) and work 1 row in st st, cont in st st (that is, knit every row) and work shapings as follows:

1st dec row: *k8, double dec (sl next 2 sts knitwise, k1, then pass the 2 sl sts over this st), k9, rep from * to end of round. Cont to dec in this manner on every alt round, each time placing the group of 3 dec sts centrally over the previous dec. When 6 sts remain, 1 row then k2tog, across next row, 1 row, then k3tog. Fasten off. Sew the base triangle to the cast-on edge matching the points to the lines of decreases. Stuff the shape with washable wadding.

Note: Three-dimensional patterns are not suited to writing in charted form. If this is necessary, it could be drawn on graph paper as three flat triangles joined to each other at the base.

The triangle can also be worked starting at the point with 1 stitch and increasing instead of decreasing.

THE BALL

Writing the pattern The pattern is written in a very similar way to the three-dimensional triangle; this is, based on the pattern for the ball in a number of sections.

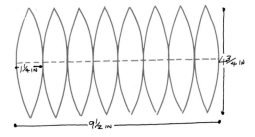

A ball in 8 sections 1. Calculate the instructions for 1 section of the work.
2. The work is started on 4 needles with 1 stitch. Double increases and decreases are worked in line with each other at 8 equal points around the work at the rate given for the pattern for one segment.

When noted down in written form, this pattern will be:

Using knitting worsted yarn and a set of No 5 needles, cast on 2 sts, inc twice in 1st row, and place 1 st on 2 needles, and 2 sts on the 3rd needles. Cont in rounds of st st, as follows:
1st row: inc in each st (8 sts).
2nd row: inc in each st (16 sts).
3rd row: *k1, inc in next st, rep from * to end (24 sts).
Work 3 rows without shaping.
7th row: *inc in next 2 sts, k1, rep from * to end (40 sts).
Work 3 rows without shaping.
11th row: *inc in next 2 sts, k3, rep from * to end (56 sts).
Work 3 rows without shaping.
14th row: *inc in next 2 sts, k5, rep from * to end (72 sts).
Work 8 rows without shaping.
23rd row: *[k2tog] x 2, k5, rep from * to end (56 sts).
Work 3 rows without shaping.
27th row: *[k2tog] x 2, k2, rep from * to end (40 sts).
Work 3 rows without shaping.
31st row: *[k2tog] x 2, k1, rep from * to end (24 sts).
Work 3 rows without shaping.
35th row: *k2tog, k1, rep from * to end (16 sts).
Now insert washable stuffing then cont as follows:
36th row: *k2tog, rep from * to end (8 sts).
37th row: *k2tog, rep from * to end (4 sts).
38th row: [k2tog] x 2 (2 sts).
39th row: k2tog. Fasten off.

Note The increases and decreases can be worked across the row at any point on that row, not necessarily in line with the previous decreases, provided that they are evenly spaced. (A better spherical shape is obtained if they are not placed in line with each other.)

THE CIRCLE A circular shape can be made either by starting at the inside edge and decreasing until there are no stitches, or by starting with one stitch and increasing to the required size. In this case, the circle must be drawn to the correct size or to scale, and increases or decreases worked to obtain to the circumferences of a number of circles drawn within the circle. The number of rows between each increase or decrease row should be the required number of rows for the depth between each circle drawn on the diagram. This is shown in the diagram below.

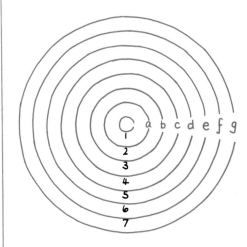

• The circles a-g are measured and increases or decreases made to correspond to each successive measurement.

• These increase or decrease rows are spaced according to the depths 1-7 which may or may not be all the same depth, as required.

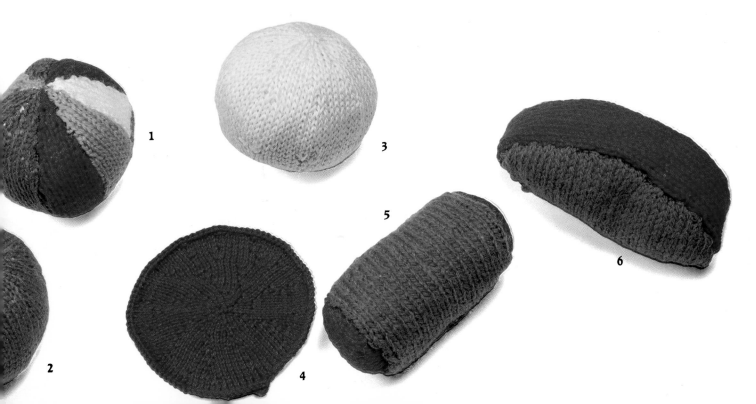

1

2

3

4

5

6

ALL ABOUT GARMENTS

GARMENTS ARE MADE from shaped pieces of knitting and now that you have learned all the skills necessary to calculate knitting patterns for any shape, writing the patterns for garments should present no difficulty provided that you have all the necessary measurements.

Measurements for a basic round-neck sweater with set-in sleeves are given in the charts below. These measurements are for a well-fitting sweater of medium length, to be worked in knitting worsted yarn. If the same garment were to be worked in a thicker yarn, the actual measurement would need to be more than 2 inches larger than the 'to fit' size and all the other measurements altered in proportion. The same garment in slightly finer yarn could have less than 2 inches added to the 'to fit' size. Garments always have this extra amount added to the 'to fit' size unless they are meant to be very bodyhugging, in which case they would probably be worked in a ribbed stitch pattern.

2. *Garments with set-in sleeves* These are usually well-fitted, but can have any style of neckline.
3. *Raglan-sleeve garments* A raglan seam is one where the armhole seam extends from the underarm point to the neckline. Most styles of neckline can be worked with this type of garment.
4. *Dolman-sleeve garments* These garments have sleeves knitted together with the body so that they have no armhole seams.

5. *Round-yoked garments* These garments usually have the yoke knitted in one piece with no seams. All the stitches across the sleeves and body pieces are picked up and worked for the depth of the yoke, making decreases so that it fits.

You will find out next how to write knitting patterns for each of these styles of garment.

CHILDREN'S MEASUREMENTS

Age	3 yrs	6 yrs	8 yrs	10 yrs	12 yrs	14 yrs	
To fit size chest	22	24	26	28	30	32	in
Actual chest	24	26	28	39	32	34	in
Length from back neck	13½	15½	17½	19½	21½	23¼	in
Armhole depth	5¼	6	6¾	7¼	7¼	7½	in
Back neck width	4½	4½	4¾	5	5¼	5½	in
Across chest	8¾	9	9½	9¾	10	10¾	in
Sleeve seam	10	11¼	12½	14¾	16¾	17¼	in
Round top of arm	9½	9¾	10	10	11¼	12½	in
Wrist	4½	4¾	4¾	5	5½	6½	in

LADIES' MEASUREMENTS

To fit size bust	30	32	34	36	38	40	in
Actual bust	32	34	36	38	40	42	in
Length from back neck	22½	23¼	24¾	25½	26½	26½	in
Armhole depth	7¼	7½	7½	8	8½	8¾	in
Back neck width	5½	5½	6½	6½	7¼	7¼	in
Across chest	12	12½	13¼	13½	14½	15¼	in
Sleeve seam	17¼	17¾	17¾	18½	18½	18¾	in
Round top of arm	12	13¼	13	14¾	15¼	15½	in
Wrist	6½	6¾	7¼	7½	8	8½	in

MEN'S MEASUREMENTS

To fit chest	36	38	40	42	44	46	in
Actual chest	38	40	42	44	46	48	in
Length from back neck	26½	26½	27¼	27¼	28	28½	in
Armhole depth	8½	8¾	9	9½	10	11¼	in
Back neck width	6½	7¼	7¼	7½	7½	8	in
Across chest	13	15¼	16	16¾	17½	18½	in
Sleeve seam	18¾	18¾	19¼	19½	19½	19½	in
Round top of arm	15¼	15½	16	16½	16¾	17	in
Wrist	7¼	8	8½	8¾	9	9½	in

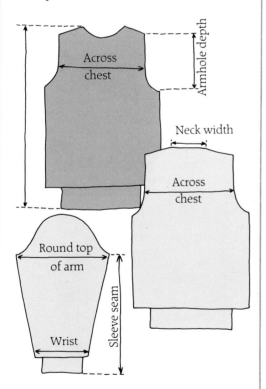

Garments come in a variety of shapes and sizes but they fall into five main groups:
1. *Square-shaped garments* These garments have little or no shaping.

Writing patterns for garments *(made from squares or rectangles)* Garments can be made entirely from square or rectangular shapes. They are knitted either in one piece or in several pieces sewn together. Writing the patterns for these garments is very simple and the resulting pattern is usually very easy to knit. These simply-shaped garments are mainly used for over-garments

SIMPLE SHAPES

Once the required measurements are known, the pattern for any of these shapes can be written according to the instructions given for the basic square or rectangle (see pages 48 to 51). A slight amount of shaping can then be added, if desired, to provide a better fit.

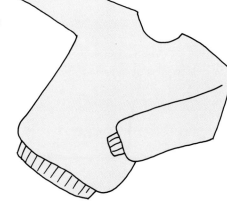

The garment can be worked in one piece, starting at the hem or the cuff, or it can be worked in several pieces, placing the seams wherever desired. The neckline can be any shape. The armhole depth needs to be deeper than that given for the set-in sleeve sweater.

Adding a rounded neckline. With ribbed cuffs and hems, this garment will be fairly well-fitted: easy to translate into a knitting pattern, easy to knit, and easy to wear.

A tabard is made from two rectangles sewn or tied together at the shoulders and side seams. It can also be worked in one piece with a slit like a large horizontal buttonhole, worked for the neck.

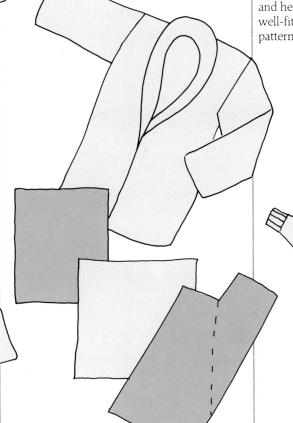

Sleeves can be added to the tabard shape by casting on extra stitches at both edges. The addition of a ribbed band worked at the cuff or hem will give the garment a better fit.

A wrap-over jacket with shawl collar can be made from very simple shapes.

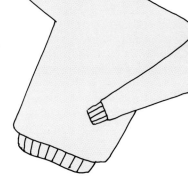

A garment with shaped sleeves is more suitable for men or boys than a garment with wide sleeves. The shaping on the sleeve is worked out according to the principles given for the triangles.

MAN'S SQUARE-SHAPED SWEATER

With shaped sleeves

① Work out the gauge for the stitch patterns using the correct needles and yarn. For this sweater, three gauge samples are needed: the gauge over single rib, using No 3 needles, for the hem and cuff; the gauge for the width of the cable pattern panel using No 5 needles; and the gauge over single rib, using No 5 needles.

② Draw a rough diagram of each of the pieces to be worked and note down the measurement for each part. Mark on the diagram the number of cable panels required.

③ Calculate the number of stitches required for the main part of the body as follows:
a) Add up the total width of all the cable panels required and deduct this figure from the total width of the piece of work. Multiply the resulting figure by the stitch gauge for the single rib on No 5 needles and divide this figure equally into the sections to go between the cable panels. Any extra stitches should be placed at the side seams, and 1 extra stitch at each of the side seam edges should be allowed.

④ The rib for the hem is worked over single rib on smaller needles. As a general rule, these hem ribs have fewer stitches than the main section of work. The correct number of stitches can be worked out by multiplying the hip measurement by the stitch gauge on the smaller needles. However, reducing the number of stitches required for the main part by an average of 10 is sufficiently accurate.

⑤ The rib at the neckline for this example has a different gauge (and therefore a different number of stitches) from the overall gauge of the main part of the work. The number of stitches must therefore be adjusted when completing the patterned section so that the width of the work remains the same.

⑥ The depth of the work is written down as a measurement so there is no need to work

GRADE ★ ★ ★ ★					
Sizes to fit	36	38	40	42	44	in
Actual size	40	42	44	46	48	in
Back length	28	28½	29	29½	30	in
Sleeve seam	17½	18	18	18½	18½	in
Materials	40	42	44	45	47	
	oz Aran thick yarn					

1 pr No 3 needles ● 1 pr No 5 needles

Suggested yarn: Phildar Pegase

Abbreviations alt – alternate ● beg – beginning ● CN – cable needle ● CN16 – cable 16 sts. thus, sl next 4 sts on to CN and hold at back *k1, p2, k1, then k1, p2, k1 from CN* slip next 4 sts on to CN and hold at front, rep from *to* ● cont – continue ● dec – decrease ● foll – following ● inc – increase ● k – knit ● patt – pattern ● p – purl ● rem – remaining ● rep – repeat ● st(s) – stitch(es) ● st st – stockinette stitch ● tog – together

out the number of rows required.

⑦ The sleeve pattern is worked out in the same manner as the body and the increases calculated as for triangles, pages 52 to 56.

GAUGE Using No 5 needles over rib, 32 sts. and 27 rows = 4in square.

BACK & FRONT (both the same) Using No 3 needles, cast on 167(173;179;185;191) sts and work in single rib as follows:
1st row: k2, *p1, k1, rep from * to last st, k1.
2nd row: k1, *p1, k1, rep from * to end.
Rep these 2 rows until work measures 3in, ending with a 1st row.
Next row: rib 24, *[inc in next st, rib 4] × 2, inc in next st, rib 25 (27;29;31;33), rep from * 2 more times, [inc in next st, rib 4] × 2, inc in next st, rib to end. 179 (185;191;197;203) sts.
Change to No 5 needles and commence st patt as follows:
1st row: k2, [p1, k1] × 9, *p3, k1, [p2, k2] × 3, p2,

k1, p3, [k1, p1] × 8 (9;10;11;12), k1, rep from * 2 more times, p3, k1, [p2, k2] × 3, p2, k1, p3, [k1, p1] × 9, k2.
2nd row: [k1, p1] × 10, *k3, p1, [k2, p2] × 3, k2, p1, k3, [p1, k1] × 8 (9;10;11;12), p1, rep from * 2 more times, k3, p1, [k2, p2] × 3, k2, p1, k3, [p1, k1] × 10.
Rep these 2 rows 2 more times.
7th row: k2, [p1, k1] × 9, *p3, C16, p3, [k1, p1] × 8 (9;10;11;12), k1, rep from * 2 more times, p3, C16, p3, [k1, p1] × 9, k2.
8th row: as 2nd row.
Rep 1st and 2nd rows once more.
These 10 rows form the patt. Cont in patt until work measures 18¾(19;19¼;19½;19¾)in from beg. Place an armhole marker at each end of last row worked. Cont in patt until work measures 24(24½;24¾;25½;25¾) in from beg, ending with a wrong side row.
Next row: k2, [p1, p1] × 11, *p2tog, [k1, p1] × 2, k2tog, [p1, p1] × 2, p2tog, [k1, p1] × 12 (13;14;15;16), k1, rep from * 2 more times, p2tog, [k1, p1] × 2, k2tog, [p1, p1] × 2, p2tog, [k1, p1] × 11, k2, 167(173;179;185;191) sts. Cont in rib until work measures 28(28¼;28¾;29¼; 29½)in from beg. Bind off ribwise placing markers for neck each side of center 63(65;67;69;71) sts.

SLEEVES Using No 5 needles, cast on 83 (85;87;89;91) sts and work in single rib as given for the back, beg with a 2nd row, until work measures 3¼ in.
Change to No 3 needles and cont in rib until work measures 6½in from beg, ending with a 2nd row.
Next row: rib 18, *[inc in next st, rib 4] × 2, inc in next st*, rib 25 (27;29;31)33), rep from * to *, rib to end. 89 (91;93;95;97) sts.
Change to No 5 needles and commence st patt as follows:
1st row: k2, [p1, k1] × 6, *p3, k1, [p2, k2] × 3, p2, k1, p3*, [k1, p1] × 8 (9;10;11;12), k1, rep from * to *, [k1, p1] × 6, k2.
Cont in patt and inc 1 st at each end of 3rd and every foll alt row until there are 167 (169;173;175;179) sts. Cont in patt without shaping until work measures 21 (21¼;21¼;22;22)in from beg. Bind off.

TO FINISH Using small backstitch, sew shoulder seams either side of markers, sew sleeve tops into armholes, sew side and sleeve seams.

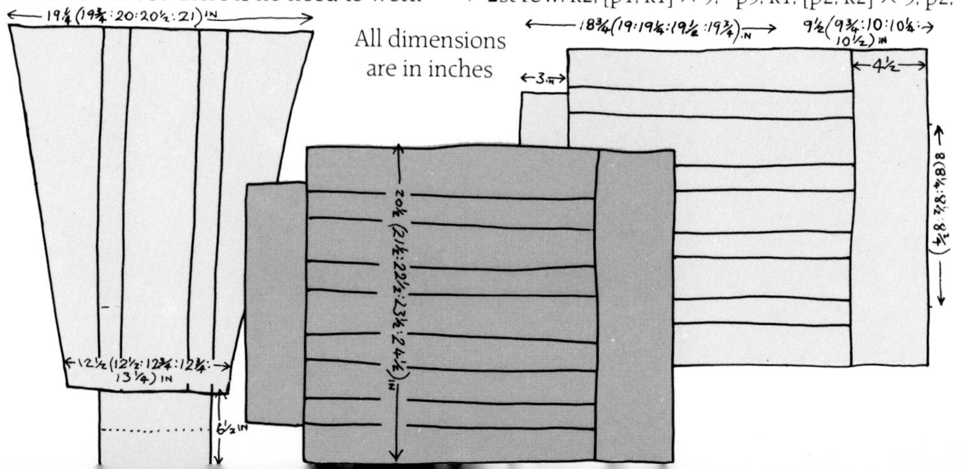

All dimensions are in inches

←—— 19¾ (19¾ : 20:20½ : 21) IN ——→

←— 18¾ (19:19¼:19½ :19¾) IN —→

←— 9½ (9¾ :10:10¼ : 10½) IN →

←—3 IN—→

←—4½—→

20½ (21¼:22½:23¾ 24½) IN

4¼ (4¼ :4¾:4¾) IN

←12½ (12½:12¾:12¼: 13¼) IN→

6½ IN

WOMAN'S FITTED ARAN SWEATER

A garment fits better and is therefore warmer if it has some shaping. Writing patterns for shaped garments requires a little more skill and experience. When first trying to write these patterns, use an existing pattern for a similar garment as a guide.

① Three gauge samples are needed for this garment, and the pattern is worked out exactly as the previous example up to the armholes. All the required shaping is worked from the armhole point.

② The number of stitches to be decreased for the armhole on the main body pieces is calculated by deducting the number of stitches required for the across-chest measurement from the number of stitches being worked for the main part of the body. The resulting number of stitches is reduced equally from each edge of the work. Make sure that the decreases do not 'cut into' any major pattern panel (ie, the pattern panel stitches should fall in line with the shoulders rather than the armholes).

③ The stitches to be reduced for the armhole of a set-in sleeve are reduced in such a way as to form a curve, beginning very sharply and ending very gradually. This curve should have an approximate depth of 2in for an adult garment, but if you are unsure, measure an existing garment. Draw this curve onto graph paper to ensure that it is a good shape.

④ When the neckline shaping is worked, the knitting is divided into two, and each half worked separately and identically. Usually, a number of stitches are bound off at the center, and then more stitches are bound off gradually to form a curve at each side of the center. Because the depth of the neckline must include the depth of the shoulder shaping, the shoulder shapings are often being worked at the same time as the neck shapings. The total number of stitches decreased or bound off for the front neckline must be the same as those decreased or bound off for the back neckline, and obviously the back and front shoulders should have an equal number of stitches.

⑤ The sleeve is worked as for the previous example up to the armholes. The sleeve head is then worked by decreasing or binding off all the stitches in such a manner as to form the curved shape shown on the diagram. Again,

following an existing garment or pattern is very helpful. For a fitted sleevehead with no gathers, the total depth of the sleevehead should be slightly shorter than the depth of the armhole and the width across the sleevehead should reduce fairly sharply in the first few rows so that the top of the sleeve fits closely. Usually the first few rows of the sleevehead are identical to the first few rows of the armhole shaping on the body.

⑥ For this garment the stitch pattern needs to be central and to match at the shoulders. Garments with horizontal stitch patterns or designs need to be matched around the body and, in particular, at the sleevehead. The design is matched at the sleevehead by ensuring that the last pattern row worked before the armhole point is the same as that worked for the body at the armhole point. To do this, it is sometimes necessary to start the sleeve pattern on a different row of the stitch pattern from the body.

⑦ When the stitches are picked up around the neck to form a border, enough stitches must be picked up around the neckline to ensure that the head can pass through the neck opening and the bound-off edge and any necessary hemming must be worked very loosely. This is particularly important for children's garments as their heads are very big in proportion to their neck size. For children's garments, it is a good idea to create some form of opening at the neck.

GRADE ★ ★ ★ ★			
Sizes to fit	32-34	36-38	40-42	in
Actual size	38	42	46	in
Back length	26½	27	27½	in
Sleeve seam	18	18½	19	in
Materials	19	21	24	
	oz knitting worsted			

1 pr No 3 needles ● 1 pr No 5 needles ● Cable needle
Suggested yarn: Pomfret Mark II by Brunswick

Abbreviations alt - alternate ● beg - beginning ● CN - cable needle ● cont - continue ● C1B - sl next st to CN and hold at back ● C2B - sl next 2 sts to CN and hold at back ● C3B - sl next 3 sts onto CN and hold at back ● C3F - sl next 3 sts onto CN and hold at front ● C4LP - C3F, p1, k3CN ● C4RP - C1B,3 p1CN ● C5LP - C3F, p2, k3CN ● C5RP - C2B, k3, p2CN ● C6LK - C3F, k3, p3CN ● C6RK - C3B, k3, k3CN ● C6RK - C3B, k3, k3CN ● dec - decrease ● foll - following ● inc - increase ● k - knit ● p - purl ● sl - slip ● st(s) - stitch(es) ● tog - together

GAUGE Using No 5 needles, patt panel (43 sts) = 5¼in, 32 rows = 4in square.

BACK Using No 3 needles, cast on 131 (145;159) sts and work in single rib as follows:
1st row: k1, *k1, p1, rep from * to last 2 sts, k2.
2nd row: k1, *p1, k1, rep from * to end.
Rep these 2 rows until work measures 3¼in, ending with a 2nd row.
Next row: rib 6 (7;8), [inc in next st, rib 8 (9;10)] × 13, inc in next st, rib to end. 145 (159;173) sts.
Change to No 5 needles and cont in st patt as follows:
1st row: (wrong side) [k1, p1] × 10 (13;16), *k2, p3, k8, p3, k6, p6, k10, p3, k2,* [p1, k1] × 9 (10;11), p1, rep from * to *, [p1, k1] × 10 (13;16).
2nd row: k20 (26;32), *p2, k3, p10, C6RK, p6, C4LP, p7, k3, p2,* k19 (21;23), rep from * to *, k20 (26;32).
3rd row: [k1, p1] × 10 (13;16), *k2, p3, k7, p3, k7, p6, k10, p3, k2,* [p1, k1] × 9 (10;11), p1, rep from * to *, [p1, k1] × 10 (13;16).
4th row: k20 (26;31), *p2, T3LP, p7, k6, p7, k3, p4, T3RP, p2*, k19 (21;23), rep from * to *, k20 (26;32).
5th row: [k1, p1] × 10 (13;16), *k5, p3, k4, p3, k7, p6, k7, p3, k5*, [p1, k1] × 9 (10;11), p1, rep from

* to *, [p1, k1] × 10 (13;16).

6th row: k20 (26;32), *p5, k3, p7. k6, p7, k3, p4. k3, p5*, k19 (21;23), rep from * to *, k20 (26;32).

7th row: as 5th row.

8th row: k20 (26;32), *p5, k3, p7, C6RK, p6, C4RP, p4, k3, p5*, k19 (21;23). rep from * to * k20 (26;32).

9th row: [k1, p1] × 10 (13;16), *k5, p3, k5, p3, k6, p6, k7, p3, k5*, [p1, k1] × 9 (10;11), p1, rep from * to *, [p1, k1] × 10 (13;16).

10th row: k20 (26;32), *p2, C6RP, p6, C4RP, C5Rp, p3, C4RP, p5, C6LP, p2*, k19 (21;23), rep from * to *, k20 (26;32).

11th row: [k1, p1] × 10 (13;16), *k2, p3, k9, [p3, k3] × 2, p3, k9, p3, k2*, [p1, k1] × 9 (10;11), p1, rep from * to *, [p1, k1] × 10 (13;16).

12th row: k20 (26;32), *p2, k3, p8, C4RP, p3, C5RP, C4RP, p9, k3, p2*, k19 (21;23), rep from * to *, k20 (26;32).

13th row: [k1, p1] × 10 (13;16), *k2, p3, k10, p6, k6, p3, k8, p3, k2*, [p1, k1] × 9 (10;11), p1, rep from * to *, (p1, k1) × 10 (13;16).

14th row: k20 (26;32), *p2, k3, p7, C4RP, p6, C6LK, p10, k3, p2*, k19 (21;23), rep from * to *, k20 (26;32).

15th row: [k1, p1] × 10 (13;16), *k2, p3, k10, p6, k7, p3, k7, p3, k2*, [p1, k1] × 9 (10;11), p1, rep from * to *, [p1, k1] × 10 (13;16).

16th row: k20 (26;32), *p2, C6LP, p4, k3, p7, k6, p7, T4RP, p2*, k19 (21;23), rep from * to *, k20 (26;32).

17th row: [k1, p1] × 10 (13;16), *k5, p3, k7, p6, k7, p3, k4, p3, k5*, [p1, k1] × 9 (10;11), p1, rep from * to *, [p1, k1] × 10 (13;16).

18th row: k20 (26;32), *p5, k3, p4, k3, p7, k6, p7, k3, p5*, k19 (21;23), rep from * to *, k20 (26;32).

19th row: as 17th row.

20th row: k20 (26;32), *p5, k3, p4, C4LP, p6, C6LK, p7, k3, p5*, k19 (21;23), rep from * to *, k20 (26;32).

21st row: [k1, p1] × 10 (13;16), *k5, p3, k7, p6, k6, (p3, k5) × 2*, [p1, k1] × 9 (10;11), p1, rep from * to *, [p1, k1] × 10 (13;16).

22nd row: k20 (26;32), *p2, C6LP, p5, C4LP, p3, C5R2P, C4LP, p6, C6LP, p2*, k19 (21;23), rep from * to *, k20 (26;32).

23rd row: as 11th row.

24th row: k20 (26;32), *p2, k3, p9, C4LP, C5RP, p3, C4LP, p8, k3, p2*, k19 (21;23), rep from * to *, k20 (26;32).

These 24 rows form the patt. Cont in patt until work measures 17½(17¾;18)in from beg, ending with a wrong side row. Keeping patt correct.

SHAPE ARMHOLES Bind off 3(4;5) sts at beg of next 4 rows. Dec 1 st at each end of next 3 rows. Dec 1 st at each end of foll 3 alt rows. 121 (131;141) sts. Cont in patt without shaping until work measures 26¾(27¼;27¾)in from beg, ending with a wrong side row.

SHAPE SHOULDERS Bind off 14(15;17) sts at beg of next 2 rows. Bind off 14(15;16) sts at beg of foll 2 rows. Bind off 13(15;16) sts at beg of next 2 rows. Bind off rem 39(41;43) sts for back neck.

FRONT Work to match the back until work measures 24¾(25¼;25¾)in from beg, ending with a wrong side row.

SHAPE NECKLINE Next row: patt 54(58;62) sts, bind off next 13(15;17) sts, patt to end. Cont on last group of sts only as follows:

1st row: patt to last 2 sts, patt 2 tog.

*2nd row: bind off 5 sts, patt to end.

3rd row: as 1st row.

4th row: bind off 3 sts, patt to end.

Dec 1 st at neck edge of every row until 44(48;52) sts remain. Dec 1 st at neck edge of foll 3 rows. Cont in patt without shaping until work measures 26¾(27¼;27¾)in from beg, ending at armhole edge.

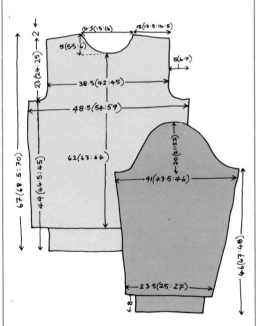

All dimensions are in inches.

SHAPE SHOULDER Bind off 14(15;17) sts at beg of next row. Bind off 14(15;16) sts at beg of foll alt row. Bind off rem 13(15;16) sts at beg of foll alt row.*

Rejoin yarn at neck edge and rep from * to *.

SLEEVES Using No 3 needles, cast on 47(51;55) sts and work in single rib as given for the back until work measures 3¼in, ending with a 2nd row.

Next row: rib 0 (2;4), [inc in next st, rib 1] × 23, inc in next st, rib to end. 71 (75;79) sts.

Change to No 5 needles and commence st patt as follows:

1st row: [k1, p1] × 7 (8;9), k2, p3, k8, p3, k6, p6, k19, p3, k2, [p1, k1] × 7 (8;9).

The position of the st patt is now set. Cont in patt and inc 1 st at each end of the 5th and every foll 4th row until there are 117 (123;129) sts. Cont in patt without shaping until work measures 18¼(18¾;19¼)in from beg, ending with a wrong side row.

SHAPE SLEEVE TOP Bind off 3(4;5) sts at beg of next 4 rows. Dec 1 st at each end of foll 6 rows. Dec 1 st at each end of every foll alt row until 43 sts remain. Bind off 9 sts at beg of next 4 rows. Bind off rem 7 sts.

NECKBAND Using small backstitch, sew right shoulder seam.

Using No 3 needles, right side facing, pick up 75 (83;91) sts evenly across front neck and pick up 40 (42;44) sts across back neck. 115 (125;135) sts.

Work in single rib as given for the back, beg with a 2nd row until neckband measures 2in. Bind off ribwise.

TO FINISH Using small backstitch, sew left shoulder/neckband seam, sew sleeve tops into armholes, sew sides and sleeve seams. Turn neckband to inside and stitch down.

CHILD'S SWEATER
with raglan seams

Fitted garments can be created not only by the use of set-in sleeves, but also by the use of raglan seaming. The armhole seam of a set-in sleeve usually has to fall exactly at the edge of the shoulder, and it can look unsightly if it does not, but with raglan seaming, any problems with the placing of the armhole seam can be avoided. Raglan seams are particularly useful for people with small or sloping shoulders and children, who very rarely conform to any 'normal' sizing. A raglan seam can be as deep or as shallow as desired.

① The pattern is worked out up to the armholes as for the first example.
② All the stitches for the body and the sleeves are reduced at a regular (but not necessarily the same) rate, following the principles given for the triangles on pages 52-56, until only the stitches of the neckline are left. However, the front neckline shaping must be commenced before the raglan seam is completed so that the raglan shaping is being worked at the same time as the neck shaping.
③ The number of rows over which the decreases are worked must be the same for the body as for the sleeves so that when sewing up, the seams are the same length. If the raglan seam on the front is shorter than the raglan seam on the back, the raglan seams on the sleeve must be of differing lengths so that all the seams fit together correctly. When this happens, the stitches at the top of the sleeve that would be part of the neckline are bound off in steps, so that tne back raglan seam on the sleeve is longer than the front raglan seam.
④ The decreases on raglan sleeves are often worked a few stitches in from the edge to form a fully-fashioned decreased edge.
⑤ Because some of the neckline stitches are picked up from the top of the sleeve, the overall length of the garment is the length of the body piece plus half the width of the top of the sleeve. Where the front raglan seam is shorter than the back raglan seam, the total length will usually be the length of the back of the work.

GRADE ★ ★ ★ ★				
Sizes to fit	24	26	28	30	in
Actual size	26	28	30	32	in
Back length	15½	16½	18	20	in
Sleeve seam	10	12	14	16	in
Materials	8	10	12	14	MC
	1	1	1	1	col A
	1	1	1	1	col B
oz knitting worsted				

1 pr No 5 needles ● 1 pr No 3 needles
Suggested yarn: Pingouin Shetland

Abbreviations alt – alternate ● beg – beginning ● cont – continue ● dec – decrease ● foll – following ● inc – increase ● k – knit ● p – purl ● patt – pattern ● psso – pass sl st over ● rem – remaining ● rep – repeat ● sl – slip ● st(s) – stitch(es) ● tog – together ● MC – main color ● A – 1st color ● B – 2nd color

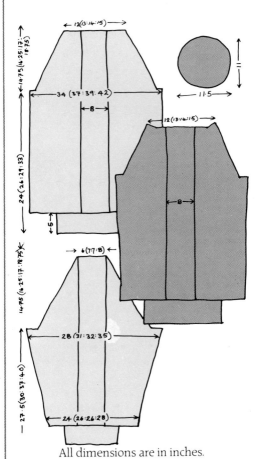

All dimensions are in inches.

GAUGE Using No 5 needles, and working in g st (every row p) 20 sts and 40 rows = 4in square.

NOTE Weave the yarn in at back of work, very loosely, where necessary.

BACK Using No 3 needles and MC, cast on 58 (62;66;74) sts and work in double rib as follows:
1st row: k2, *p2, k2, rep from * to end.
2nd row: p2, *k2, p2, rep from * to end.
Rep these 2 rows 6 more times, then rep the 1st row once more.
Next row: rib 4 (1;3;2) sts, *rib 2 (2;2;3) sts, inc in next st, rib 2 (2;2;3) sts, rep from * to last 4 (1;3;2) sts, rib to end. 68 (74;78;84) sts.
Change to No 5 needles and work in patt as follows:
1st row: using MC p25 (28;30;33) sts, k1, using A k16, using MC k1, 25 (28;30;33) sts.
2nd row: using MC p26 (29;31;34) sts, using A k16, using MC p26 (29;31;34) sts.
3rd row: using MC p25 (28;30;33), k18, p25 (28;30;33) sts.
4th row: using MC p to end.
5th row: as 1st row but using B.
6th row: as 2nd row but using B.
7th & **8**th row: as 3rd and 4th rows.
These 8 rows form the patt. Cont in patt until work measures 9½ (10¼; 11½; 13) in, ending with a wrong side row.

SHAPE RAGLANS Cont in patt and dec 3 sts at beg of next 2 rows, then dec 1 st at each end of next and every foll 3rd row 19 (21;22;24) times. Bind off rem 24 (26;28;30) sts loosely.

FRONT Work as given for the back until 16 (18;19;21) dec rows have been worked, and there are 30 (32;34;36) sts.

SHAPE NECKLINE Cont to dec on every 3rd row and on next row bind off center 18 (20;22;24) sts. And at the same time, turn and work on last group of sts as follows:
* Cont to dec on every 3rd row at raglan edges. And at the same time, dec at neck edge on the same 3rd row until all sts have been decreased. Fasten off*.
Rejoin yarn to rem sts at neck edge and work 2nd side to match 1st side as given from * to *

SLEEVES Using No 3 needles and MC, cast on 42(46;46;50)sts and work in double rib as given for the back for 15 rows. Next row: rib 0 (2;2;1) sts, *rib 3, inc in next st, rib 3 (3;3;4), rep from * to last 0 (2;2;1) sts, rib to end. 48 (52;52;56) sts.

Change to No 5 needles and cont in patt as for the back, the 1st row being:
1st row: using MC, p15 (17;17;19) sts, k1; using A, k16; using MC, k1, p15 (17;17;19) sts. Cont in patt k16 and inc 1 st at each end of every foll 8th row until there are 56 (62;64;70) sts, then cont in patt until work measures 11 (12;14½;15¾) in, ending with a wrong side row.

SHAPE RAGLANS Work as for the back raglan shaping until 12 (14;14;16) sts remain. Bind off loosely.
Work second sleeve to match.

NECKBAND Join three raglan seams using small backstitch.
Using No 3 needles and MC and working from the right side, pick up 86 (90;90;94) sts and work in double rib as for the back, starting with a 2nd row and working for 16 rows. Bind off on next row ribwise, loosely.

PATCHES (make 4) Using No 3 needles and MC, cast on 18 sts and work in single rib. Inc 1 st at each end of every row for 6 rows, then inc 1 st at each end of every alt row 6 times. Work 2 rows without shaping, then dec 1 st on next and every foll alt row 6 times, then dec 1 st at each end of next 6 rows. Bind off rem 18 sts.

TO FINISH Using small backstitch, sew rem raglan seam. Sew underarm seam from wrist to cuff using small backstitch. Pin patches into place on shoulders and at elbows and sew round edge using small backstitch. Turn neckband to inside and hem down loosely.

WOMAN'S DOLMAN SWEATER

Dolman-sleeve garments are very similar to square and rectangular-shaped garments in that they are loose-fitting. They can be knitted in one piece or with a seam at the shoulders, either from cuff to cuff or from the hem. The extra stitches for the sleeve are usually cast on gradually to form a curve.

① Work out the number of stitches to be cast on as for the first example.
② It is necessary to work out the number of rows required between the hem and the lower edge of the wrist, for the depth of the wrist and the depth of the shoulder shaping, if any. It is also necessary to work out the depth of the neckline in rows.
③ The sleeve increases must be worked at varying rates to fit exactly into the depth of the work, from the hem to the lower edge of the wrist. To calculate the rate of the increases, the work is treated in the same manner as for the circle shown on pages 58-59. In the example given here, the diagram shows the various trianglar segments used to form the shaping.
⑤ Any stitch or color pattern should be kept fairly simple or shown in chart form as it is virtually impossible to write the instructions for a complex pattern, since each row for the whole garment would need to be written down, to take the shapings into account.
⑥ Usually the back and front are identical, except for the neckline, so the pattern will match at the seams automatically.

GRADE ★ ★ ★ ★				
Sizes to fit	32-34	36-38	40-42	in
Actual size	38	42	46	in
Back length	24	24½	25	in
Materials	12	14	15	A
	8	10	12	B
	oz standard bulky			

1 pr No 6 needles • 1 pr No 8 needles
Suggested yarn: Phildar Vizir

Abbreviations alt – alternate • beg – beginning • cont – continue • dec – decrease • foll – following • inc – increase • k – knit • klwl – knit next st winding yarn around needle 3 times • p – purl • patt – pattern • psso – pass sl st over • rem – remaining • rep – repeat • sl – slip • st(s) – stitch(es) • st st – stockinette stitch • tog – together • A – 1st color • B – 2nd color • C – 3rd color • D – 4th color

GAUGE Using No 8 needles over st st, 15 sts and 20 rows = 4in square.

NOTE Use separate balls of yarn for each diagonal strip and twist yarns at color changes.

BACK Using No 6 needles and A, cast on 62 (70;78) sts and work in double rib as follows:
1st row: *k2, p2, rep from * to last 2 sts, k2.
2nd row: *p2, k2, rep from * to last 2 sts, p2.
Rep these 2 rows until work measures 2¾in, ending with a 1st row.
Next row: rib 0 (4;2), [inc in next st, rib 4 (5;8)] × 12 (10;8), inc in next st, rib to end. 75 (81;87) sts.
Change to No 8 needles and cont in st patt as follows:
3rd size only:
1st row: k10B, k1w1B, k13A, k1w1A, K13B,

k1w1B, k9A, k1w1B, K13B, K1w1A, k13A, k1w1B, k10B.
2nd row: p10B, sl1, p13A, sl1, p13B, sl1, p9A, sl1, p13B, sl1, p13A, sl1, p10B.
2nd & 3rd sizes only:
Next row: k6 (9) B, k1A, sl0 (1), k13 (12) A, k1B, sl 1p, k12B, k1A, sl 1p, k9A, sl1, k1A, k12B, sl1, k1B, k13 (12) A, sl0 (1), k1A, k6 (9) B.
Next row: p5 (8) B, p2A, sl0 (1), p12 (11) A, p2B, sl1, p11B, p2A, sl1, p9A, sl1, p2A, p11B, sl1, p2B, p12 (11) A, sl0 (1), p2A, p5 (8) B.
All sizes:
Next row: k0 (3;6) B, k1w1B, k13A, k1w1A, k13B, k1w1B, k17A, k1w1B, k13B k1w1A, k13A, k1w1B, k0 (3;6) B.
Next row: p0 (3;6) B, sl1, p13A, sl1, p13B, sl1, p17A, sl1, p13B, sl1, p13A, sl1, p0 (3;6) B.
Next row: k0 (2;5) B, k0 (1;1) A, sl1, k12A, k1B, sl1, k12B, k1A, sl1, k17A, sl1, k1A, k12B, sl1, k1B, k12A, sl1, k0 (1;1) A, k0 (2;5) B.
Next row: p0 (1;4) B, p0 (2;2) A, sl1, p11A, p2B, sl1, p11B, p2A, sl1, p17A, sl1, p2A, p11B, sl1, p2B, p11A, sl1, p0 (2;2) A, p0 (1;4) B.
Next row: k0 (0;2) B, k0 (0;1) w1B, k10 (13;13) A, k1w1A, k13B, k1w1B, k25A, k1w1B, k13B, k1w1A, k10 (13;13) A, k0 (0;1) w1B, k0 (0;2) B.
Next row: p0 (0;2) B, sl0 (0;1), p10 (13;13) A, sl1, p13B, sl1, p25A, sl1, p13B, sl1, p10 (13;13) A, sl0 (0;1), p0 (0;2) B.
Next row: k0 (0;1) A, k0 (0;2) B, sl0 (0;1), k9 (12;12) A, k1B, sl1, k12B, k1A, sl1, k12A, k1B, k12A, sl1, k1A, k12B, sl1, k1B, k9 (12;12) A, sl0 (0;1), k0 (0;1) B, k0 (0;1) A.
Next row: p0 (0;2) A, sl0 (0;1), p8 (11;11) A, p2B, sl1, p11B, p2A, sl1, p11A, p3B, p11A, sl1, p2A, p11B, sl1, p2B, p8 (11;11) A, sl0 (0;1), p0 (0;2) A.
Next row: k6 (9;12) A, k1w1A, k13B, k1w1B, k13A, k1w1A, k5B, k1w1A, k13A, k1w1B, k13B, k1w1A, k6 (9;12) A.
Next row: p6 (12;13) A, sl1, p13B, sl1, p13A, sl1, p5B, sl1, p13A, sl1, p13B, sl1, p6 (9;12) A.
Cont working diagonal stripes and long sts as before and shape sleeves as follows:
Inc 1 st at each end of next and every foll 4th row, 4 times in all.
Inc 1 st at each end of every foll alt row, 8 times in all.
Inc 1 st at each end of every foll row, 10 times in all.
Cast on 4 sts at beg of next 10 rows.
Cast on 8 (8;7) sts at beg of next 2 rows.
Cast on 8 sts at beg of foll 2 rows. 191 (197;201) sts.
Work 28 rows in patt without shaping.

All dimensions are in inches

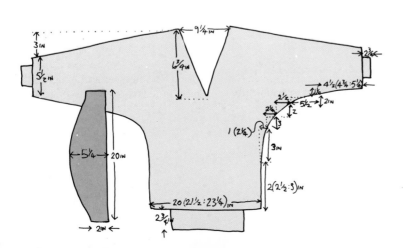

SHAPE SLEEVE TOPS AND SHOULDERS
Bind off 13(15:16) sts at beg of next 2 rows.
Bind off 10(11:12) sts at beg of foll 2 rows. Bind off 11 sts at beg of next 10 rows. Bind off rem 35 sts for back neck.

FRONT Work as given for the back until 10 rows have been worked at the wrist edge.

SHAPE NECKLINE Next row: patt 93 (96:98) sts, sl1, k2tog, psso, k2tog, patt to end. Now turn and work on last group of sts as follows: *Dec 1 st at neck edge of every foll alt row 16 times in all AND at the same time, when 29 rows have been worked at the wrist edge, ending at wrist edge, cont shoulder shaping as follows:

Bind off 13(15:16) sts at wrist edge of next row. Bind off 10(11:12) sts at wrist edge of foll alt row. Bind off 11 sts at wrist edge of next 5 alt rows. Fasten off.
Rejoin yarn to rem sts at neck edge and work 2nd side to match 1st side as given from *.

COLLAR Using No 5 needles and MC, cast on 10 sts and work in double rib as given for the back, for 6 rows, then cont in double rib, and inc 1 st at left edge only, of next and every foll 3rd row until there are 25 sts. Work 28 rows, then dec at shaped edge only of every foll 3rd row, until 10 sts remain. Work 2 rows on these sts.
Next row: rib 4, bind off 2 sts loosely, rib 4.
Next row: rib 4, cast on 2 sts, rib 4.
Work 2 rows, then bind off.

CUFFS Using small backstitch, sew both shoulder/sleeve top seams.
Using No 5 needles and A, right side facing, pick up 30 sts across wrist edge. Work 2¾ in double rib as given for the back, beg with a 2nd row. Bind off ribwise.

TO FINISH Pin the cast on edge of the collar neatly around the neckline and short sides along either side of front 'V', sew collar in place. Using small backstitch, sew side/underarm seams.

WOMAN'S ROUND YOKED SWEATER

Because these garments are worked on a three-dimensional basis, they are complex to write, and should not be attempted by the inexperienced pattern-writer. The addition of a stitch or color pattern will make them more complex so any patterning should be kept to a minimum.

① The pattern is worked out up to the armholes as for the first example.

② Shapings are worked to form a gently rounded curve in the center of the work, and raglan seamings at the armhole edge of the work. The center curve can be bound off to form the shaping or worked by partial knitting. The raglan seams on the sleeve must be the same length as those on the body as they have to be sewn together.

③ All the stitches of the yoke are picked up around all the pieces of the work, and knitted on a circular needle or set of 4 needles. These stitches must then be reduced gradually until the yoke is the correct depth and only the required number of stitches for the neckline remain. The decreases are not always worked at a regular rate as the shoulders do not slope at a regular rate, so it is a good idea to use an existing pattern as a guide. The decreases must be worked so that they do not disturb any patterning.

④ Any color or stitch pattern must match at the yoke and underarm seams which can make writing the pattern very complicated.

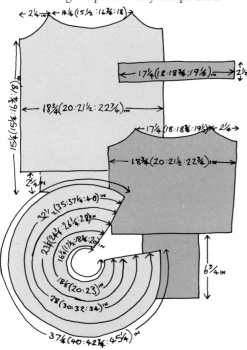

GRADE ★ ★ ★					
Sizes to fit	32	34	36	38	in
Actual size	36¼	39	41¾	44	in
Back length	15¼	15¼	16¾	18	in
Sleeve seam	18	18	19½	19½	in
Material	21	22	22	24	
	oz knitting worsted				

1 pr No 3 needles ● 1 pr No 5 needles ● 1 circular No 5 needle

Suggested yarn: Aree by Lion Brand used in double strand

Abbreviations alt – alternate ● beg – beginning ● cont – continue ● dec – decrease ● foll – following ● inc – increase ● k – knit ● p – purl ● patt – pattern ● psso – pass sl st over ● rem – remaining ● rep – repeat ● sl – slip ● st(s) – stitch(es) ● st st – stockinette stitch ● tog – together ● yo – yarn over needle

GAUGE Using No 5 needles over st patt, 24 sts and 34 rows = 4in square.

BACK & FRONT (both the same) Using No 3 needles, cast on 99,(107;115;123) sts and work in single rib as follows:
1st row: k2, *p1, k1, rep from * to last st, k1.
2nd row: k1, *p1, k1, rep from * to end.
Rep these 2 rows until work measures 2½in ending with a 1st row.
Next row: rib 3 (1;5;2), [inc in next st, rib 6 (7;8;8)] × 13, inc in next st, rib to end. 113 (121;129;137) sts.
Change to No 5 needles and cont in st patt as follows:
1st row: *k1, p1, rep from * to last st, k1.
Rep this row 5 more times.
7th row: *k1, yo, sl1, k1, psso, k3, k2tog, yo rep from * to last st, k1.
8th, 10th & 12th rows: p to end.
9th row: *k2, yo, sl1, k1, psso, k1, k2tog, yo k1, rep from * to last st, k1.
11th row: *k3, yo, sl1, k2tog, psso, yo, k2, rep from * to last st, k1.
These 12 rows form the patt. Cont in patt until work measures approximately 15¼(15¼;16¾;18)in from beg to st patt, ending with a 12th patt row.

SHAPE RAGLANS & YOKE Keeping patt correct.
** Bind off 4 sts at beg of next 2 rows, Dec 1 st at each end of the next and foll 3 alt rows. Patt 1 row.
1st row: k2tog, patt 33 (33;38;38) sts, turn.
2nd row & every alt row: sl1, patt to end.
3rd row: k2tog, patt 28 (28;33;33) sts, turn.
5th row: k2tog, patt 23 (23;28;28) sts, turn.
7th row: k2tog, patt 18 (18;23;23) sts, turn.
9th row: k2tog, patt 12 (13;18;18) sts, turn.
11th row: k2tog, patt 8 (8;13;13) sts, turn.
13th row: k2tog, patt 3 (3;8;8) sts, turn.
1st & 2nd sizes only:
Break yarn.

All dimensions are in inches

3rd & 4th sizes only:
15th row: k2tog, patt 3 (3) sts, break yarn.
All sizes:
sl next 51 (59;61;69) sts onto right hand needle, rejoin yarn, patt 33 (33;38;38), k2tog.
1st row: patt 30 (30;35;35) sts, turn.
Cont on these sts to match left side of front, working 5 sts less on each wrong side row and ending with a right side row.**
Next row: p9 (7;7;3), [p2tog, p1] × 21 (25;27;31), p2tog, p to end.
Leave rem 61 (65;69;73) sts on a spare needle for the yoke.

SLEEVES Using No 3 needles, cast on 57 (61;65;69) sts and work in single rib as given for the back until work measures 6³⁄₄in, ending with a 1st row.
Next row: inc in every st to last st, k1. 113 (121;129;137) sts.
Change to No 5 needles and cont in st patt as given for the back until work measures 18 (18;19¹⁄₂;19¹⁄₂)in from beg, ending with 12th patt row.
Rep from ** to ** as given for the back.
Next row: p10 (10;11;11), [p2tog] × 32 (36;38;42), p to end.
Leave rem 51 (55;59;63) sts on a spare needle for yoke. Do not break yarn at end of 2nd sleeve.

YOKE Using circular No 5 needle, [k1, p1] across the 2nd sleeve to last st, k1; [p1, k1] across the front to the last st, p1; [k1, p1] across the other sleeve to last st, k1; [p1, k1] across the back to the last st, p1. 224 (240;256;272) sts.
Work yoke in rows as follows:
2nd row: *p1, k1, rep from * to end.
3rd row: *k1, p1, rep from * to end.
Rep these 2 rows once more and 2nd row once again.

7th-**11**th rows: k to end.
12th row: k3, *k2tog, k6, rep from * to last 5 sts. k2tog, k3. 196 (210;224;238) sts.
Rep rows 1-11 once again.
24th row: k2, *k2tog, k5, rep from * to last 5 sts. k2tog, k3. 168 (180;192;204) sts.
Rep rows 1-11 once again.
36th row: k2, *k2tog, k4, rep from * to last 4 sts. k2tog, k2. 140 (150;160;170) sts.
Rep rows 1-11 once again.
48th row: k1, *k2tog, k3, rep from * to last 4 sts. k2tog, k2. 112 (120;128;136) sts.
Rep rows 1-11 once again.
60th row: k3, *k2tog, k6, rep from * to last 5 sts. k2tog, k3. 98 (105;112;119) sts.
1st & 3rd sizes only:
Rep rows 1-5 once again.
2nd & 4th sizes only:
61st row: p2tog, k1, *p1, k1, rep from * to end.
Rep rows 1-4 once again.
All sizes:
Bind off loosely in patt.

COLLAR Using 3¹⁄₄mm needles, cast on 105 (109;113;117) sts. Rep 1st row of st patt as given for the back until work measures 2 ¹⁄₂in. Bind off in patt.

TO MAKE UP Using small backstitch, sew raglan seams, sew side and sleeve seams. Pin collar around the neckline with the opening at the center front, stitch in place.

BOW Using No 5 needles, make a loop and k into front and back of this loop. 2 sts.
1st row: inc in 1st st, k1.
2nd row: k1, p1, k1.
3rd row: inc in 1st st, p1, k1.
4th row: [k1, p1] × 2
5th row: inc in 1st st, k1, p1, k1.
6th row: [k1, p1] × 2, k1.
7th row: inc in 1st st, [p1, k1] × 2
8th row: [k1, p1] × 3
9th row: inc in 1st st, k1, [p1, k1] × 2

10th row: [k1, p1] × 3, k1.
11th row: inc in 1st st, [p1, k1] × 3
12th row: [k1, p1] × 4. Leave these 8 sts on a spare needle.
Make another loop and k into front and back of this loop. 2 sts.
1st row: k1, inc in last st.
2nd row: k1, p1, k1.
3rd row: k1, p1, inc in last st.
Cont in this manner keeping moss st patt correct to:
12th row: [p1, k1] × 4.
Next row: [k1, p1] × 4, work across 1st group of 8 sts as follows:
Inc in 1st st, k1, [p1, k1] × 3, 17 sts.
Rep this row until work measures 17¹⁄₄in from beg. Shape end as follows:
1st row: [k1, p1] × 4, turn and cont on these 8 sts only as follows:
2nd row: k2tog, [p1, k1] × 3.
3rd row: [k1, p1] × 3, k1.
4th row: p2tog, k1, [p1, k1] × 2.
Cont in this manner keeping moss st patt correct to:
12th row: p2tog, k1.
13th row: k2tog. Fasten off.
Rejoin yarn to rem 9 sts and cont as follows:
1st row: p2tog, k1, [p1, k1] × 3.
2nd row: [k1, p1] × 3, k2tog.
3rd row: [k1, p1] × 3, k1.
4th row: [k1, p1] × 2, k1, p2tog.
Cont in this manner keeping moss st patt correct to:
12th row: k1, p2tog.
13th row: k2tog. Fasten off.
Using No 5 needles, cast on 7 sts and rep 1st row of st patt as given for the back until work measures 2³⁄₄in. Bind off.

TO FINISH Fold the long strip to form a bow. Wrap the short strip around the center and stitch firmly. Fasten the completed bow to the center of the front neckline.

MAKING ALTERATIONS

ALL PATTERNS CAN be altered in size and shape, but if a number of alterations are to be made, it's probably better to start completely from scratch. In order to make alterations to a pattern it is sometimes necessary to know the exact measurement of a specific part of the pattern. To do this, divide the number of stitches or rows for any section by the stitch or row gauge. The result will be the measurement of that particular section of the work. There are two main principles that govern the altering of patterns:
a) Where possible all alterations should be worked on unshaped sections of the work.
b) When two sections of the work are to be seamed together, if one section is altered, the second section should be altered so that the seams remain the same length. This also applies to edges from which the stitches are to be picked up: the number of stitches to be picked up should also be altered.

1 LENGTHENING THE WORK
a) Length can be added to the body of a garment simply by working a few extra rows. This extra length should be added before the armhole shaping as shown in the diagram by the line AB. If there is a stitch or color pattern that matches horizontally, make sure that it will continue to match both at the side seams and at the underarm point with the sleeves.
b) Length can also be added to the sleeve in the same manner as shown by the line EF. If the sleeve has shapings (ie, increases), the spacing between these shapings must be recalculated so that the edge of the work remains in a good, smooth line.
c) If the armhole depth is to be made longer then the top of the sleeve must also be lengthened to correspond; that is, if depth is added at the line CD on the body, it must also be added at the line CD on the sleeve.

2 SHORTENING THE WORK
This is done in the same manner as for lengthening the work, except that the number of rows is reduced.

3 ADDING WIDTH
a) Small amounts of extra width can be added by working a few extra stitches at each edge of the work. These extra stitches should then be decreased in the armhole. This is shown by the lines AB in the diagram. In theory, the same number of stitches should also be added to the sleeve and bound off at the armhole in the same manner but, in practice, if the body needs to be widened by only a small amount it is not absolutely necessary to alter the sleeves to match.
b) Where the garment needs to be widened by a fairly large amount, the extra stitches are added equally at each edge as before, but they are bound off in equal amounts between the armholes, shoulders and neck, as shown by the lines AB, CD and EF.
c) Width should only be added to the sleeve when the lines AB correspond with the body. Otherwise, if extra stitches are added to the middle of the work, the sleevehead will be gathered into the armhole (unless the armhole is altered to correspond). It is also possible to add width at the wrist edge and then alter the increases or decreases so that the final number of stitches remains the same at the armhole point. This is shown by the dotted line in the diagram.
d) Any extra stitches added to the width should not disturb any color or stitch pattern. It is best to add stitches in the same multiple as any stitch pattern.

4 REDUCING WIDTH
This is done in the same manner as adding width to the work, except that the number of stitches is reduced.

5 OTHER GARMENT SHAPES
The examples shown here are for the round neck sweater with set-in sleeves, but the principles apply to all other shaped pieces of work. It is not advisable to alter an adult pattern to fit a child as the body proportions are not the same, although it can be done if referring to an existing well-fitting garment.

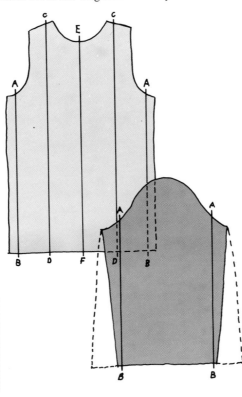

DESIGNER KNITS

The following designer patterns comprise a complete range of garments for all the family. There's In The Bleachers for the active boy, the Topsy for the growing girl who is growing up fast and The Silver Lining for the go-ahead granny.

For men, there is the Modern-day Mao Chinese-style jacket, The Hunter, The Country Gentleman dogtooth waistcoat and the Tile Style patchwork sweater. And for the fashion-conscious woman, there is Cool Accord, The Cape Cod and The East Egg Coolie. Patterns range from exotic Suzy Wong to the radical chic of Manhattan. There's the sophistication of the Cocktails For Two angora dress, the Elizabethan elegance of the Prithee Maid and the warm practicality of The Nantucket. Whether you're in search of Mohair Magic or Amazing Lace, traveling on the Trans-Siberian Express or planning to summer in Cap d'Antibes, sampling a Winter Warmer or going out to the Ritz – in 'Ritzy Knit' – there is something here for you.

THE CAPE COD
Chunky sweater with a fishy pattern

GAUGE Using No 10 needles over st st 14 sts and 20 rows = 4in square.

BACK Using No 6 needles and MC cast on 62 (70;78) sts and work in double rib as follows:
1st row: *k2, p2, rep from * to last 2 sts, k2.
2nd row: *p2, k2, rep from * to last 2 sts, p2.
Cont in double rib until work measures 3¼in, ending with a 2nd row, and inc 6 sts evenly across last row. 68 (76;84) sts.
Change to No 10 needles and cont in st st working from the chart, until chart is completed. Work the shoulder shapings as follows:

SHOULDER SHAPINGS Bind off 10 (12;14) sts at beg of next 2 rows. Bind off 11 (12;13) sts at beg of foll 2 rows. Bind off rem 26 (28;30) sts.

FRONT Work as given for back to the 76th chart row, then commence neck shaping as follows:

SHAPE NECKLINE Patt across 1st 27 (31;35) sts, bind off center 14 sts, then patt rem 27 (31;35) sts. Work on this last group of sts as follows:
* Cont in patt from the chart to row 106, ending at the neck edge.
Next row: bind off 2 sts, patt to end.
Next row: patt to end.
Rep these 2 rows once more, then dec 1 st at neck edge of next 2 (3;4) rows. Cont working from the chart to shoulder shapings, ending at armhole edge.

SHOULDER SHAPINGS Bind off 10 (12;14) sts at beg of next row, and 11 (12;13) sts at beg of foll alt row. Fasten off.*
Rejoin yarn to rem sts and work from the chart, and working the shapings to match 1st side as given from * to *

SLEEVES Using No 6 needles and MC cast on 34 sts, and work in double rib as given for the back, until work measures 3¼in, ending with a 2nd row. Inc 8 (10;12) sts evenly across the last row. 42 (44;46) sts.
Change to No 10 needles, and cont in st st. and working from the chart inc 1 st at each end of every foll 4th row until there are 68 (76;84) sts, then cont without shaping until work measures 17¾(18¼;18¾)in from the beg. Bind off.

GRADE ★ ★				
Sizes to fit	32-34	36-38	40-42	in
Actual size	38	42	46	in
Back length	25½	26	26¼	in
Sleeve seam	17¾	18¼	18¾	in
Materials	16	18	20	
	6	7	8	
	4	4	4	
	4	4	4	
	oz bulky yarn			

1 pr No 6 needles ● 1 pr No 10 needles ● 6 buttons
Suggested yarn: Wendy Shetland Chunky

Abbreviations alt – alternate ● beg – beginning ● cont – continue ● dec – decrease ● foll – following ● inc – increase ● k – knit ● p – purl ● patt – pattern ● rem – remaining ● rep – repeat ● st(s) – stitch(es) ● st st – stockinette stitch ● tog – together ● MC – main color ● A – 1st color ● B – 2nd color ● C – 3rd color

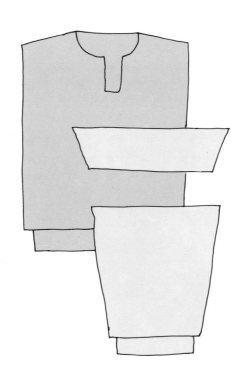

All dimensions are in inches

BUTTONBAND Using No 6 needles and MC cast on 18 sts, and work in double rib for 30 rows. Bind off ribwise

BUTTONHOLE BAND Work as given for buttonband for 2 rows.
Next row: rib 2, bind off 3 sts, rib 8 sts, bind off 3 sts, rib 2 sts.
*Next row: rib 2 sts, cast on 3 sts, rib 8 sts, cast on 3 sts, rib 2 sts.
Work 10 more rows rep from * once more, then work 2 more buttonhole rows, then 2 rows. Bind off.

COLLAR Using No 6 needles and MC cast on 154 (162;170) sts and work in double rib as given for the back. At the same time inc 1 st at each end of every 3rd row, 2 sts in from the edge (so that the right side edge sts are 2 knit stitches for the length of the edge). Cont in this manner until work measures 6in. Bind off.

TO FINISH Sew buttonband and buttonhole band into neck opening. Using small backstitch sew shoulder seams. Sew collar around neckline. Sew sleeves into armholes, placing half the sleeve top equally each side of the shoulder seam. Sew underarm seams from wrist to hem. Sew buttons into place.

MAYAN MOHAIR

Mohair sweater with a mysterious pyramid motif

GAUGE Using No 8 needles over st st 15 sts and 20 rows = 4in square.

NOTE Do not strand yarns, but use a separate ball of yarn for each color area.

BACK Using No 5 needles and MC, cast on 65 (71;77) sts and work in single rib as follows:
1st row: k1, *k1, p1, rep from * to last 2 sts, k2.
2nd row: k1, *p1, k1, rep from * to end.
Rep these 2 rows until work measures 3in, ending with a 2nd row and inc 7 (9;11) sts evenly across last row worked. 72 (80;88) sts.
Change to No 8 needles and cont in st st and working from the chart, to shoulder shapings, work should measure 24¾(25¼;25¾)in.

SHAPE SHOULDERS Bind off 7 (8;10) sts at beg of next 2 rows, bind off 7 (9;10) sts at beg of next 2 rows, bind off 8 (9;10) sts at beg of next 2 rows. Bind off rem 28 sts for back neck loosely.

FRONT Work as given for the back, to position of neck shaping as shown on the chart, ending with a wrong side row. Work should measure 23½(24;24½)in.

SHAPE NECKLINE Patt across 1st 29 (33;37) sts, turn and work on these sts as follows:
*Dec 1 st at neck edge of every foll row until 22 (26;30) sts remain. Cont without shaping until work measures 24¾(25¼;25¾)in, ending at armhole edge.

SHAPE SHOULDERS Bind off 7 (8;10) sts at beg of next, row, 7 (9;10) sts at beg of foll alt row. Then bind off rem 8 (9;10) sts at beg of next alt row.*
Rejoin yarn to rem sts at center, bind off 1st 14 sts. Then work 2nd side to match 1st side as given from * to *.

GRADE ★ ★			
Sizes to fit	32-34	36-38	40-42	in
Actual size	38	42	46	in
Back length	25½	26	26½	in
Sleeve seam	17¾	18¼	18¾	in
Materials	10	12	14	MC
	1	1	1	A
	1	1	1	B
	1	1	1	C
	oz mohair thick			

1 pr No 5 needles ● 1 pr No 8 needles
Suggested yarn: Anny Blatt Mohair

Abbreviations alt – alternate ● beg – beginning ● cont – continue ● dec – decrease ● foll – following ● inc – increase ● k – knit ● p – purl ● patt – pattern ● rem – remaining ● rep – repeat ● st(s) – stitch(es) ● st st – stockinette stitch ● tog – together ● MC – main color ● A – 1st color ● B – 2nd color ● C – 3rd color

SLEEVES Using No 5 needles and MC cast on 41 (43;45) sts and work in single rib as given for the back, until work measures 2¾in, ending with a 2nd row, and inc 7 sts evenly across the last row. 48 (50;52) sts.
Change to No 8 needles and cont in st st working from the chart, and inc 1 st at each end of every foll 6th row, until there are 70 (74;76) sts. Then cont without shaping until work measures 17¾(18¼;18¾)in, from beg, ending with a wrong side row. Bind off.

COLLAR Using No 5 needles and MC cast on 73 (77;81) sts and work in single rib as given for the back for 8 rows.
Change to No 8 needles for 8 rows and cont in single rib and inc 1 st at each end of every alt row, working the inc 1 st in from the edge. Cont in this manner until work measures 6in. Bind off ribwise loosely.

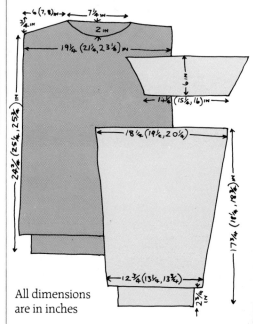

All dimensions are in inches

TIE Using No 8 needles and MC cast on 7 sts and work in single rib as given for the back until work measures 59in. Bind off ribwise.

TO FINISH Using small backstitch, sew both shoulder seams, sew sleeves to armhole, placing half the top of the sleeve to each side of the shoulder seam. Sew side seam from wrist to hem, sew collar around neckline with opening at center front, sew tie into place at center front.

MAYAN MOHAIR

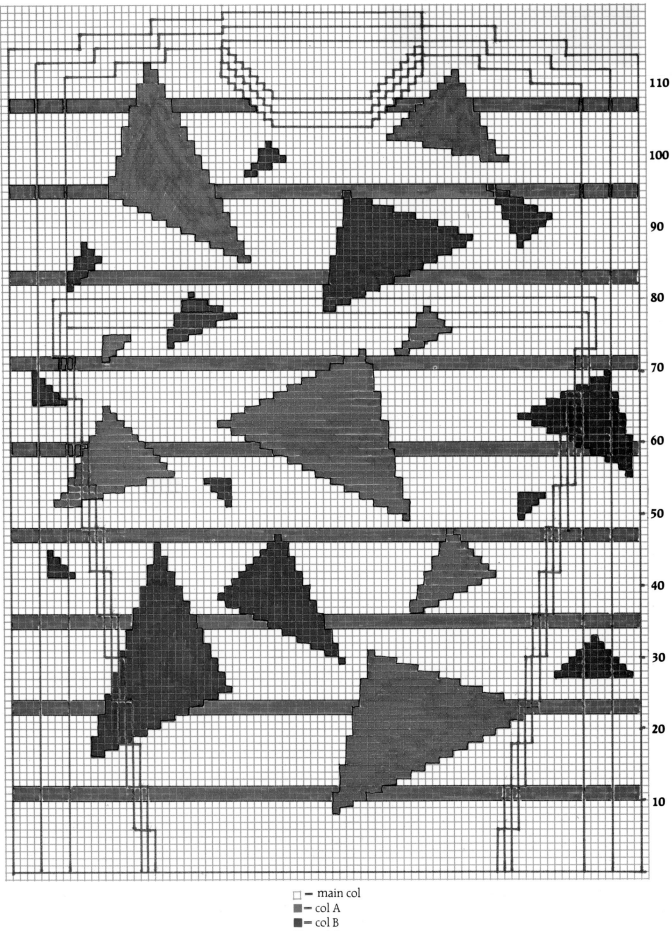

□ = main col
▦ = col A
◼ = col B
◼ = col C

TOWNSWOMAN'S TRAWL

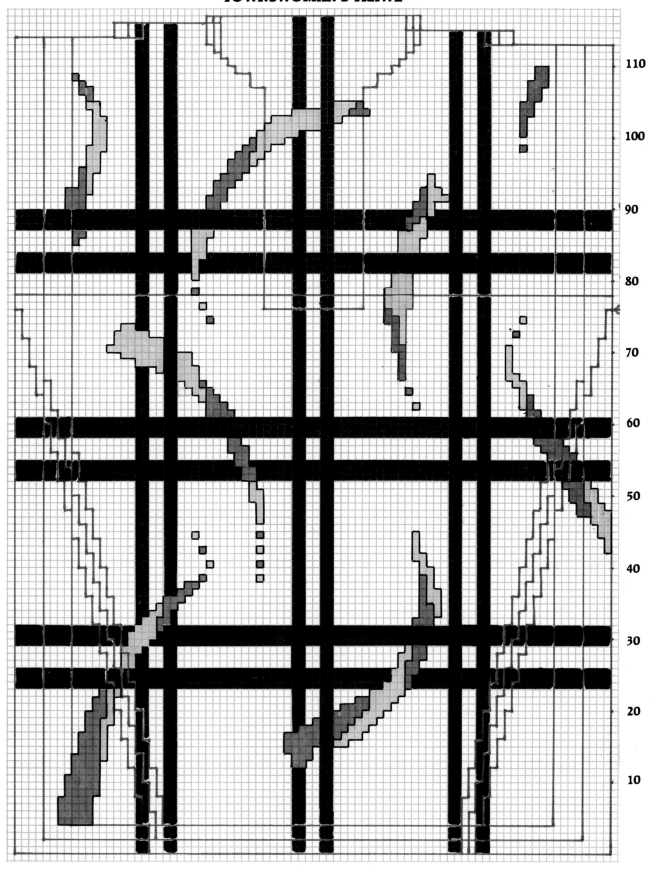

◯= Make bobble in the color indicated thus:
(k1 p1 k1) into stitch, turn work, p3, turn work,
s1 k2 tog, psso.

☐ main col
■ col A
▨ col B
▨ col C

TILE STYLE

Man's patchwork-style sweater

GAUGE Using No 5 needles, over moss rib for square A, 24 sts and 32 rows = 4in square. Using No 5 needles, over cable patt for square B, 33 sts and 32 rows = 4 in square.

SQUARE A Worked over 19 sts.
1st row: k19.
2nd row: p2, [k1, p1] × 8, p1.
Rep rows 1 & 2 12 more times. (26 rows).

SQUARE B Worked over 26 sts.
1st row: (right side) [p2, k1] × 4, p2.
2nd row: [k2, p4] × 4, k2.
Rep rows 1 & 2 once more.
5th row: [p2, C4] × 4, p2.
6th row: as 2nd row.
Rep 1st 2 rows once more.
Rep rows 3-8 twice more. (26 rows)

BACK Using No 3 needles cast on 123 sts and work in single rib as follows:
1st row: k2, *p1, k1, rep from * to last st, k1.
2nd row: k1, *p1, k1, rep from * to end.
Rep these 2 rows until work measures 2¾in, ending with a 1st row and inc 1 st in the last st worked. (124 sts)
Next row: rib 2, *rib 1, inc in next st, rib 2, rep from * to last 2 sts, rib to end. (154 sts)
Change to No 5 needles and cont in patt as follows:
Work rows 1-26 of the patt squares A & B, alternating them, and starting with a square A.
27th-29th row: Work in reverse st st.
30th row: *k3, [inc in next st, k1] × 7, k5, [k2tog, k1] × 7, rep from * to last 19 sts, k3, [inc in next st, k1] × 7, k2. (161 sts)
Now work rows 1-26 of the patt squares A & B, alternating them, and starting with a square B.
57th-59th row: work in reverse st st.
60th row: *k3, [k2tog, k1] × 7, k5, [inc in next st, k1] × 7, k2, rep from * to last 26 sts, k3, [k2tog, k1] × 7, k2. (154 sts)
These 60 rows form the patt. Cont in patt until work measures 28¼in, ending with a 57th patt row. Bind off on next row.
Place neckline marker each side of the center 53 sts.

GRADE ★ ★ ★		
Sizes to fit	36-40	in
Actual size	44	in
Back length	28¼	in
Sleeve seam	17½	in
Materials	22oz knitting worsted	

1 pr No 3 needles ● 1 pr No 5 needles ● 3 buttons
Suggested yarn: Phildar Détente

Abbreviations alt – alternate ● beg – beginning ● cont – continue ● dec – decrease ● foll – following ● inc – increase ● k – knit ● p – purl ● patt – pattern ● rem – remaining ● rep – repeat ● st(s) – stitch(es) ● st st – stockinette stitch ● tog – together

FRONT Using No 3 needles, cast on 123 sts and work in single rib as given for the back (for 2¾in, ending with a 1st row).
Next row: rib 4 *rib 1, inc in next st, rib 1, rep from * to last 5 sts, rib to end. (161 sts)
Change to No 5 needles and cont in patt starting with row 3. Shape neckline when work measures approximately 20¾in, ending with a 28th patt row.

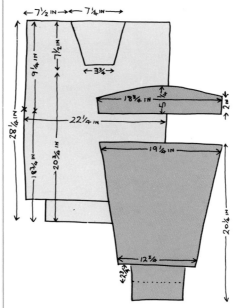

7½ in — 7¼ in
7½ in
9¼ in
3¾
28¼ in
18¾ in
2 in
22¼ in
18¾ in
20⅜ in
19¼ in
20¼ in
12¾
2¾ in

All dimensions are in inches

SHAPE NECKLINE Patt across next row, and bind off center 26 sts. Work on the last group of sts only as follows:
**Cont in patt and dec 1 st at neck edge of every foll 3rd row, until 17 sts have been decresed in this manner, then cont without shaping until work measures same as back to shoulders, ending with the same patt row. Bind off.
Rejoin yarn to rem sts and work 2nd side of neck to match 1st side as given from **.

SLEEVES Using No 3 needles, cast on 55 sts and work in single rib as given for the back, for 5½in, ending with a 1st row.
Next row: rib 10 sts, inc in each of next 35 sts, rib 10 (90 sts).
Change to No 5 needles and work in patt as given for the back, starting with a square A. At the same time inc 1 st at each end of every foll 5th row and incorporate the sts into the patt, cont in this manner until one extra pattern square has been increased at each side of work. Cont in patt without shaping until work measures approximately 20¼in, ending with a 59th patt row. Work 2 more rows in reverse st st. Bind off loosely.

COLLAR Using No 3 needles, cast on 15 sts and work in single rib as given for the back, for 4 rows.

BUTTONHOLES *Rib 1st 4 sts of next row, turn and work 2 more rows on these sts, break yarn and rejoin to rem sts. Work 3 rows on these sts. Work 6 rows across all the sts. Rep from * once more, then work 1 more buttonhole. At the same time, inc 1 st at the left hand edge of the work, on every 3rd row from the beg, 19 times in all, then cont in rib for a further 54 rows. Now dec 1 st at left edge of every 3rd row 19 times in all. Bind off ribwise.

TO FINISH Using small backstitch sew shoulder seams. Sew sleeves to armholes matching patt squares as far as possible. Sew 1st 3¼in of cuff on right side, then sew underarm seam from cuff to hem on inside. Sew shaped edge of collar to neckline, with buttons on left side. Sew cast on and bind off edges of collar to cast off stitches at center front, so that they overlap with button edge at front. Sew button into place.

COOL ACCORD

Cool lacy top with a twist cord pattern

GAUGE Using No 5 needles over st pattern. 25 sts and 28 rows = 4in square.

BACK & FRONT (both the same) Using No 3 needles, cast on 93 (97;103;107) sts and work in single rib as follows:
1st row: k2, *p1, k1, rep from * to last st, k1.
2nd row: k1, *p1, k1, rep from * to end.
Rep these 2 rows until work measures 2¼in, ending with a 1st row.
Next row: rib 3 (5;2;4) sts, *rib 3 (3;4;4) sts, inc in next st, rib 4, rep from * to last 2 (4;2;4) sts, rib to end. 104 (108;114;118) sts.
Change to No 5 needles and cont in patt as follows:
1st row: pl (3;1;3) sts *RT, pl, sl1, k1, psso, yo, k2, yo, k2tog, p1, rep from * to last 3 (5;3;5;) sts, RTK, p to end.
2nd row and all alt rows: k1 (3;1;3), *p2, k1, p6, k1, rep from * to last 3 (5;3;5) sts, p2, k to end.
3rd row: pl (3;1;3), *RTK, p1, C6, p1, rep from * to last 3 (5;3;5) sts, RTK, p to end.
5th, **7**th, **9**th and **11**th rows: as 1st row.
12th row: as 2nd row.
These 12 rows form the patt. Cont in patt until work measures 18¾(19¼;19½;20)in, ending with a wrong side row.

SHAPE ARMHOLES Bind off 4 sts at beg of next 2 rows. Bind off 3 sts at beg of next 2 rows. Dec 1 st at each end of next and foll alt row. Work 1 row without shaping. 86 (90;96;100) sts.
SHAPE NECKLINE Next row: k2tog, patt 28 (30;32;34) sts, turn work.
Next row: patt to end.
Next row: k2tog, patt to last 7 (7;8;8) sts, turn work.
Next row: patt to end.
Rep the last 2 rows two more times.
Slip to 1st 52 (54;58;60) sts onto stitch holder and work on rem 30 (32;34;36) sts as follows:
Next row: patt to last 2 sts, k2tog.
Next row: patt to last 7 (7;8;8) sts, turn work.
Rep the last 2 rows two more times.
Next row: patt to last 2 sts, k2tog.
Leave all 78 (82;88;92) sts on stitch holder.

COLLAR Using No 3 circular needle, starting at center front and working from the right side, pick up 39 (41;44;46) sts from front. Cast on 62 (65;66;69) sts, pick up 78 (82;88;92) sts from back, cast on 62 (65;66;69) sts, pick up rem 39 (41;44;46) sts of front. 280 (294;308;322) sts.

GRADE ★ ★				
Sizes to fit	32	34	36	38	in
Actual size	32	34	36	38	in
Side seam	18¾	19¼	19½	20	in
Materials	15	17	19	21	
	oz knitting worsted				

1 pr No 3 needles ● 1 pr No 5 needles ● 1 No 3 circular needle ● 1 button
Suggested yarn: Pingouin Coton Naturel 8 Fils

Abbreviations alt – alternate ● beg – beginning ● cont – continue ● dec – decrease ● foll – following ● inc – increase ● k – knit ● C6 – cable 6, C3B. k3, k3CN ● CN – cable needle ● LN – left needle ● C3B – sl next 3 sts to CN and hold at back ● k3CN – k3 sts from CN ● RTk – right twist knitwise: k2tog but do not remove from LN k into 1st of the 2 sts. then remove both sts from LN tog ● p – purl ● patt – pattern ● psso – pass sl st over ● rem – remaining ● rep – repeat ● sl – slip ● st(s) – stitch(es) ● st st – stockinette stitch ● tog – together ● yo – yarn over needle ●

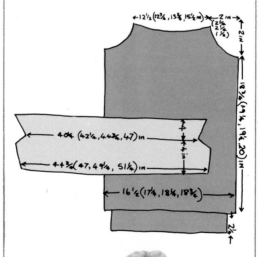

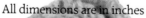

All dimensions are in inches

Work in rounds of single rib for 10 rows.
Next row: *rib 19 (20;21;22) sts, dec ribwise in each of next 2 sts, rib 19 (20;21;22) sts, rep from * to end of rounds. 266 (280;294;308) sts.
Work in rounds of single rib for 10 rows.
Next row: *rib 18 (19;20;21) sts, dec ribwise in each of next 2 sts, rib 18 (19;20;21) sts, rep from * to end of round. 252 (266;280;294) sts.
Work in single rib for 6 rounds.
Now begin working in rows of single rib by turning the work at the end of each row and working the shapings as follows (with the wrong side row worked on the right side of the garment so that when the collar is folded over the right side is on the outside).
Next row (wrong side row): k1, p2, inc in next st, rib to last 4 sts, inc in next st, p2, k1.
Next row (right side row): k3, inc in the next st, rib to last 4 sts, inc in next st, k3.
Rep these 2 rows two more times, then still working the increases at the edge in this manner, work a row of increases by increasing 14 sts evenly across the row, placing double increases in line with the double increases previously worked. Cont working in rib and increasing at the edge as before for a further 7 rows.
Next row: k1, p2, work 2 sts tog ribwise, rib to last 5 sts, work 2 sts tog ribwise, p2, k1.
Next row: k3, work 2 sts tog ribwise, rib to last 5 sts, work 2 sts tog ribwise, k3.
Rep the 1st of these 2 rows once more, then work another inc row as before, by increasing 14 sts evenly around the row, placing the double increases in line with the double increases previously worked. Cont working in rib and dec at the edge in the manner given, for a further 10 rows. Bind off loosely, ribwise.

TO FINISH Using small backstitch, sew side seams. Sew button into place on front collar.

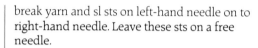

PRITHEE MAID

Fluffy sweater with Elizabethan ribbon ties

GAUGE Using No 5 needles over moss st. 20 sts and 37 rows = 4in square.

BACK & FRONT (both the same) Using No 3 needles, cast on 83 (87;91;95) sts and work in single rib as follows:
1st row: k2, *p1, k1, rep from * to last st, k1.
2nd row: k1, *p1, k1, rep from * to end.
Rep these 2 rows until work measures 2¼, ending with a 1st row.
Next row: rib 5 (7;4;6), [inc in next st, rib 7 (7;8;8)] × 9, inc in next st, rib to end. 93 (97;101;105) sts.
Change to No 5 needles and cont in st patt as follows:
1st row: [p1, k1] × 7 (8;9;10), *k6, [p1, k1] × 12, rep from * to last 19 (21;23;25) sts, k6, [p1, k1] × 6 (7;8;9), p1.
2nd row: [p1, k1] × 7 (8;9;10), *p1, k3, [p1, k1] × 13, rep from * to last 19 (21;23;25) sts, p1, k3, [p1, k1] × 7 (8;9;10), p1.
3rd row: [p1, k1] × 7 (8;9;10), *k2, yo, k2tog, k2, [p1, k1] × 12, rep from * to last 19 (21;23;25) sts, k2, yo, k2tog, k2, [p1, k1] × 6 (7;8;9), p1.
4th row: as 2nd row.
Rep rows 1 and 2, 4 more times.
These 12 rows form the patt. Cont in patt until work measures 9½(10;10¼;10½)in from beg, ending with a right side row. Keeping patt correct, shape sleeves as follows:

SLEEVES Inc 1 st at each end of the next and every foll 4th row 3 times in all.
Inc 1 st at each end of every foll alt row 6 times in all.
Inc 1 st at each end of every foll row 7 times in all. 125 (129;133;137) sts.
Cast on 3 sts at beg of next 16 rows.
Cast on 6 sts at beg of next 4 rows.
Cast on 9 sts at beg of next 8 rows.
269 (273;277;281) sts.
Work a further 40 (42;44;46) rows in patt without shaping.
Next 2 rows: patt to last 13 (13;12;12) sts, turn.
Next 2 rows: patt to last 26 (26;24;24) sts, turn.
Next 2 rows: patt to last 39 (39;36;36) sts, turn.
Next 2 rows: patt to last 52 (52;48;48) sts, turn.
Next 2 rows: patt to last 65 (65;60;60) sts, turn.
Next 2 rows: patt to last 78 (78;72;72) sts, turn.
Next 2 rows: patt to last 90 (91;84;84) sts, turn.
3rd & 4th sizes only:
Next 2 rows: patt to last 95 (96) sts, turn.

All sizes:
Next row: patt to last 102 (104;106;108) sts, turn.
Next row: patt to last 102 (104;106;108) sts,

GRADE ★ ★					
Sizes to fit	32	34	36	38	in
Actual size	34	36	38	40	in
Back length (from nape approx)	21	21½	22	22½	in
Materials	17	19	21	22	
	oz knitting worsted				

1 pr No 3 needles ● 1 pr No 5 needles ● ribbon
Suggested yarn: Wendy Dolcé

Abbreviations alt – alternate ● beg – beginning ● cont – continue ● foll – following ● inc – increase ● k – knit ● p – purl ● patt – pattern ● ● rep – repeat ● st(s) – stitch(es) ● tog – together ● yo – yarn over needle

break yarn and sl sts on left-hand needle on to right-hand needle. Leave these sts on a free needle.

FRILLS Using No 5 needles, cast on 403 (409;415;421) sts.
1st and **2**nd rows: k to end.
3rd row: k1 (4;3;2) *yo, k2tog, k6, rep from * to last 2 (5;4;3) sts, yo, k2tog, k0 (3;2;1).
4th row: k to end.
5th row: *k1, p1, rep from * to last st, k1.
Rep the 5th row 6 more times.
Next row: k1, *k2tog, k1, rep from * to end. 269 (273; 277;281) sts.

JOIN FRILLS (both the same) With right side of garment facing and frill in front, working 1 st from frill and 1 st from garment tog, k to end. Bind off knitwise.

CUFFS With right side facing, pick up 24 (25;26;27) sts across wrist edge of back and 23 (24;25;26) sts across wrist edge of front. 47 (49;51;53) sts. Work in single rib as given for the back and front beg with a 2nd row until cuff measures 2¼in. Bind off ribwise.

TO FINISH Using small backstitch, sew underarm seam. Thread ribbon through holes in vertical stripes. Fasten off ribbon in center front and center back stripes. Tie remaining ribbons leaving approximately 2in to 4in gap between front and back.

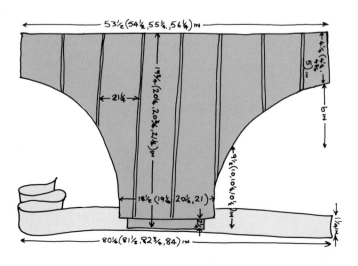

All dimensions are in inches

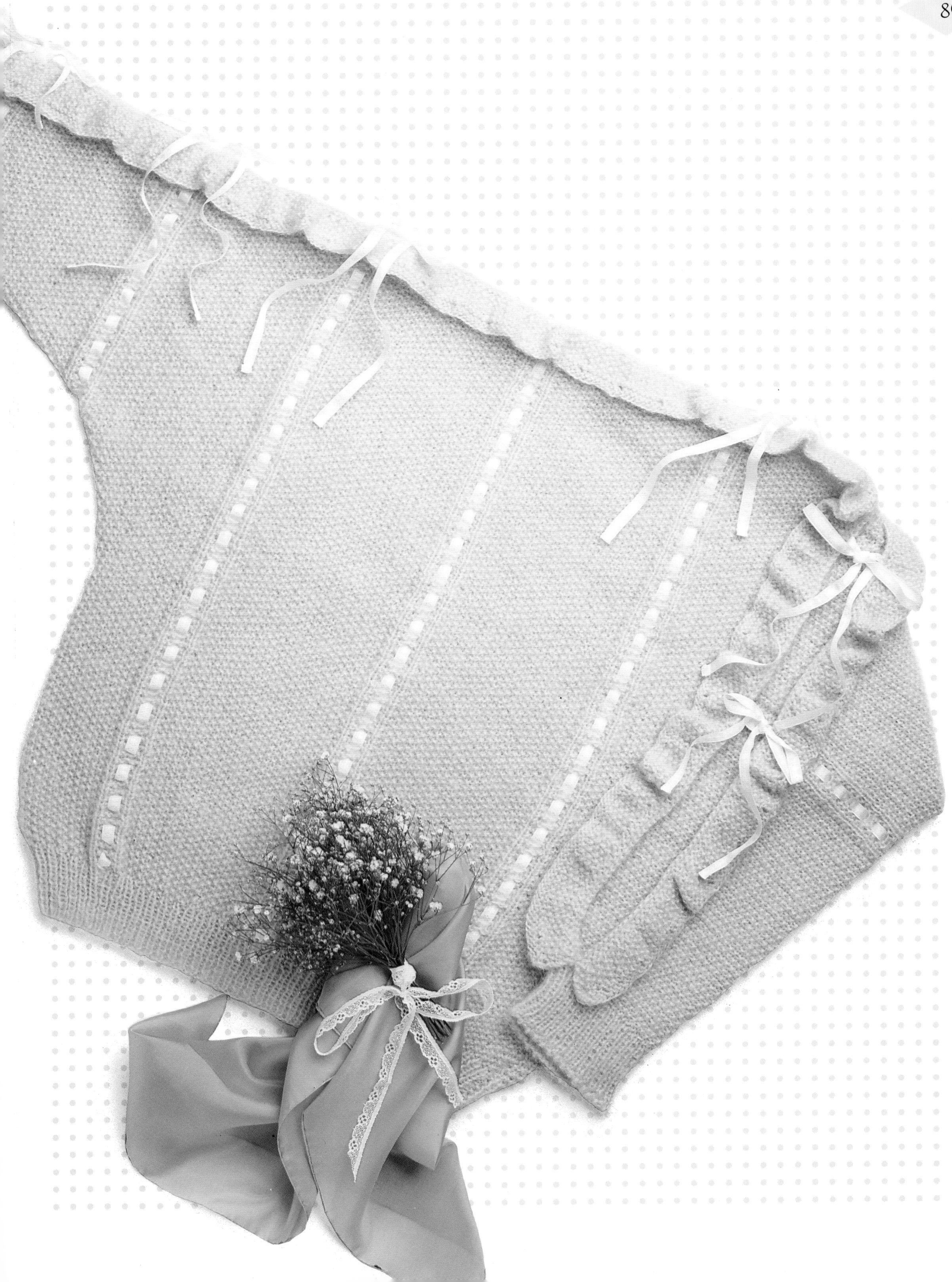

LITTLE LEAGUER
Child's sweater in brioche rib

GAUGE Using No 5 needles and working in brioche rib patt 26 sts and 40 rows = 4in square.

BACK No 3 needles and MC, cast on 83 (89;95;101) sts and work in single rib as follows:
1st row: k2, *p1, k1, rep from * to last st, k1.
2nd row: k1, *p1, k1, rep from * to end.
Rep these 2 rows until work measures 2in ending with a 1st row.
Next row: rib 2 (5;3;1), *rib 3 (3;4;4) sts, inc in next st, rib 4 (4;4;5) sts, rep from * to last 1 (4;2;0) sts, rib to end. 93 (99;105;111) sts.
Change to No 5 needles and cont in patt as follows:
1st row: k1, p1, *k1, p1, rep from * to last 3 sts, k1B, p1, k1.
2nd row: k to end.
These 2 rows form the patt. Cont in patt until work measures 8 (9¾;11¼;12¼)in, ending with a wrong side row. Change to A and work 6 rows in patt, then work 6 rows B, then a further 6 rows A. Work 1 row B.

SHAPE RAGLANS Cont working in B as follows:
1st row (wrong side): k4, p1, k to last 5 sts, p1, k to end.
2nd row: k1, p1, k1, k2tog, *p1, k1, rep from * to last 6 sts, p1, sl1, k1, psso, k1, p1, k1.
3rd row: k2, p2, k to last 4 sts, p2, k2.
4th row: k1, p1, k2tog, *p1, k1, rep from * to last 5 sts, p1, sl1, k1, psso, p1, k1.
Rep rows 1-4 until 31 (33;35;37) sts remain. Bind off.

FRONT Work as given for the back, until 43 (45;51;53) sts remain.

SHAPE NECKLINE Cont to dec at raglan edges as before.
Next row: patt to center 9 (9;11;11) sts. Bind these sts off and cont in patt to end of row.
**Working on this last group of sts only, cont in patt and raglan shaping and dec 1 st at neck edge of every row 10 (11;11;12) times in all. Cont shaping at raglan edge only until 1 st rem. Fasten off.
Rejoin yarn to rem sts at neck edge and work 2nd side of neck to match 1st side as given from **

GRADE ★ ★				
Sizes to fit	26	28	30	32	in
Actual size	28	30	32	34	in
Back length	16¼	18	20¼	21¼	in
Sleeve seam	12	13½	14¾	16	in
Materials	7	8	8	10	MC
	1	1	1	1	A
	oz knitting worsted				
	5	5	7	7	B
	oz knitting worsted				

1 pr No 3 needles ● 1 pr No 5 needles
Suggested yarn: Candide, Pomfret Mark II by Brunswick

Abbreviations alt – alternate ● cont – continue ● dec – decrease ● foll – following ● inc – increase ● k – knit ● k1b – knit into st on row below (dropping stitch on needle) ● p – purl ● patt – pattern ● psso – pass sl st over ● rem – remaining ● rep – repeat ● sl – slip ● st(s) – stitch(es) ● tog – together ● MC – main color ● A – 1st color ● B – 2nd color

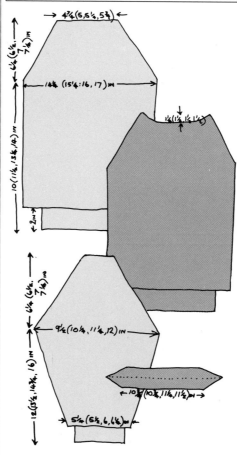

All dimensions are in inches

SLEEVES Using No 3 needles and MC, cast on 35 (37;39;41) sts and work in single rib as for the back until work measures 2in ending with a 2nd row.
Change to No 5 needles and cont in patt as given for the back. Also inc 1 st at each end of every foll 6th row until there are 63 (67;75;79) sts. At the same time, when work measures 10 (11½;12½;14)in, work stripes as follows: 6 rows A, 6 rows B, 6 rows A, then 1 row B. Cont working in B as follows:

SHAPE RAGLANS Starting with a wrong side row, work the 4 rows of decreases as for the back raglan shaping, repeating them until 7 (7;9;9) sts rem. Bind off.

NECKBAND Using No 3 needles and A, cast on 69 (71;73;75) sts and work in single rib for 8 rows. And inc 1 st at each end of every row. Work next row as a p row, then work a further 8 rows in single rib decreasing 1 st at each end of every row.

TO FINISH Using small backstitch, sew all raglan seams, then sew underarm seam from wrist to hem. With right sides together, sew shaped edge of neckband to neckline, overlapping the ends approximately 1in each side of center (overlapping on right side, to the right for a boy and the left for a girl). Turn neckband to inside and sew other edge to inside.

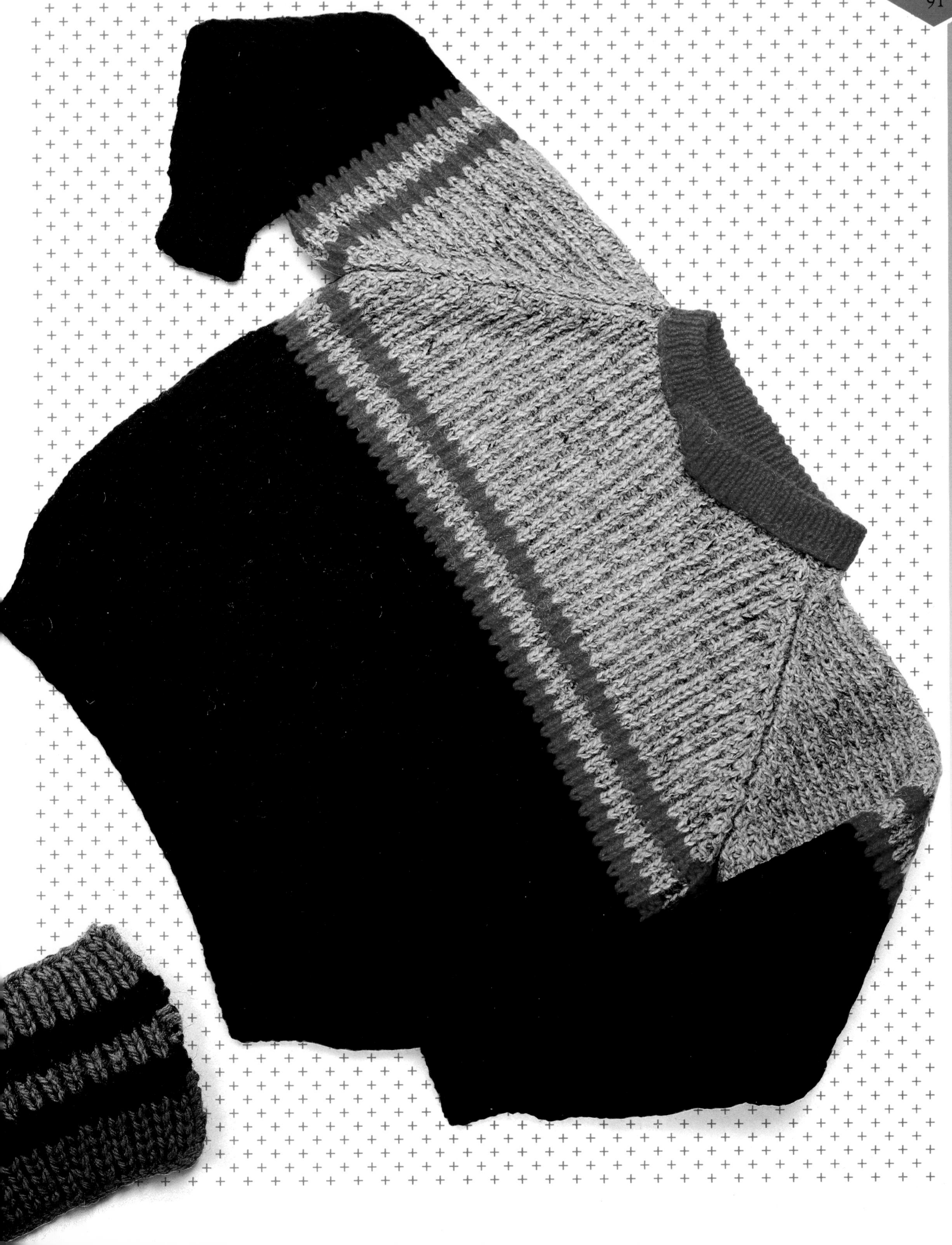

COUNTY GALWAY

Aran-style sweater

GAUGE Using No 5 needles over stitch patt 25 sts and 31 rows = 4in square.

BACK Using No 3 needles, cast on 105 (117;131) sts and work in single rib as follows:
1st row: k2, *p1, k1, rep from * to last st, k1.
2nd row: k1, *p1, k1, rep from * to end.
Rep these 2 rows until work measures 2¼in, ending with a 1st row.
Next row: rib 3 (4;1) sts, *rib 4 (4;6) sts, inc in next st. rib 4 (5;6) sts, rep from * to last 3 (3;0) sts, rib to end. 116 (128;141) sts.

Change to No 5 needles and cont in patt st as follows:
1st row: p2 (8;2), RTK *p1, C6, p1, RTK, p13, RTK, rep from * to last 12 (18;12) sts, p1, C6, p1, RTK, p2 (8;2).
2nd row: k2 (8;2), p2, *k1, p6, k1, p2, k13, p2, rep from * to last 12 (18;12) sts, k1, p6, k1, p2, k2 (8;2) sts.
3rd row: p2 (8;2), RTK *p1, k2, RTK, k2, p1, RTK, p6, MB, p6, RTK, rep from * to last 12 (18;12) sts, p1, k2, RTK, k2, p1, RTK, p2 (8,2) sts.
4th row: k2 (8;2), p2, *k1, p6, k1, p2, k6, p1 tbl, k6, p2, rep from * to last 12 (18;12) sts, k1, p6, k1, p2, k2 (8;2) sts.
5th row: p2 (8;2), RTK *p1, C6, p1, RTK, p3, MB, p2, k1 tbl, p2, MB, p3, RTK, rep from * to last 12 (18;12) sts, p1, C6, p1, RTK, p2 (8;2).
6th row: k2 (8;2), p2, *k1, p6, k1, p2, k3, p1 tbl, k2, p1, k2, p1 tbl, k3, p2, rep from * to last

GRADE ★ ★ ★ ★			
Sizes to fit	32-34	36-38	40-42	in
Actual size	36	40	44	in
Back length	24	25	26	in
Sleeve seam with cuff turned back	17	17½	18	in
Materials	24	28	33	
	oz knitting worsted			

1 pr No 5 needles ● 1 pr No 3 needles ● 2 buttons
Suggested yarn: Pomfret Mark II by Brunswick

Abbreviations alt - alternate ● BC - back cross:- C1B. k1. plcn ● beg - beginning ● Cb - C1F. k2. K1CN. C2B. k1. k2CN ● CN - cable needle ● cont - continue ● dec - decrease ● F - (k1 yo) x 2 k1) all into next st. turn. k5. turn. p2tog. pl. p2tog. turn sl 1.k2tog. psso ● FC - front cross:- c1F. pl. K1CN ● foll - following ● inc - increase ● k - knit ● MIP - make 1 st purlwise, lift running thread between the sts. p into back of this st ● MB - make bobble ● p - purl ● RTK - right twist. knitwise. k2tog. do not remove from LN. k into 1st of the 2 sts. then remove both from LN tog ● st(s) - stitches ● tbl - through back of loop ● tog - together

12 (18;12) sts, k1, p6, k1, p2, k2 (8;2) sts.
7th row: p2 (8;2), RTK * p1, k2, T2, k2, p1, RTK, p1, MB, p1, FC, p1, k1 tbl, p1, BC, p1, MB, p1, RTK, rep from * to last 12 (18;12) sts, p1, k2, RTK, k2, p1, RTK, p2 (8;2) sts.
8th row: k2 (8;2), p2, *k1, p6, k1, p2, k1, p1 tbl, k2, (p1, k1) × 3, k1, p1 tbl, k1, p2, rep from * to last 12 (18;12) sts, k1, p6, k1, p2, k2 (8;2).
9th row: p2 (8;2) sts, RTK, *p1, C6, p1, RTK, p1, FC, p1, FC, k1 tbl, BC, p1, BC, p1, RTK, rep from *

to last 12 (18;12) sts, p1, C6, p1, RTK, p2 (8;2) sts.
10th row: k2 (8;2), p2, *k1, p6, k1, p2, k2, BC, k1, p3, k1, FC, k2, p2, rep from * to last 12 (18;12) sts, k1, p6, k1, p2, k2 (8;2) sts.
11th row: p2 (8;2), RTK, *p1, k2, RTK, k2, p1, RTK, p3, FC, M1p, sl1, k2tog psso, M1p, BC, p3, RTK, rep from * to last 12 (18;12) sts, p1, k2, RTK, k2, p1, RTK, p2 (8;2).
12th row: k2 (8;2), p2, *k1, p6, k1, p2, k4, BC, p1, FC, k4, p2, rep from *to last 12 (18;12) sts, k1, p6, k1, p2, k2 (8;2) sts.
13th row: p2 (8;2), RTK, *p1, C6, p1, RTK, p4, p into front and back of next st, sl1, k2tog, psso, p into front and back of next st, p4, RTK, rep from * to last 12 (18;12) sts, p1, cable 6, p1, RTK, p2 (8;2).
14th row: k2 (8;2), p2, *k1, p6, k1, p2, k6, p1, k6, p2, rep from * to last 12 (18;12) sts, k1, p6, k1, p2, k2 (8;2).
15th row: p2 (8;2), RTK, *p1, k2, RTK, k2, p1, RTK, p13, RTK, rep from * to last 12 (18;12) sts, p1, k2, RTK, k2, p1, RTK, p2 (8;2).
16th row: k2 (8;2), p2, *k1, p6, k1, p2, k13, p2, rep from * to last 12 (18;12) sts, k1, p6, k1, p2, k2 (8;2) sts.

These 16 rows form the patt. Cont in patt until **work measures 14 (14¾;15½)in, ending with a** wrong side row. Place a marker for armhole at each end of this last row, then cont without **shaping until work measures 23 (24;25)in.** ending with a wrong side row.

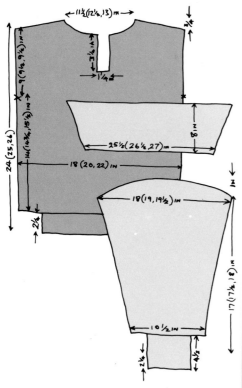

←11¾(12¼,13)in→

←25½(26¼,27)in→

←18(20,22)in→

←18(19,19½)in→

←10½in→

24(25,24)in

17(17½,18)in

All dimensions are in inches

SHAPE SHOULDERS & NECKLINE Bind off 7 (8;9) sts at beg of next row. Patt 23 (26;29) sts. Bind off center 56 (60;65) sts, patt rem 30 (34;38) sts, turn and work on this last group of sts as follows:
Next row: bind off 7 (8;9) sts, patt to last 2 sts, K2tog.
Next row: bind off 2 sts, patt to end.
Rep these 2 rows once more.
Next row: bind off 7 (9;11) sts, patt to last 2 sts, k2tog.
Next row: bind off rem 2 sts.
Rejoin yarn to rem sts at neck edge and work as follows:
Next row: bind off 3 sts, patt to end.
Next row: bind off 7 (8;9) sts, patt to last 2 sts, k2tog.
Next row: bind off 2 sts, patt to end.
Next row: bind off 7 (9;11) sts, patt to last 2 sts, k2tog.
Next row: bind off rem 2 sts.

FRONT Work as for the back until work measures 18 (19;20)in, ending with a wrong side row.

DIVIDE FOR NECK Next row: patt 54 (60;66) sts, turn and cont in patt on these sts for a further 3¼in, ending at the neck edge.

***SHAPE NECKLINE** Next row: bind off 4 sts, patt to end.
Next row: patt to last 2 sts, k2tog.
Rep these 2 rows once more.
Next row: bind off 3 sts, patt to end.
Next row: patt to last 2 sts, k2tog.
Rep the last 2 rows 2 more times.
Next row: bind off 2 sts, patt to end.
Next row: patt to last 2 sts, k2tog.
Now dec 1 st at neck edge of every row 3 (5;7) times. AND at the same time, when work measures 23 (24;25)in ending at armhole edge. Cont to dec 1st at neck edge of every row for a further 5 rows, and at the same time, commence shoulder shaping as follows:

SHAPE SHOULDERS Bind off 7 (8;9) sts at beg of next and foll alt row. Bind off 7 (9;11) sts at beg of foll alt row.
Rejoin yarn to rem sts at neck edge. Bind off 8 (8;9) sts, then cont on rem sts for 3¼in, ending at neck edge.
Complete neck shaping to match first side as from*.

SLEEVES Using No 3 needles, cast on 55 sts and work in single rib as for the back until work measures 4¾in, ending with a 1st row.
Next row: *rib 2, inc in next st, rib 2, rep from * to end. 66 sts.
Change to No 5 needles and cont in patt as for the back, foll instructions given for the 1st size. Also inc 1 st at each end of every foll 3rd row until there are 118 (122;128) sts, then cont without shaping until work measures 19½ (20;20½)in, from beg, ending with a wrong side row.

SHAPE SLEEVE TOPS Cont in patt and bind off 14 (15;15) sts at beg of next 8 rows. Bind off rem 12 (10;14) sts.

BUTTONBAND Using No 3 needles, cast on 11 sts and work in single rib for 24 rows. Leave sts on safety pin.

BUTTONHOLE BAND Using No 3 needles, cast on 11 sts and work in single rib for 6 rows.
Next row: rib 4, bind off 3, rib 4.
Next row: rib 4 cast on 3, rib 4.
Work 8 rows in rib then work another buttonhole over next 2 rows. Work a further 6 rows and leave sts on safety pin.

COLLAR Using small backstitch sew both shoulder seams.
Using No 3 needles and working from the wrong side, pick up 11 sts from buttonband, 179 (187;191) sts evenly around neck, then 11 sts from buttonhole band. Work in single rib as given for the back, starting with a 1st row, until work measures 2¼in. Use alternate No 3 and No 5 needles over the next 8 rows, then cont on No 5 needles until collar measures 8in. Bind off loosely ribwise.

TO FINISH Using small backstitch throughout, sew sleeves to armhole between markers, sew underarm seam from middle of cuff to hem, sew remainder of cuff on the outside. Sew buttonband and buttonhole band to neck. Sew buttons into place.

BLOOMING BUTTON UP
Cardigan with a floral pattern in diamond cable

GAUGE Using No 5 needles over st patt 26 sts and 30 rows = 4in square.

NOTE Omit working floral motif into partial diamonds. These can be embroidered on when making up.

BACK Using No 3 needles and MC, cast on 115 (121;127;133) sts and work in single rib as follows:

1st row: k2, *p1, k1, rep from * to last st, k1.
2nd row: k1, *p1, k1, rep from *to end.
Rep these 2 rows until work measures 2¼in. ending with a 1st row.
Next row: rib 7 (5;8;5), [inc in next st, rib 8 (9;9;10)] × 11, inc in next st, rib to end. 127 (133;139;145) sts.
Change to No 5 needles and cont in st patt as follows:

1st row: p0 (3;6;0), *p7, T2R, p6, rep from * to last 1 (4;7;1) sts, p1 (4;7;1).
2nd row: k0 (3;6;0), *k7, p2, k1, p2, k6, rep from * to last 1 (4;7;1) sts, k1 (4;7;1).
3rd row: k0 (0;1;0), p0 (3;5;0), *p6, C2R, p1, C2L, p5, rep from * to last 1 (4;7;1) sts, p1 (4;6;1), k0 (0;1;0).
4th row: p0 (0;1;0), k0 (3;5;0), *k6, p2, k3, p2, k5, rep from * to last 1 (4;7;1) sts, k1 (4;6;1), p0 (0;1;0).

1st, 2nd & 4th sizes only:
5th row: p0 (3;0), *p5, C2R, p3, C2L, p4, rep from * to last 1 (4;1) sts, p1 (4;1).

3rd size only:
5th row: C1LK, *p9, C2R, p3, C2L, rep from * to last 11 sts, p9, C1RK.

All sizes:
6th row: p0 (0;2;0), k0 (3;4;0), *k5, p2, k5, p2, k4, rep from * to last 1 (4;7;1) sts, k1 (4;5;1), p0 (0;2;0).

1st, 2nd & 4th sizes only:
7th row: p0 (3;0), *p4, C2R, p2, yo, MLs, yf, p2, C2L, p3, rep from * to last 1 (4;1) sts, p1 (4;1).

3rd size only:
7th row: C2L, *p7, C2R, p2, yo, MLs, yf, p2, C2L, rep from * to last 10 sts, p7, C2R.

All sizes:
8th row: k0 (0;1;0), p0 (0;2;0), k0 (3.3.0), *k4, p2, k3, yf, sl 3pdl, k4, p2, k3, rep from * to last 1 (4;7;1) sts, k1 (4;4;1), p0 (0;2;0), k0 (0;1;0).

1st, 2nd & 4th sizes only:
9th row: k0 (1;0), p0 (2;0), *p3, C2R, p1, yb, CAR, sl1, yfd, CAL, C2L, p2, rep from * to last 1 (4;1) sts, p1 (3;1), k0 (1;0).

3rd size only:
9th row: p1, C2L, *p5, C2R, p1, yb, CAR, sl1, yf, CAL, C2L, rep from * to last 9 sts, p5, C2R, p1.

All sizes:
10th row: k0 (0;2;0), p0 (1;2;0), k0 (2;2;0), *k3, p2, [k1, yf, sl1, k2] × 3, p2, k2, rep from * to last 1 (4;7;1) sts, k1 (3;3;1), p0 (1;2;0), k0 (0;2;0).

1st & 4th sizes only:
11th row: *p2, C2R, [p2, yb, sl1, p1] × 3, C2L, p1, rep from * to last st, p1.

2nd size only:
11th row: C1LK, *p3, C2R, [p2, yb, sl1, p1] × 3, C2L, rep from * to last 5 sts, p3, C1RK.

3rd size only:
11th row: p2, C2L, *p3, C2R, [p2, yb, sl1, p1] × 3, C2L, rep from * to last 8 sts, p3, C2R, p2.

All sizes:
12th row: k0 (0;3;0), p0 (2;2;0), k0 (1;1;0), *k2, p2, k2, [yf, sl1, k3p] × 3, p2, k1, rep from * to last 1 (4;7;1) sts, k1 (2;2;1), p0 (2;2;0), k0 (0;3;0).

1st & 4th sizes only:
13th row: *p1, C2R, [p8, yb, sl1] × 3, p2, C2L, rep from *to last st, p1.

2nd & 3rd sizes only:
13th row: p0 (3), C2L, *p1, C2R, [p3, yb, sl1] × 3, p2, C2L, rep from * to last 4 (7) sts, p1, C2R,

p0 (3).
All sizes:
14th row: k0 (1;4;0), p0 (2;2;0), *k1, p2, [k3, yf, sl1] × 3, k4, p2, rep from * to last 1 (4;7;1) sts, k1, p0 (2;2;0), k0 (1;4;0).

1st & 4th sizes only:
15th row: p1, k2, *p3, yb, MB, p3, yb, sl1, p2, yb, MB, p3, T2R, rep from * to last 19 sts, p3, yb, MB, p3, yb, sl1, yb, MB, p3, k2, p1.

2nd & 3rd sizes only:
15th row: p1 (4), *T2R, p3, yb, MB, p3, yb, sl1, p2, yb, MB, p3, rep from * to last 6 (9) sts, T2R, p1 (4).

All sizes:
16th row: k0 (1;4;0), p0 (2;2;0), *k1, p2, k6, yf, sl1, k7, p2, rep from * to last 1 (4;7;1) sts, k1, p0 (2;2;0), k0 (1;4;0).

1st & 4th sizes only:
17th row: *p1, C2L, p5, yb, MB, p5, C2R, rep from * to last st, p1.

2nd & 3rd sizes only:
17th row: p0 (3), *C2R, p1, C2L, p5, yb, MB, p5, rep from * to last 7 (10) sts, C2R, p1, C2L, p0 (3).

All sizes:
18th row: k0 (0;3;0), p0 (2;2;0), k0 (1;1;0), *k2, p2, k11, p2, k1, rep from * to last 1 (4;7;1) sts, k1 (2;2;1), p0 (2;2;0), k0 (0;3;0).

1st & 4th sizes only:
19th row: *p2, C2L, p9, C2R, rep from * to last st, p1.

2nd size only:
19th row: C1P, *p3, C2L, p9, C2R, rep from * to last 5 sts, p3, C1LP.

3rd size only:
19th row: p2, *C2R, p3, C2L, p9, rep from * to last 11 sts, C2R, p3, C2L, p2.

All sizes:
20th row: k0 (0;2;0), p0 (1;2;0), k0 (2;2;0), *k3, p2, k9, p2, k2, rep from * to last 1 (4;7;1) sts, k1 (3;3;1), p0 (1;2;0), k0 (0;2;0).

1st, 2nd & 4th sizes only:
21st row: pl (4;1), *p2, C2L, p7, C2R, p2, yo, MLs, yf, rep from * to last 18(21;18) sts, p2, C2L, p7, C2R, p3 (6;3).

3rd size only:
21st row: pl, C2R, p5, *C2L, p7, C2R, p2, yo, MLs, yf, p2, rep from * to last 22 sts, C2L, p7, C2R, p5, C2L, p1.

1st, 2nd & 4th sizes only:
22nd row: k4 (7;4), *p2, k7, p2, k3, yf, sl 3pdl, K4, rep from * to last 15 (18;15) sts, p2, k7, p2, k4 (7;4).

3rd size only:
22nd row: k1, p2, k5, *p2, k7, p2, k3, yf, sl 3pdl,

GRADE ★ ★ ★ ★				
Sizes to fit	34	36	38	40	in
Actual size	38	39½	41½	43½	in
Back length	27	27½	28	28½	in
Sleeve seam	17½	18	18	18½	in
Materials	15	17	19	21	MC
	3	3	3	5	Col A
	5	5	5	7	Col B
					oz knitting worsted

1 pr No 3 needles ● 1 pr No 5 needles ● 1 No 3 circular needle ● 4 buttons
Suggested yarn: Pingouin Mohair 70

Abbreviations alt – alternate ● beg – beginning ● CAL – sl next st onto CN and hold at front, p3, yb, sl 1 from CN ● CAR – sl next 3 sts onto CN and hold at back sl 1. p3 from CN. yb ● CN – cable needle ● cont – continue ● ClLP – sl next st onto CN and hold at front. pl. kl from CN ● ClP – sl next st onto CN and hold at back pl. kl from CN ● ClRK – sl next st onto CN and hold at back. kl. kl from CN● ClLK – sl next st onto CN and hold at front kl. kl. from CN ● C2RK – sl next 2 sts onto CN and hold at front K2. K2 from CN ● dec – decrease ● foll – following ● inc – increase ● k – knit ● MB – make bobble in color B, into next to 2 sts together (kl. pl) x 2. kl. turn. p5. MC around needle sl the 5 color B sts over the MC loop ● MLS – in color A.kl.pl. k into next wnding yarn around needle 4 times on each st ● p – purl ● sl – slip ● sl 2pdl – sl next 3 sts dropping extra loops ● st(s) – stitches ● st st – stockinette stitch ● tbl – through back of loop ● tog – together ● T2R – sl next 3 sts onto CN and hold at back K2.pl and k2 from CN ● yb – yarn back ● yf – yarn forward ● yo – yarn over needle ● MC – main color ● A – 1st color ● B – 2nd color

k4, rep from * to last 21 sts, p2, k7, p2, k7, p2, k1.

1st, 2nd & 4th sizes only:

23rd row: p4 (7;4), *C2L, p5, C2R, p1, yb, CAR, sl1, yf, CAL, rep from * to last 15(18;15) sts, C2L, p5, C2R, p4 (7;4).

3rd size only:

23rd row: C2R, p7, *C2R, p1, yb, CAR, sl1, yf, CAL, rep from * to last 21 sts, C2L, p5, C2R, p7, C2L.

All sizes:

24th row: p0(0;2;0), k5(8;9;5), *p2, k5, p2, [k1, yf, sl1, k2] × 3, rep from * to last 14(17;20;14) sts, [p2, k5] × 2, k0 (3;4;0), p0 (0;2;0).

1st, 2nd & 4th sizes only:

25th row: p5 (8;5), *C2L, p3, C2R, [p2, yb, sl1, p1] × 3, rep from * to last 14 (17;14) sts, C2L, p3, C2R, p5 (8;5).

3rd size only:

25th row: C1P, p9, *C2L, p3, C2R, [p2, yb, sl1, p1] × 3, rep from * to last 20 sts, C2L, p3, C2R, p9, C1LP.

All sizes:

26th row: p0 (0;1;0), k6 (9;11;6), *p2, k3, p2, k2, [yf, sl1, k3] × 3, rep from * to last 13 (16;19;13) sts, p2, k3, p2, k6 (9;11;6), p0 (0;1;0).

27th row: p6 (9;12;6), *C2L, [p3, yb, sl1] × 3, p2, rep from * to last 13 (16;19;13) sts, C2L, p1, C2R, p6 (9;12;6).

28th row: k7 (10;13;7); *p2, k1, p2, [k3, yf, sl1] × 3, k4, rep from * to last 12 (14;18;12) sts, p2, k1, p2, k7 (10;13;7).

29th row: p7 (10;13;7), *T2R, p3, yb, MB, p3, yb, sl1, p2, yb, MB, p3, rep from * to last 12 (15;18;12) sts, T2R, p7 (10;13;7).

30th row: k0 (3;6;0), *k7, p2, k1, p2, k6, yf, sl1, rep from * to last 19 (22;25;19) sts, k7, p2, k1, p2, k7 (10;13;7).

31st row: k0 (0;1;0), p6 (9;11;6), *C2R, p1, C2L, p5, yb, MB, p5, rep from * to last 13 (16;19;13) sts, C2R, p1, C2L, p6 (9;11;6), k0 (0;1;0).

32nd row:- as 4th row.

18¼(18¾;19¼;19½)in from beg. Place an armhole marker at each end of the last row worked.

Cont in patt until work measures 27 (28;28¾;29½)in from beg, ending with a wrong side row. Bind off, placing neckline markers in st 47 (49;51;53) and st 81 (85;89;93).

LEFT FRONT Using No 3 needles and MC, cast on 55 (57;61;63) sts and work in single rib as given for the back for 2¼in ending with a 1st row.

Next row: rib 4 (4;5;4), (inc in next st, rib 8 (7;9;8) × 5 (6;5;6)), inc in next st, rib to end. 61 (64;67;70) sts.

Change to No 5 needles and cont in st patt as follows:

1st, 2nd & 3rd sizes only:

1st row: p0 (3;6), *p7, T2R, p6, rep from * to last 7 sts, p7.

4th size only:

1st row: *p7, T2R, p6, rep from * to last 16 sts, p7, T2R, p4.

Position of the st patt is now set. Cont in patt until work measures 18¼(18¾;19¼;19½)in from beg, ending with a right side row. Place an armhole marker at the beg of the last row worked.

SHAPE NECKLINE Dec 1 st at beg of next and every foll 4th row until 46 (48;50;52) sts remain. Cont in patt without shaping to the same patt row as back at binding off. Bind off.

RIGHT FRONT Work to match left front, reversing shaping and patt placement.

SLEEVES Using No 3 needles and MC, cast on 59 (63;63;67) sts and work in single rib as given for the back for 2¼in ending with a 1st row.

Next row: rib 4 (3;3;5) sts, [inc in next st, rib 6 (7;7;7)] × 7, inc in next st, rib to end. 67 (71;71;75) sts.

Change to No 5 needles and cont in st patt as follows:

1st row: p4 (6;6;8), *T2R, p13, rep from * to last 9 (11;11;13) sts, T2R, p4 (6;6;8).

Position of st patt is now set. Cont in patt and inc 1 st at each end of the 3rd and every foll 4th row until there are 115 (121;127;133) sts. Cont in patt without shaping until work measures 17¾(18¼;18¼;18¾)in from beg, ending with wrong side row. Bind off.

FRONT BANDS & COLLAR Using small backstitch, sew both shoulder seams. Using No 3 circular needle and MC, with right side facing, beg at bottom edge of right front, pick up 124 (127;130;133) sts to beg of neckline shaping, pick up 70 (72;74;76) sts to right shoulder seam, pick up 33 (35;37;39) sts across back neck, pick up 70 (72;74;76) sts to

end of left front neckline shaping and pick up 124 (127;130;133) sts to bottom left edge. 421 (433;445;457) sts.

Working in single rib as given for the back, beg with a 2nd row, shape collar as follows:

1st row: rib 213 (219;225;231) sts, turn.

2nd row: rib 9 sts, turn.

3rd row: rib 13 sts, turn.

Cont ribbing an additional 4 sts on each row until the row rib 145 sts, turn has been worked.

Next row: rib 149 (150;151;152) sts, turn.

Next row: rib 153 (155;157;150) sts, turn.

Next row: rib 157 (160;163;166) sts, turn.

Next row: rib 163 (167;171;175) sts, turn.

Next row: rib 167 (172;177;182) sts, turn.

Next row: rib 173 (179;185;191) sts, turn.

Next row: rib to end.

Work 3 rows rib across all sts.

Next row: rib 299 (308;317;326) sts, [bind off next 4 sts, rib 34 (35;36;37)] × 3, bind off next 4 sts, rib 4.

Next row: rib 4, [cast on 4 sts, rib 34 (35;36;37)] × 3, cast on 4 sts, rib to end.

Work 4 more rows in rib across all sts, bind off ribwise.

TO FINISH Using small backstitch, sew sleeve tops into armholes, sew side and sleeve seams. Embroider florets where appropriate. Sew on buttons.

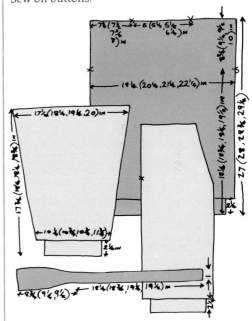

All dimensions are in inches

NO SQUARE

Mohair jacket in a square style with a square motif

GAUGE Using No 8 needles over patt st 16 sts and 22 rows – 4in square.

BACK Using No 5 needles cast on 81 (89;96) sts and work in g st (k every row), until work measures ¾in from beg, ending with a wrong side row.
Change to No 8 needles and work in patt as follows:
1st row: k.
2nd row: p0 (4;1), *k3, p10, rep from * to last 3 (7;4) sts, k3, p0 (4;1).
Rep the 1st and 2nd rows 7 more times.
17th row: k.
18th row: k.
19th row: k.
20th row: k.
These 20 rows form the patt. Cont in patt until work measures 14 (14¼;14½)in from beg. Mark each end of the last row with a contrast thread to indicate the start of the armholes. Cont in patt until the armhole measures 11¼ (11½;12)in from the marker.

SHAPE SHOULDERS Bind off 10 (11;12) sts at the beg of the next 4 rows. Bind off rem 40 (45;48) sts.

LEFT FRONT Using No 5 needles cast on 42 (46;50) sts and work ¾in in g st, ending with a wrong side row.
Change to No 8 needles, and commence patt as follows:
1st row: k.
2nd row: p0 (4;1), *k3, p10, rep from * to last 3 (3;10) sts, k3, p0 (0;7).
Rep rows 1 and 2, 7 more times.
17th to **20**th rows: k.
These 20 rows form the patt. Cont in patt until work measures 14 (14½;14¾)in from beg, mark armholes. Cont in patt until armhole measures 9¼ (9½;10)in from marker ending at neck edge

SHAPE NECKLINE Next row: bind off 18 sts patt to end. Dec 1 st at neck edge on the next and every foll alt row until 20 (22;24) sts remain. Cont straight until armhole measures same as back ending at armhole edge.

SHAPE SHOULDER Beg at armhole edge, bind off 11 (13;15) sts at the beg of the next and foll alt row 10 (11;12).

GRADE ★				
Sizes to fit	32-34	36-38	40-42	in
Actual size	40	43½	47½	in
Back length	24½	25½	26½	in
Sleeve seam	17½	18	18½	in
Materials				
Jacket	16	17	19	A
	2	2	2	B
	2	2	2	C
Scarf	5	5	5	B
	oz mohair thick			

1 pr No 5 needles ● 1 pr No 8 needles ● 1 button
Suggested yarn: Anny Blatt Mohair

Abbreviations alt – alternate ● cont – continue ● dec – decrease ● foll – following ● g st – garter stitch ● inc – increase ● k – knit ● patt – pattern ● p – purl ● rem – remaining ● rep – repeat ● st(s) – stitch(es) ● st st – stockinette stitch ● A – 1st color ● B – 2nd color ● C – 3rd color

RIGHT FRONT Using No 5 needles cast on 42 (46;50) sts and work ¾in in g st, ending with a wrong side row.
Change to No 8 needles, and commence patt as follows:
1st row: knit.
2nd row: p0 (0;7), *k3, p10, rep from * to last 3 (7;4) sts, k3, p0 (4;1).
Rep the 1st and 2nd rows 7 more times.
17th to **20**th rows: k.
These 20 rows form the patt. Complete right front as given for the left front until the armhole measures 8½ (8¾;9¼)in from the marker.

MAKE BUTTONHOLE With right side facing patt 3 sts, bind off 3 sts patt to end.
2nd row: patt to last 3 sts, cast on 3 sts, patt to end.
Cont as given for the left front to end, reversing the neck shaping.

SLEEVES Using No 5 needles cast on 68 (72;76) sts and work ¾in in g st, ending with a wrong side row.
Change to No 8 needles and commence patt as follows:
1st row: k.
2nd row: p0 (2;4), *k3, p10, rep from * to last 3 (5;7) sts, k3, p0 (2;4).
Rep 1st and 2nd rows 7 more times.
17th to **20**th rows: k.

Cont in patt until work measures ·17¾(18¼;18¾)in from beg AND at the same time inc 1 st at each end of the 7th (9th;11th) row, and then at each end of every foll 8th (10th;12th) row until there are 89 (93;97) sts. Bind off.

NECKBAND Join both shoulder seams. With right side of work facing pick up and k 34 sts from right front neck, 40 (45;48) sts from back neck, and 34 sts from left front neck. 108 (113;116) sts. Work ¾in in g st, ending with a wrong side row. Bind off, purlwise.

FRONT EDGINGS (make 2) Cast on 7 sts and work 23¼ (24;24¾)in in g st, pulling slightly. Bind off.

SCARF Using No 8 needles cast on 55 sts and work in k1 p1 rib as follows:
1st row: k1, *k1, p1, rep from * to last 2 sts, k2.
2nd row: *p1, k1, rep from * to last st, k1.
When work measures 80in, bind off.

EMBROIDERY Using photograph as a guide A and B, work cross stitches in the small square formed by the knitted patt.

TO FINISH Set in sleeves. Using small backstitch, sew side and sleeve seams, sew front edgings to front. Sew button to correspond to buttonhole.

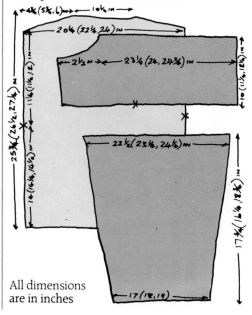

All dimensions are in inches

WINTER WARMER
Chunky, textured loose coat

GAUGE Using No 10 needles over st patt, 20 sts and 16 rows = 4in square.

BACK Cast on 113 (121;129) sts and p1 row. Commence st patt as follows:
1st row: (wrong side) k2, *p5, k3, rep from * to last 7 sts, p5, k2.
2nd row: p2, *k1, into next 3 sts tog – p1, k1, p1, then k1, p2.
These 2 rows form the patt. Cont in patt until work measures 21½(23;24½)in. Place armhole markers at each end of the last row. Cont in patt until work measures 35½(37½;39½)in from beg. Bind off placing neckline markers in sts 44 (47;50) and sts 71 (75;81).

POCKET BAGS Cast on 33 sts and commence st patt as follows:
1st size only:
p2, *k2, p5, rep from * to last 7 sts, k3 p4.
2nd size only:
*p5, k3, rep from * to last st, p1.
3rd size only:
As given for the back.
Cont in st patt until work measures 6in ending with a right side row. Leave sts on free needle.

LEFT FRONT Cast on 57 (61;65) sts and p1 row. Commence st patt as follows:
1st & 3rd sizes:
As given for the back.
2nd size only:
1st row: p3, *k3, p5, rep from * to last 2 sts, k2.
Cont in patt until work measures 10in from beg, ending with a wrong side row.
Next row: patt 12 (14;16) sts, bind off next 33 sts, patt to end.
Next row: patt 12 (14;16) sts, patt across a pocket bag, patt to end.
Cont in patt until work measures 21½(23¼.24¾)in from beg, ending with a right side row. Place an armhole marker at the armhole edge of the last row.

SHAPE COLLAR Cast on 5 sts at beg of neck and foll 3 alt rows. Work these 25 sts in single rib to end. Cont in patt and rib without shaping until work measures 35½(37½;39½)in from beg, ending at armhole edge. Bind off 43 (46;49) sts at armhole edge and then continue in patt for a further 2¼(2;3)in. Bind off.

GRADE ★ ★				
Sizes to fit	32-34	36-38	40-42	in
Actual size	44	47	50	in
Back length	35	37	39	in
Sleeve seam	16	16½	17	in
Materials	54	58	61	
	oz bulky			

1 pr No 10 needles
Suggested yarn: Pomfret Mark II by Brunswick

Abbreviations alt – alternate ● beg – beginning ● cont – continue ● dec – decrease ● foll – following ● k – knit ● p – purl ● patt – pattern ● rem – remaining ● rep – repeat ● st(s) – stitch(es) ● st st – stockinette stitch ● tog – together

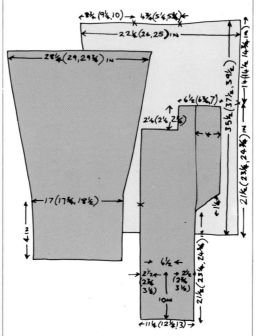

All dimensions are in inches

RIGHT FRONT Work to match left front, reversing patt placement and neckline shaping.

SLEEVES Cast on 85 (89;93) sts and p1 row. Commence st patt as follows:
1st & 3rd sizes only:
1st row: *p5, k3, rep from * to last 5 sts, p5.
2nd size only:
As given for the back.
Cont in patt until work measures 4in ending with a right side row. K1 row. Cont in patt, beg with a 1st (wrong side) row and inc 1 st at each end of the 9th and every foll alt row until there are 141 (145;149) sts. Cont in patt without shaping until work measures 20¼(20¾;21¼)in from beg. Bind off.

TO FINISH Using small backstitch, sew shoulder seams, sew sleeve tops into armholes, sew side and sleeve seams, reversing seam for the cuffs, sew center back seam of collar. Turn collar to inside, and hem cast on edges together, turn back to outside so that this hem is enclosed. Make 4 × 6 in cords and 4 tassels, sew the tassels to ends of the cords, sew the cords to collar as shown in photograph.

POCKET TOPS With right side facing, pick up 22 sts evenly across pocket top. Bind off knitwise.

FRONT EDGES With right side facing, pick up 92 (96;100) sts between beg of the collar and the bottom edge of the front. Bind off knitwise.

AMAZING LACE
Two-color lacy cardigan with maze pattern

GAUGE Using No 5 needles over st patt, 22 sts and 46 rows = 4in square.

BACK Using No 3 needles and MC, cast on 118 sts and work in double rib as follows:
1st row: k2, *p2, k2, rep from * to end.
2nd row: p2, *k2, p2, rep from * to end.
Rep these 2 rows 3 more times and dec 1 st in last st worked. 117 sts.
Change to No 5 needles and cont in patt from the chart, the 1st row being:
1st chart row: using col A, k3, *sl1, k1, sl1, k17, sl1, k1, rep from * to last 4 sts, sl1, k3.
Cont in patt until work measures 14³⁄₄in, place armhole marker at each end of this last row, then cont in patt until work measures 25¹⁄₄in ending with a wrong side row.

SHAPE SHOULDERS Bind off 19 sts at beg of next 2 rows. Bind off 18 sts at beg of foll 2 rows. Bind off rem 43 sts.

POCKET BAGS (make 2) Using No 5 needles and MC, cast on 31 sts and work in st st for 4in. Leave sts on stitch holder.

LEFT FRONT Using No 3 needles and MC, cast on 58 sts and work in double rib as given for the back for 8 rows, and inc 1 st in last st worked. 59 sts.
Change to No 5 needles and cont in patt from the chart, the 1st row being:
1st chart row: using A, k3, *sl1, k1, sl1, k17, sl1, k1, rep from * to last 12 sts, sl1, k1, sl1, k9.
Cont in patt until work measures 5in ending with a wrong side row.

PLACE POCKET Next row: patt 14 sts, bind off 31 sts, patt rem 14 sts.
Next row: patt 14 sts, with wrong side of pocket bag facing, patt across 31 sts of pocket bag, patt rem 14 sts.
Cont in patt until work measures 14³⁄₄in, ending with a right side row at the center front edge. Place an armhole marker at beg of this last row.

SHAPE NECKLINE Cont in patt and dec 1 st at beg of next row, and at neck edge only of every foll 5th row until 22 sts have been decreased in all, then cont without shaping until work measures 25¹⁄₂in ending at armhole edge.

GRADE ★ ★		
Sizes to fit	34-38	in
Actual size	42	in
Back length	25	in
Sleeve seam	17	in
Materials	17	MC
	14	A
		oz knitting worsted

1 pr No 3 needles ● 1 pr No 5 needles ●1 circular No 3 needle ● 5 buttons
Suggested yarn: Pingouin Fil d' Ecosse No 3

Abbreviations alt – alternate ● beg – beginning ● cont – continue ● dec – decrease ● foll – following ● inc – increase ● k – knit ● p – purl ● patt – pattern ● rem – remaining ● rep – repeat ● st(s) – stitch(es) ● st st – stockinette stitch ● tog – together ● MC – main color ● A – 1st color

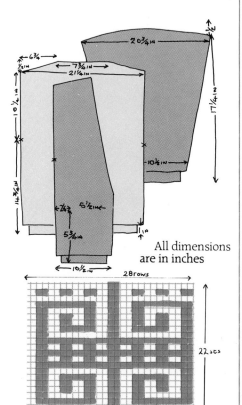

All dimensions are in inches

Method of working the chart
Alternate col A and MC, working 2 rows of each throughout the pattern, each time working from the chart only that color shown. Slip all remaining stitches with yarn at back on right side rows, and yarn at front on wrong side rows. Work every row as a knit row.

SHAPE SHOULDERS Bind off 19 sts at beg of next row, and 18 sts at beg of foll alt row.

RIGHT FRONT Work as given for left front, reversing shaping and pattern, the 1st chart row of pattern being:
1st row: using A, k9, sl1, k1, *sl1, k1, sl1, k17, sl1, k1, rep from * to last 4 sts, sl1, k3.

SLEEVES Using No 3 needles and MC cast on 58 sts and work in double rib as given for the back, for 8 rows and inc 1 st in last st worked. (59 sts)
Change to No 5 needles and cont in patt from the chart, the 1st row being:
1st chart row: using A, k5, sl1, k1, *sl1, k1, sl1, k17, sl1, k1, rep from * to last 8 sts, sl1, k1, sl1, k5.
Cont in patt and inc 1 st at each end of every foll 6th row until there are 115 sts, then cont without shaping until work measures 17¹⁄₄in.

SHAPE SLEEVE TOPS Cont in patt and bind off 23 sts at beg of next 5 rows. Fasten off. Work second sleeve to match.

NECKBAND Using small backstitch, sew both shoulder seams. Using long No 3 circular needle and working from the right side, pick up 82 sts between lower edge of right front and beg of neck shaping, pick up 158 sts round neckline to end of left front neck shaping, pick up 82 sts between this point and lower edge of left front. 322 sts.
Working in rows, work in double rib as given for the back, starting with a 2nd row for 3 rows.
Next row: rib 3 sts *bind off 3 sts, rib 16, rep from *3 more times, bind off 3 sts, rib to end of row.
Next row: work in rib, casting on 3 sts over each group of bound off sts.
Work for 2 more rows in rib. Bind off ribwise on next row.

POCKET TOPS (make 2) Using No 3 needles and MC, pick up 30 sts from right side of pocket top, and work in double rib for 7 rows. Bind off ribwise on next row.

TO FINISH Using small backstitch sew sleeves into armholes between markers, sew underarm seam from wrist to hem, sew pocket bags to inside front, sew buttons into place.

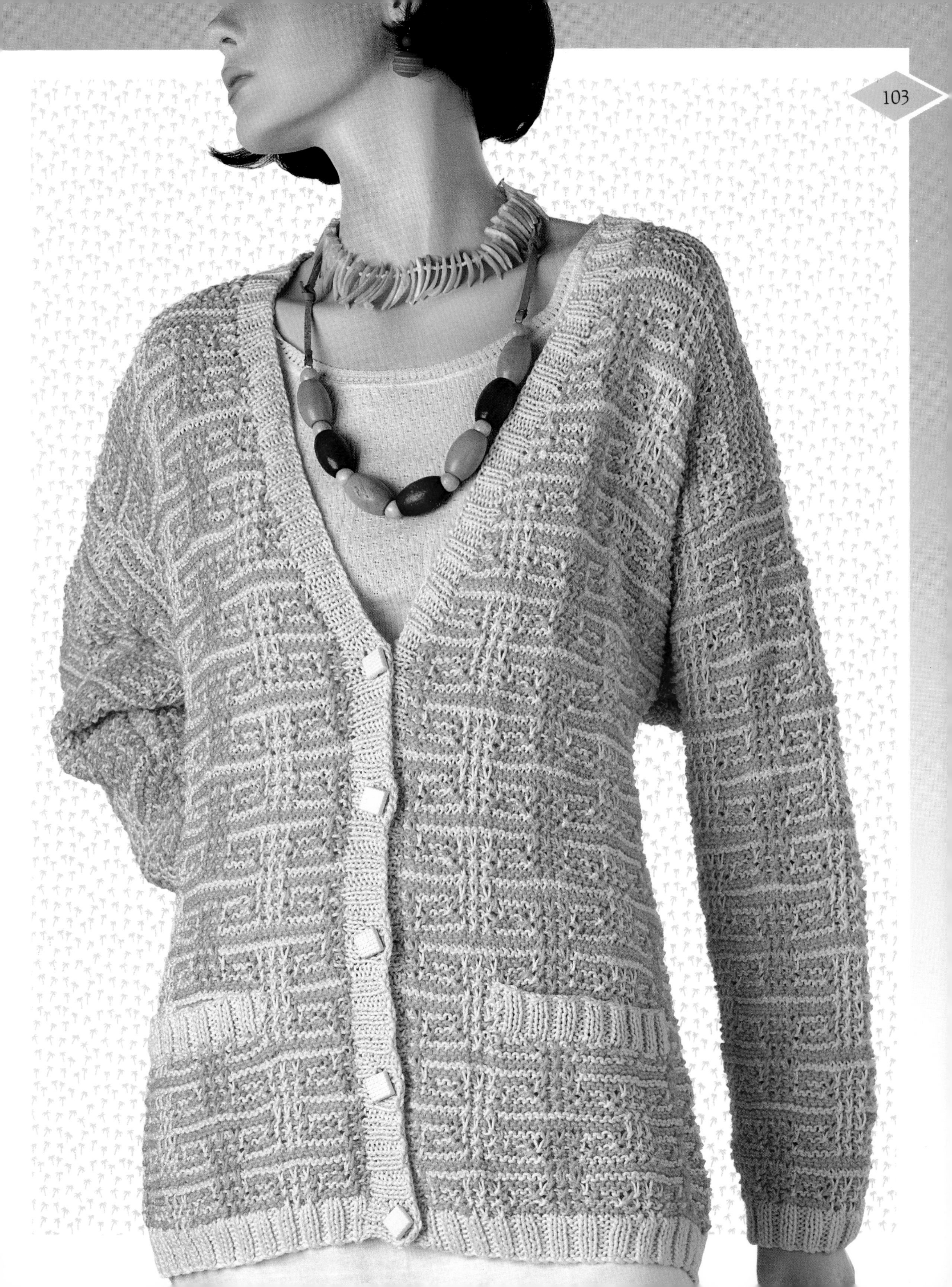

MODERN-DAY MAO

Man's chunky Chinese-style jacket

GAUGE Using No 7 needles over st st, 18 sts and 24 rows = 4 in square

BACK Using No 5 needles and MC, cast on 93 (95;101;107) sts and work in single rib as follows:
1st row: k2, *p1, k1, rep from * to last st, k1.
2nd row: k1, *p1, k1, rep from * to end.
Rep these 2 rows once more then rep the 1st row once again. K1 row. Work 5 more rows in single rib as given.
Next row: rib 6 (3;6;3), [inc in next st, rib 7 (7;7;8)] × 10 (11;11;11), inc in next st, rib to end. 104 (107;113;119) sts.
Change to No 7 needles and cont in st patt as follows:
1st row: *k2C, k1A, rep from * to last 2 sts, k2C.
2nd row: *p2C, p1A, rep from * to last 2 sts, p2C.
Rep these 2 rows 8 more times.
19th row: *k2MC, k1A, rep from * to last 2 sts, k2MC.
20th row: *p2MC, p1A, rep from * to last 2 sts, p2MC.
Rep these last 2 rows 8 more times.
These 36 rows form the patt. Cont in patt until work measures 18 (18;18¼;18¼)in from beg. Place armhole markers at each end of the last row. Cont in patt until work measures 29½ (30;30¼;30¾)in from beg. Bind off.

LEFT POCKET BAG Using No 7 needles and MC, cast on 38 sts and work 1¼in of st patt as given for the back ending with a wrong side row. Leave sts on a stitch holder.

GRADE ★ ★					
Sizes to fit	38	40	42	44	in
Actual size	44	46	48	50	in
Back length	28	28½	29	29½	in
Sleeve seam	18	18½	19	19½	in
Materials	17	19	22	24	MC
	14	15	17	19	A
	12	14	15	17	B
	oz Aran thick				

1 pr No 5 needles ● 1 pr No 7 needles ● 1 open-ended 24 (26; 28) in zipper ● 2 buckles
Suggested yarn: Phildar Pegase

Abbreviations alt – alternate ● beg – beginning ● cont – continue ● dec – decrease ● foll – following ● inc – increase ● k – knit ● p – purl ● patt – pattern ● rem – remaining ● rep – repeat ● st(s) – stitch(es) ● st st – stockinette stitch ● tog – together ● MC – main color ● A – 1st color ● B – 2nd color

LEFT FRONT **Using No 5 needles and MC, cast on 47 (49;53;55) sts and work 5 rows in single rib as given for the back. K1 row. Work a further 5 rows in single rib.
Next row: rib 3, [inc in next st, rib 7 (6;8;7)] × 5 (6;5;6), inc in next st, rib to end. 53 (56;59;62) sts.**
Change to No 7 needles and cont in st patt as given for the back until work measures 3½in from beg, ending with a wrong side row.
Next row: patt 15 (18;21;24) sts, (leave rem sts on a free needle), patt across pocket bag, Cont in patt on these sts until work measures 9½in ending with a wrong side row.
Next row: patt 15 (18;21;24) sts, bind off the next 38 sts.

Break yarn and rejoin to rem 38 sts on the free needle. Cont patt on these sts to the same patt row as the side section (right side row).
Next row: patt across the 38 sts, patt across rem 15 (18;21;24) sts of side section.
Cont in patt across these 53 (56;59;62) sts until work measures 13¼(13¼;13¼;12¼)in from beg.

SHAPE FRONT FLAP Keeping patt correct, inc 1 st at center front edge of next and every foll 5th row until 18 (18;18;19) sts have been increased. At the same time, place an armhole marker at the side edge on the same patt row as markers on the back. Cont in patt until work measures 27½in from beg, ending with a right side row.

SHAPE NECKLINE 1st row: bind off 18 (18;18;19) sts, place a center front marker in st on right hand needle, bind off 4 (4;5;5) sts, patt to end.
*2**nd row: patt to last 2 sts, patt 2 tog.
3rd row: bind off 2 (3;3;4) sts, patt to end.
Dec 1 st at neck edge of next 4 rows. Dec 1 st at neck edge of foll 2 alt rows.
Cont on rem 40 (42;44;46) sts to the same patt row as the back at bind off.
Bind off.*

RIGHT POCKET BAG Using No 7 needles and MC, cast on 38 sts and work in patt as given for the back for 1¼in, ending with a right side row. Leave sts on a st holder.

RIGHT FRONT Using No 5 needles and MC, cast on 46(49;53;55) sts and rep from ** to ** as given for the left front.
Change to No 7 needles and cont in st patt as given for the back until work measures 3½in from beg, ending with a right side row.
Next row: patt 15(18;21;24) sts, (leave rem sts on a free needle), patt across pocket bag.
Cont in patt on these sts until work measures 9½in ending with a right side row.
Next row: patt 15(18;21;24) sts, bind off the next 38 sts.
Break yarn and rejoin to the rem 38 sts on the free needle. Cont in patt on these sts to the same patt row as the side section (wrong side row).
Next row: patt across the 38 sts, patt across the rem 15(18;21;24) sts of the side section.
Cont in patt on these 53(56;59;62) sts to the same patt row as the back at armhole markers. Place an armhole marker at the side edge and cont in patt to the patt row before the last row of the left front at neckline shaping (wrong side row).

SHAPE NECKLINE Next row: bind off 4(4;5;5;) sts, patt to end.
Rep from * to * as given for the left front.

SLEEVES Using No 5 needles and MC, cast on 41(43;47;49) sts and work 5 rows in single rib as given for the back. K1 row. Work 5 more rows in rib.
Next row: rib 2(2;5;5), [rib 1, inc in next st, rib 1] × 12(13;12;13), rib rem 3(2;6;5) sts. 53(56,59;62) sts.
Change to No 7 needles and cont in patt as given for the back and inc 1 st at each end of the 3rd and every foll 4th row until there are 105(108;113;118) sts. Cont in patt without shaping until work measures 19½(20;20¼;20¾)in from beg. Bind off.

LEFT FRONT FACING Using No 5 needles and MC, cast on 23(23;23;25) sts and work in single rib as given for the back and dec 1 st at end of 3rd row and at the same edge on every foll 5th row until 2 sts remain. K2 tog. Fasten off.

TO FINISH Using small backstitch, sew shoulder seams, sew sleeve tops into armholes, sew side and sleeve seams. Fold bottom rib to the inside and stitch down. Fold cuffs to the inside and stitch down.

LEFT FRONT BANDS Pin facing to the wrong side of the left front, matching shaped edges, and slip st along center front line.
Using 4mm needles and MC, right side facing, pick up 157 sts from point of front flap to fold of bottom edge. *Work 5 rows in single rib as given for the back beg with a 2nd row and inc 1 st at flap point on every row. P1 row. Work 5 more rows in rib and dec 1 st at flap point on every row. Bind off ribwise.*
Using No 5 needles and MC, right side facing, beg at neckline center front marker, pick up 23(23;23;25) sts to flap point. Rep from * to *.
Sew miters and fold bands to inside and stitch down.

COLLAR Using No 5 needles and MC, right side facing, beg at center front edge of right front, pick up 25(31;31;37) sts along right front neckline, pick up 25(27;29;33) sts across back neck, pick up 25(31;31;37) sts along left front neckline to center front marker. Work 12 rows in single rib as given for the back beg with a 2nd row. K1 row. Work 12 more rows in rib. Bind off ribwise. Fold collar to the inside and slip st down. Join to flap band on left front.

POCKET EDGES Using No 5 needles and MC, right side facing, pick up 33 sts along pocket edge. Work 5 rows in single rib as given for the back beg with a 2nd row. P1 row. Rib 5 more rows. Bind off ribwise. Fold to the inside and stitch down. Stitch down pocket bag.

BUCKLE TABS (make 2) Using No 5 needles and MC, cast on 7 sts. Work 4in in single rib as given for the back. Bind off ribwise.
Sew tabs on right side of left front as shown in the picture and sew buckles to right front to match.
Sew in zipper along center front line of left front and the edge of the right front.

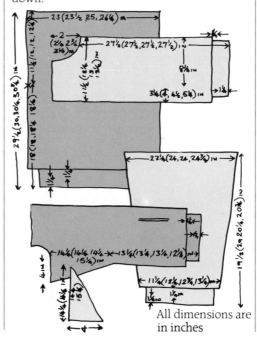

All dimensions are in inches

THE EAST EGG COOLIE
Woman's chunky herringbone jacket

GAUGE Using No 8 needles over st st, 18 sts and 24 rows = 4in square.

BACK Using No 8 needles and B, cast on 92 (102:112) sts and commence st patt as follows:
1st row: k1A, *k2B, k2A, k1B, k1A, k2B, k2A, rep from * to last st, k1B.
2nd row: p1B, *p1B, [p2A, p2B] × 2, p1A, rep from * to last st, p1B.
3rd row: k1B, *k2A, k2B, k1A, k1B, k2A, k2B, rep from * to last st, k1A.
4th row: p1A, *p1A, [p2B, p2A] × 2, p1B, rep from * to last st, p1A.
These 4 rows form the patt. Cont in patt until work measures 18½(19½:20)in from beg, ending with a p row.

SHAPE RAGLANS Keeping patt correct, dec 1 st at each end of next and every foll alt row until 16 (20:24) sts remain ending with a p row. Bind off.

POCKET BAGS (make 2) Using No 8 needles and B, cast on 21 (22:23) sts and work 4in in st st ending with a k row. Leave sts on a free needle.

RIGHT FRONT Using No 8 needles and B, cast on 47 (52:57) sts and commence st patt as follows:
1st row: *1st & 3rd sizes only* K1B, k1A, k2B, k2A, k1B, *k1B, k2A, k1B, k1A, k2B, k2A, k1B, rep from * to end.
1st row: *2nd size only* as given for the back patt until work measures 8¾in from beg

ending with a p row.
Next row: patt 13 (15:17) sts, bind off next 21 (22:23) sts, patt to end.
Next row: patt 13 (15:17) sts, patt across pocket bag, patt to end.
Cont in patt until work measures 18½(19½:20)in from beg, ending with a p row.

SHAPE NECKLINE Dec 1 st at neck edge of next and every foll 3rd row until 17 (20:23) sts have been decreased then cont straight. At the same time,

SHAPE RAGLAN Dec 1 st at armhole edge of next and every foll alt row until 2 sts remain, ending with a p row. K2tog. Fasten off.

LEFT FRONT Work to match the right front, reversing shapings and working st patt as follows:
1st row: *1st & 3rd sizes only* k1A, *k2B, k2A, k1B, k1A, k2B, k2A, rep from * to last 6 sts, k2B, k2A, k1B, k1A.
1st row: *2nd size only* as given for the back.

SLEEVES Using No 8 needles and B, cast on 78 (80:88) sts and work in st patt as follows:
1st row: k2 (0:2)B, k2 (0:2)A, *k2B, k2A, k1B, k1A, k2B, k2A, rep from * to last 4 (0:4) sts, k2 (0:2)B, k2 (0:2)A.
The position of the patt is now set. Cont in patt and inc 1 st at each end of every foll 3rd row until there are 130 (138:148) sts, then cont without shaping until work measures 15 (15½:16)in ending with a wrong side row.

SHAPE RAGLAN Dec 1 st at each end of every row, except every foll 5th row until 56 (60:64) rows have been worked and there are 40 (42:44) sts rem.

SHAPE SLEEVE TOPS 1st row: bind off 3 sts at beg of row, patt to last 2 sts, k2tog.
2nd row: p2tog, patt to end.
Rep the last 2 rows 3 (2:2) more times.
Next row: bind off 2 sts at beg of row. Patt to last 2 sts, k2tog.
Next row: p2tog, patt to end.
Rep the last 2 rows 3 (5:5) more times.
Work 0 (1:1) more row without shaping. Dec 1 st at right hand edge only on next 4 (3:5) rows. Fasten off.

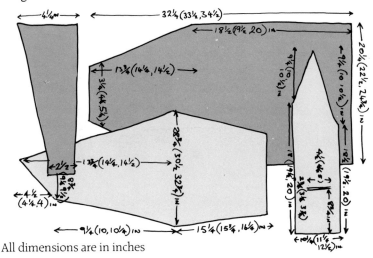

All dimensions are in inches

RIGHT COLLAR Using small backstitch, sew raglan seams.
Using No 8 needles and B, cast on 20 sts and commence st patt as follows:
1st row: *k1B, k2A, k1B, k1A, k2B, k2A, k1B, rep from * to end.
Cont in patt and dec 1 st at beg of 3rd and every foll 8th row until 8 sts have been decreased. Cont in patt until collar fits neatly to center back of neck. Bind off.

LEFT COLLAR Work to match right collar reversing shaping.

CUFFS Using No 6 needles and B, with right side facing, pick up 78 (80;88) sts across sleeve edge. *Work 8 rows in st st, beg with a p row. K1 row. Work 8 rows in st st beg with a k row. Bind off.*

POCKET TOPS (make 2) Using No 6 needles and B, right side facing, pick up 21 (22;23) sts across pocket top. Rep from * to * as given for the cuffs.

RIGHT FRONT EDGING Using small backstitch, sew center back seam of collar and sew collar to garment.
Using No 6 needles and B, with right side facing, beg at bottom of right front, pick up 88 (92;94) sts to 1¼in from beg of collar, cast on 4 sts miss ¾in, pick up sts to beg of collar. Work 8 rows in st st beg with a p row and inc 1 st at beg of 2nd and foll 3 alt rows. K1 row. Work 8 rows in st st beg with a k row and dec 1 st at beg of 1st and foll 3 alt rows. Bind off.

LEFT FRONT EDGING Work to match right front band, omitting buttonhole and reversing shaping.

COLLAR EDGING Using No 6 needles and B, with right side facing, beg at start of left collar, pick up 18 sts across bottom edge of collar, pick up 84 (86;90) sts to center back of collar, pick up 84 (86;90) sts to point of right collar, pick up 18 sts along bottom of right collar. 204 (208;216) sts.
1st row: p to end.
2nd row: k17, inc in next 2 sts, k to last 19 sts, inc in next 2 sts, k17.
3rd row: as 1st row.
4th row: k18, inc in next 2 sts, k to last 20 sts, inc in next 2 sts, k18.
Cont in st st increasing as before at collar corners for 4 more rows. K1 row. Work 8 rows in st st beg with a k row and dec 2 sts at collar corners on 1st and foll 3 alt rows. Bind off.

BOTTOM EDGING Using small backstitch, sew side and sleeve seams.
Using No 6 needles and B, right side facing, beg at left center front, pick up 45 (50;55) sts to left side seam, pick up 90 (100;110) sts across bottom of back, pick up 45 (50;55) sts across bottom of right front. 180 (200;220) sts. Work 8 rows in st st beg with a p row and inc 1 st at each end of the 2nd and foll 3 alt rows. Bind off.

RAGLAN TRIMS Using No 6 needles and B, right side facing, beg at neck end of left back raglan, pick up 120 (128;136) sts along raglan seam to sleeve seam, and up along left front raglan seam to collar. Work 7 rows in st st, beg with a p row. Bind off knitwise. Work right side to match, picking up sts from front to back.

SLEEVE TRIM Using No 6 needles and B, right side facing, beg at center of sleeve at right neck, pick up 130 (134;138) sts along center of sleeve to cuff. Work 7 rows in st st beg with a p row. Bind off knitwise. Work left sleeve trim to match, picking up sts from cuff to neck.

TO FINISH Join miters and turn edgings to wrong side. Slip st down edgings leaving the buttonhole opening on the right front. Sew edgings tog at bottom of collar. Sew on button.

SHOULDER PADS Using No 8 needles and A, cast on 22 sts and work 28 rows in st st. Bind off.
Using No 8 needles and A, cast on 18 sts.
1st row: k to last 2 sts, k2tog.
2nd row: p2tog, p to end.
3rd row: k to end.
4th row: as 2nd row.
5th row: as 1st row.
6th row: as 2nd row.
7th row: as 3rd row.
8th row: as 2nd row.
9th row: as 1st row.
10th row: p to end.
11th row: as 1st row.
12th row: as 2nd row.
13th row: as 1st row.
14th row: as 10th row.
Rep rows 1-9 once more. P2tog. Fasten off. Place the triangle on the wrong side of one half of the square and fold the square over the triangle. Sew the unfolded sides tog. Secure the pads to the inside of the sleeves at the 3 points.

MY OLD FLAME
Paisley sweater with flaming design

GAUGE Using No 5 needles over st st. 24 sts and 32 rows = 4in square

BACK Using No 3 needles and MC, cast on 101 (113;127) sts and work in moss st as follows:
1st row: k2, *p1, k1, rep from * to last st, k1.
Rep this row until work measures 1¼in
Next row: patt 2 (8;7) sts, [inc in next st, patt 5 (5;6)] × 16, inc in next st, patt to end. 118 (130;144) sts.
Change to No 5 needles and, working in st st, and commence the following chart:
1st row: k3 (3;0)MC, k1A, k1MC, *k2MC, k3A, k5MC, k1A, k1MC, rep from * to last 5 (5;2) sts, k2MC, k3 (3;0)A.
Cont to follow the chart until work measures 14¾(15;15¼)in from beg. Place armhole markers at each end of the last row. Cont in patt until work measures 26¼(27;27½)in from beg. Bind off.

FRONT Work as for the back until work measures 16¾(17;17¼)in from beg, ending with a wrong side row.

SHAPE NECKLINE Next row: patt 59 (65;72) sts, turn.
Cont in patt on these sts only and dec 1 st at each end of the next and every foll 4th row until 44 (49;55) sts remain. Cont in patt without shaping until work measures 26¼(27;27½)in from beg. Bind off. Rejoin yarn at neck edge and complete 2nd side to match 1st side.

SLEEVES Using No 3 needles and MC, cast on 55 (57;61) sts and work 1¼in in moss st as for the back.
Next row: patt 2 (3;5), (inc in next st, patt 4) × 10, inc in next st, patt to end. 66 (68;72) sts.
Change to No 5 needles and commence following the chart:
1st row: k2 (1;0)MC, k1 (1;0)A, k1 (1;1)MC, *k2MC, k3A, k5MC, k1A, k1MC, rep from * to last 3 (4;0) sts, k2 (2;0)MC, k1 (2;0)A.
Cont in patt and inc 1 st at each end of every 3rd row until there are 142 (148;152) sts. Cont in patt without shaping until work measures 17¾(18½;18¾)in from beg. Bind off.

COLLAR Using No 3 needles and MC, cast on 157 (163;169) sts. Working in moss st as for the back, shape the collar as follows:
1st row: patt 94 (102;104) sts, turn.

GRADE ★ ★ ★ ★			
Sizes to fit	32-34	36-38	40-42	in
Actual size	38	42	46	in
Back length	26	26½	27	in
Sleeve seam	17½	18	18½	in
Materials	12	14	14	MC
	7	8	8	A
	7	8	8	B
	oz knitting worsted			

1 pr No 3 needles ● 1 pr No 5 needles
Suggested yarn: Pomfret Mark II by Brunswick

Abbreviations alt – alternate ● beg – beginning ● cont – continue ● dec – decrease ● foll – following ● inc – increase ● k – knit ● p – purl ● patt – pattern ● rem – remaining ● rep – repeat ● st(s) – stitch(es) ● st st – stockinette stitch ● MC – main color ● A – 1st color ● B – 2nd color

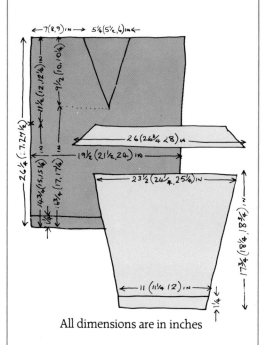

All dimensions are in inches

2nd row: patt 9 (13;13) sts, turn.
3rd row: patt 19 (23;24) sts, turn.
Cont in patt working an additional 10 (10;11) sts on each row until:
Next row: patt 169 (173;189), turn is completed.
Next row: patt to end.
Cont in moss st across all sts and dec 1 st at each end of the next and every foll 3rd row 12 times in all. patt 1 row. Bind off in patt.

TO FINISH Using small backstitch, sew shoulder seams, sew sleeve tops into armholes, sew side and sleeve seams. Pin cast-on edge of collar around neckline and stitch down.

20 rows

12 sts

☐ main col
☐ col A
■ col B

THE HUNTER
Man's chunky sweater

GAUGE Using No 10½ needles over st st, 14 sts and 19 rows = 4in square.

BACK AND FRONT (both the same) Using No 8 needles, cast on 66 (70;74;78;78) sts and work in rib as follows:
1st row: k2, *p2, k2, rep from * to end.
2nd row: p2, *k2, p2, rep from * to end.
Rep these 2 rows until work measures 2¼in ending with a 1st row.
Next row: rib 2 (4;6;6;2), [inc in next st, rib 9 (9;11;12;8)] × 6 (6;5;5;8), inc in next st, rib to end. 73 (77;80;84;87) sts.
Change to No 10½ needles and cont in st st until work measures 16½(16½;16½;17;17)in from beg. Place armhole markers at each end of the last row worked. Cont in st st until work measures 26½(26¾;27¼;27½;28) in from beg, ending with a p row. Bind off.

SLEEVES Using No 8 needles, cast on 38 (38;38;46;46) sts and work in rib as given for the back until work measures 2¼in ending with a 2nd row.
Change to No 10 ½ needles and cont as follows:
1st row: k10 (10;10;14;14), [p2, k2] × 4, p2, k to end.
2nd row: p10 (10;10;14;14), [k2, p2] × 4, k2, p to end.
Keeping ribbed panel correct, inc 1 st at each end of next and every foll 3rd row until there are 88 (90;92;92;94) sts. Cont without shaping until work measures 18¼(18¾;19¼;19½;20)in from beg, ending with a wrong-side row. Bind off 35 (36;37;38;39) sts at beg of next 2 rows. Cont in rib on rem 18 sts until work measures 24½(25½;26½;27;28)in from beg.

GRADE ★					
Sizes to fit	36	38	40	42	44	in
Actual size	40	42	44	46	48	in
Back length	26¼	26¾	27¼	27½	28	in
Sleeve seam	18	18½	19	19½	20	in
Materials	31	33	37	37	40	
	oz bulky					

1 pr No 8 needles • 1 pr No 10½ needles
Suggested yarn: Wendy Shetland Chunky

Abbreviations beg – beginning ● cont – continue ● dec – decrease ● foll – following ● inc – increase ● k – knit ● p – purl ● rem – remaining ● rep – repeat ● st(s) – stitch(es) ● st st – stockinette stitch ● tog – together

Next row: rib 6 sts, bind off next 6 sts rib to end. Cont on last group of sts as follows:
1st row: rib to last 2 sts, rib 2tog.
2nd row: rib 2tog, rib to end.
Rep these 2 rows once more.
5th row: rib to end.
6th row: as 2nd row.
Rep rows 5 and 6 once more. Fasten off. Rejoin yarn to rem sts and complete 2nd side to match 1st side.

COLLAR Using No 8 needles and some waste yarn of equal thickness, cast on 23 sts and work as follows:
1st row: *k2, p2, rep from * to last 3 sts, k2, p1.
2nd row: k1, *p2, k2, rep from * to last 2 sts, p2.
Rep these 2 rows 2 more times.
Change to main yarn and cont in rib until main yarn work measures 24 (24¾;24¾;25½;25½)in Work 6 more rows in waste yarn and bind off.

TO FINISH Using small backstitch, sew sleeve tops into armholes and sew shoulder ribs along top edges of back and front. Graft tog the ends of the collar and remove the waste yarn. Sew on the collar. Sew side and sleeve seams.

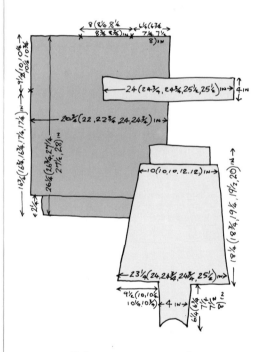

All dimensions are in inches

THE SILVER LINING

The sun breaks through a cloudy sky on this mohair jacket

GAUGE Using No 8 needles over patt 16 sts and 21 rows = 4in square.

NOTE When working the color pattern, the yarns must be woven in very loosely across the back of the work so that the tension is not affected and the weaving in should not be noticeable from the right side.

POCKET BAGS (make 2) Using No 8 needles and MC, cast on 28 sts and work in st st for 5½in, leave on a stitch holder.

BACK & FRONT (worked in one) Using No 8 needles and MC, cast on 162 (180) sts and work in color patt from the chart as follows:
1st row: *k6MC, k4A, k8MC, rep from * to end.
Cont in color patt from the chart and inc 1 st at each end of every foll 7th row (incorporating these extra sts into color patt). At the same time, when work measures 6in ending with a wrong side row, place pockets.

POCKETS (make 2) Patt across 8 sts, bind off next 28 sts, patt across rem sts to last 36 sts. Bind off next 28 sts, patt rem 8 sts.
Next row: patt across 8 sts, patt across top of pocket, patt to last 36 sts, patt across top of next pocket bag, patt rem 8 sts.
Cont in patt working shaping on these sts until work measures 14¾(15¼)in, ending with a wrong side row.

DIVIDE FOR ARMHOLES Divide work into 3 sections with 80 (90) sts in the middle back section. Work on left front only as follows:
**Cont to inc at front edge only, as before, until 16 increases have been worked in all, then cont without shaping until work measures 22¾(24)in, ending at front edge.

SHAPE NECKLINE Bind off 20 sts, patt to end.
Next row: patt to last 2 sts, p2tog.
Next row: bind off 4 sts, patt to end.
Now dec 1 sts at neck edge only of next 7 (6) rows, then cont in patt on rem 25 (30) sts until work measures 24¼(25½)in. Bind off.
Rejoin yarn to right front and work to match left front as given from **. At the same time work buttonhole, 2 rows below beg of neck shaping by binding off 3 sts, 2 sts in from the edge on the next row, and then binding these

GRADE ★ ★ ★ ★			
Sizes to fit	32-34	36-38	in
Actual size	40	44	in
Back length	24	25	in
Sleeve seam	17	17½	in
Materials	11	12	MC
	8	9	A
	2	3	B
	oz mohair thick yarn		

1 pr No 8 needles ● 1 pr No 6 needles ● 1 button
Suggested yarn: Anny Blatt Mohair

Abbreviations alt – alternate ● beg – beginning ● cont – continue ● dec – decrease ● foll – following ● inc – increase ● k – knit ● p – purl ● patt – pattern ● rem – remaining ● rep – repeat ● st(s) – stitch(es) ● st st – stockinette stitch ● tog – together ● MC – main color ● A – 1st color ● B – 2nd color

3 sts on over the bound-off sts on foll row. Rejoin yarn to 80 (90) sts for back and work in patt until work measures 24¼(25½)in. Bind off.

SLEEVES Using No 8 needles and MC, cast on 54 sts and work in patt, the 1st row being as for the back. At the same time, inc 1 st at each end of every foll 7th (5th) row until there are 78 (86) sts, then cont without shaping until work measures 17¼(17½)in. Bind off.

HEM EDGING Using No 6 needles and working from the right side using B, pick up 174 (192) sts evenly around hem. Bind off knitwise on next row.

FRONT EDGES Using No 6 needles and B, pick up 92 (96) sts from right side of front edge. Bind off knitwise on next row.

NECK EDGE Using small backstitch sew shoulder seams. Using No 6 needles and B, pick up 76 (80) sts from right side of neck edge. Bind off knitwise on next row.

SLEEVE EDGE Using No 6 needles and B, and working from right side, pick up 56 sts evenly along lower edge of sleeve. Bind off knitwise on next row.

POCKET EDGE Using No 6 needles and B, pick up 30 sts from right side of pocket top. Bind off knitwise on next row.

TO FINISH Using small backstitch, sew sleeve seams, sew sleeves into armholes, sew pocket bags to inside. Sew button into place. Using B, work French knots at random over garment.

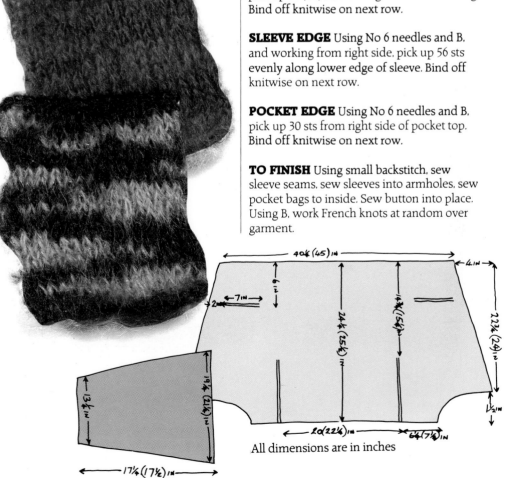

All dimensions are in inches

COCKTAILS FOR TWO
Angora dress with diamante

GAUGE Using No 4 needles, over st st 26 sts and 34 rows = 4in square.

DRESS FRONT Using No 4 needles, cast on 140 (156;170) sts and work in st st until work measures 24in, ending with a wrong side row.

**SHAPE SLEEVES Inc 1 st at each end of next and every foll 8th row 4 times in all. Inc 1 st at each end of next and every foll 4th row 7 times in all. Inc 1 st at each end of next and every foll alt row 5 times in all. Inc 1 st at each end of next 12 (10;8) rows. Cast on 4 sts at beg of next 28 rows. Cast on 10 sts at beg of foll 6 rows. 368 (380;390) sts.
Work a further 24 (28;32) rows without shaping.

DIVIDE FOR NECKLINE Knit 183 (189;194) sts, bind off next 2 sts, knit rem 183 (189;194) sts. Cont on this last group of sts only, as follows:
1st row: p to last 2 sts, p2tog.
2nd row: bind off 10 sts, k to end.
Rep the last 2 rows 2 more times.
7th row: as 1st row.
8th row: bind off 6 sts, k to end.
9th row: as 1st row.
10th row: bind off 3 sts, k to end.
Rep rows 9 and 10 0 (1;2) more times.
Dec 1 st at neck edge of next 4 rows. Dec 1 st at neck edge of next 4 alt rows.

SHAPE SHOULDER Next row: bind off 25 (26;26) sts, p to end.
Next row: k to last 2 sts, k2tog.
Rep these 2 rows 3 more times.
Bind off rem 27 (25;26) sts.
Rejoin yarn to rem sts at neck edge and work 2nd side to match 1st side of neck, reversing shapings.

DRESS BACK Using No 4 needles, cast on 70 (78;85) sts and work in st st until work measures 8in. Leave these sts on a stitch holder.
Work 2nd piece to match, then place all the sts on needle and work across them all. Cont in st st, completing the back to match the dress front.

<table>
<tr><td colspan="5" align="center">GRADE ★</td></tr>
<tr><td>Sizes to fit</td><td>32-34</td><td>36-38</td><td>40-42</td><td>in</td></tr>
<tr><td>Actual size</td><td>42</td><td>46½</td><td>51</td><td>in</td></tr>
<tr><td>Back length</td><td></td><td></td><td></td><td></td></tr>
<tr><td>dress</td><td>43</td><td>43¼</td><td>43½</td><td>in</td></tr>
<tr><td>sweater</td><td>23¼</td><td>23½</td><td>23¾</td><td>in</td></tr>
<tr><td>Materials</td><td>18</td><td>20</td><td>21</td><td></td></tr>
<tr><td></td><td colspan="4">oz sports yarn</td></tr>
</table>

1 pr No 1 needles ● 1 pr No 4 needles
Suggested yarn: Rubertin by Nevada

Abbreviations alt – alternate ● beg – beginning ● cont – continue ● dec – decrease ● foll – following ● inc – increase ● k – knit ● p – purl ● rem – remaining ● rep – repeat ● st(s) – stitch(es) ● st st – stockinette stitch ● tog – together

NECK EDGING Using No 1 needles and working from the right side, pick up 142 (146;150) sts evenly around front neck. Bind off purlwise on next row. Work neck back to match.

CUFFS Using small backstitch, sew both shoulder seams.
Using No 1 needles, and working from the right side, pick up 77 (83;89) sts and work in single rib for 1in. Bind off ribwise, work 2nd cuff to match.

TO FINISH Using small backstitch, sew both side seams from wrist to hem.

HEM Using No 1 needles and working from the right side, pick up 286 (320;340) sts evenly around lower edge. Work next row as a k row, then, starting with a k row, work 9 rows in st st. Bind off loosely.

BACK OPENING EDGES (make 2) Using No 1 needles and working from the right side, pick up 60 sts evenly along 1 side of back slit. Bind off purlwise on next row.

SHOULDER STRAPS Using No 1 needles, cast on 4 sts and work as follows:
1st row: k4.
2nd row: k1, p2, k1.
Rep these 2 rows until work measures 7in. Bind off.
Work 2nd piece to match. Sew into place on each side of neckline, approximately 6½in from center of neck.

TO FINISH Sew diamanté all round neck, edge and over straps. Tack lines at center-front to match lines of diamanté shown in photograph. Sew diamanté along these lines, then remove basting.

JUMPER BACK & FRONT (both the same) **Alternative Sweater version** Cast on 139 (155;169) sts using No 1 needles and work in single rib until work measures 1in inc 1 st in last st worked. 140 (156;170) sts.
Next row: change to No 4 needles and cont in st st for 2in then work as given for dress from ** to end.

All dimensions are in inches

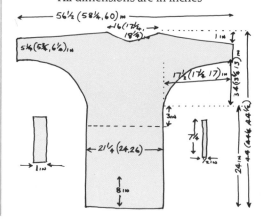

TRANS-SIBERIAN EXPRESS
Chunky winter traveling dress

GAUGE Using No 10 needles over st st, 13 sts and 20 rows = 4in square.

FRONT Using No 8 needles, cast on 63 (71;79) sts and work in single rib as follows:
1st row: k2, *p1, k1, rep from * to last st, k1.
2nd row: k1, *p1, k1, rep from * to end.
Rep these 2 rows until work measures 4in ending with a 2nd row.
Change to No 10 needles and cont in st st until work measures 36 (37;38)in from beg, ending with a p row. Place markers at each end of the last row.

SHAPE RAGLANS *1st row: k3, k2tog, k to last 5 sts, k2tog tbl, k3.
2nd row: p to end.*
Rep these 2 rows until 37 (41;45) sts remain.

SHAPE NECKLINE Next row: k3, k2tog, k5 (6;7), bind off the next 17 (19;21) sts, k5 (6;7), k2tog tbl, k3.
Next row: p9 (10;11), turn.
Next row: bind off 6 (7;8) sts, k1, k2tog tbl.
Next row: p2, turn.
Next row: k2tog, fasten off.
Rejoin yarn at neck edge and complete left side to match the right side.

LEFT BACK Using No 8 needles, cast on 35 (39;43) sts and work in single rib as given for the front until work measures 4in, ending with a 2nd row.
Change to No 10 needles and work 2 rows in st st.

MAKE BUTTONHOLE Next row: k3, bind off next 3 sts, k to end.
Next row: p to end casting on 3 sts over bound off sts of previous row.
Cont in st st until work measures 35½ (36½;37½)in from beg, ending with a p row and make additional buttonholes over the last buttonhole every 5 (5¼;4¾)in. Place a marker at beg of last row. Keeping buttonholes to the same spacings

SHAPE RAGLANS Next row: k to last 5 sts, k2tog tbl, k3.
Next row: p to end.
Rep these 2 rows 12 (14;16) more times.

GRADE ★			
Sizes to fit	32-34	36-38	40-42	in
Actual size	38	42	46	in
Back length	43	44½	46	in
Sleeve seam	17½	18	18½	in
Materials	15	17	19	
	oz bulky			

1 pr No 8 needles ● 1 pr No 10 needles ● 9 (9; 10) buttons
Suggested yarn: Venetian Bernat

Abbreviations alt – alternate ● beg – beginning ● cont – continue ● dec – decrease ● foll – following ● inc – increase ● k – knit ● p – purl ● rem – remaining ● rep – repeat ● st(s) – stitch(es) ● st st – stockinette stitch ● tbl – through back of loop ● tog – together

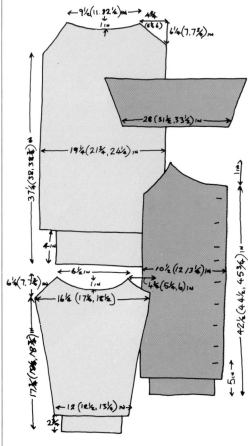

All dimensions are in inches

SHAPE NECKLINE Next row: bind off 12 (13;14) sts, k to last 5 sts, k2tog tbl, k3.
Next row: p to end.
Next row: bind off 6 (7;8) sts, k1 k2tog tbl.
Next row: p2.
Next row: k2tog, fasten off.

RIGHT FRONT Work to match left front, omitting buttonholes and reversing shapings.

SLEEVES Using No 8 needles, cast on 33 (35;37) sts and work in single rib as given for the front until work measures 3in ending with a 1st row.
Next row: rib 3 (2;3), [inc in next st, rib 4 (5;5)] × 5, inc in next st, rib to end. 39 (41;43) sts.
Change to No 10 needles and cont in st st and inc 1 st at each end of the 7th and every foll 8th row until there are 53 (57;61) sts. Cont in st st without shaping until work measures 17¾ (18¼;18¾)in from beg, ending with a p row. Place markers at each end of the last row.

SHAPE RAGLANS Rep from * to * as given for the front until 27 sts remain.
Next row: k3, k2tog, k4, bind off next 9 sts, k4, k2tog tbl, k3.
Next row: p8, turn.
Next row: bind off 5 sts, k1, k2tog tbl.
Next row: p2.
Next row: k2tog, fasten off.
Rejoin yarn to rem 9 sts and work other side to match 1st side.

COLLAR Using small backstitch, sew raglan seams matching markers.
Using No 8 needles, right side facing, beg 4 sts from center back edge of left back neckline, pick up 22 (24;26) sts to 1st raglan seam, pick up 19 sts across top of left sleeve, pick up 45 (49;53) sts across front neckline, pick up 19 sts across top of right sleeve, pick up 22 (24;26) sts across right back neckline to 4 sts from center back edge. 127 (135;143) sts. Work in single rib as given for the front, beg with a 2nd row until collar measures 8in. Bind off loosely ribwise.

TO FINISH Using small backstitch, sew side and sleeve seams.
Using No 8 needles, right side facing, pick up 150 (156;162) sts along center back edge. Bind off knitwise on next row. Work other center back edge to match. Sew on buttons.

THE NANTUCKET
Baggy textured skirt and jacket with hood

GAUGE Using No 5 needles over moss rib 21 st and 31 rows = 4in square. Using No 5 needles over double rib 32 sts and 31 rows = 4in square.

JACKET BACK & FRONT CENTER PANEL
Using No 5 needles cast on 59 (65) sts and work in patt as follows:
1st row: (right side) k1, *p1, k1, rep from * to end.
2nd row: p to end.
These 2 rows form the patt. Cont in patt until work measures 21 (21½)in, ending with a wrong side row.

SHAPE SLEEVES Cont in patt and cast on 115 (116) sts at beg of next 2 rows, then cont in patt on these 289 (297) sts until work measures 25½(26¼)in, ending with a wrong side row.

DIVIDE FOR NECK Patt 1st 127 (130) sts, bind off center 35 (37) sts, patt rem 127 (130) sts. Work in patt on this last group of sts only as follows:
**Work 6 rows without shaping, then work 5 rows increasing 1 st at neck edge of each row (ending at neck edge). Cast on 4 sts at beg of next and foll alt row. Cast on 6 sts at beg of foll 2 alt rows. Cast on 14 (16) sts at beg of foll alt row.
Cont in patt until work measures 4¼(5)in, from neck divide, ending at armhole edge.

GRADE ★ ★ ★			
Jacket			
Sizes to fit	32-34	36-38	in
Actual size	42	46	in
Back length	25	26	in
Skirt (hips)	34	38	in
Skirt (length)	10¾	30¼	in
Materials			
Jacket	30	35	
Skirt	15	19	
Hood	12	12	
		oz knitting worsted	

1 pr No 3 needles ● 1 pr No 5 needles ●1 circular No 3 needle ● 4 small buckles for jacket ● elastic to fit waist for skirt
Suggested yarn: Candide No 5

Abbreviations alt – alternate ● beg – beginning ● cont – continue ● dec – decrease ● foll – following ● inc – increase ● k – knit ● p – purl ● patt – pattern ● rem – remaining ● rep – repeat ● st(s) – stitch(es) ● st st – stockinette stitch ● tog – together

SLEEVE SHAPING Bind off 115 (116) sts at beg of next row, then cont in patt on rem 51 (55) sts until work measures 25½(26¼)in from neck divide. Bind off.
Rejoin yarn to rem sts at neck edge and work 2nd side to match 1st side as given from ******

SIDE PANEL FOR BODY (make 2) Using No 5 needles cast on 86 (98) sts and work in double rib as follows:
1st row: k2, *p2, k2, rep from * to end.
2nd row: p2, *k2, p2, rep from * to end.

These 2 rows form the patt. Cont in patt until work measures 15¾(15¼)in, ending with a wrong side row.

DIVIDE FOR SHAPING Next row: patt 43 (49) sts, turn and work on this 1st group of sts as follows:
1st row: p2, k2tog, keeping continuity of rib, work in rib patt as before.
2nd row: work in rib to last 4 sts, p2tog, k2.
Rep these 2 rows 21 (24) times in all. Fasten off.
Rejoin yarn to rem sts at center and work as follows:
1st row: k2, p2tog, work in rib, as before, to end.
2nd row: rib to last 4 sts, k2tog, p2.
Rep these 2 rows 21 (24) times in all. Fasten off.

SIDE PANEL FOR SLEEVE (make 2) Using No 5 needles cast on 70 (82) sts and work in double rib as given for side panel, until work measures 16¼(16)in, ending with a wrong side row.

DIVIDE FOR SHAPING Next row: patt 35 (41) sts, turn and work on this 1st group of sts as follows:
1st row: p2, k2tog, work in rib as before to end.
2nd row: rib to last 4 sts, p2tog, k2.
Cont decreasing in this manner on every row except on every 6th row, until 1 st rem. Fasten off. Rejoin yarn to rem sts at center and work as follows:
1st row: k2, p2tog, work in rib as before to end.
2nd row: rib to last 4 sts, k2tog, p2.

Cont decreasing in this manner on every row, except on every foll 6th row, until 1 st remains. Fasten off.

POCKETS (make 2) Using No 5 needles cast on 63 (67) sts and work in moss rib patt as given for center panel, until work measures 6½in, ending with a wrong side row. Work 2 rows in reverse st st, bind off knitwise.

TABS (work 2) Using No 3 needles cast on 10 sts and work in double rib, as given for side panel, until work measures 3¼in. Bind off ribwise.

TO FINISH Using small backstitch throughout, sew shaped edge of side panel for body, to shaped edge of side panel for sleeve. Sew the outside edges of these 2 pieces to main panel at side edges and sleeve edges. At the same time insert side edge of pocket panel in front and back seams at lower edge. With garter stitch rows of pocket at top.

SLEEVE EDGE Using No 3 circular needle, and working from the right side, pick up 140 (160) sts evenly around lower edge of sleeve. Work 3 rounds in p, then bind off purlwise.

HEM EDGE Using No 3 needles and working from the right side (and through both layers of pocket section), pick up 304 (328) sts evenly around lower edge. Work 2 rows in reverse st st. Bind off knitwise on next row.

CENTER FRONT EDGES Using No 3 needles, and working from the right side, pick up 140 (144) sts evenly along edge and work as given for hem edge.

NECK EDGE Using No 3 needles and working from the right side, pick up 122 (124) sts evenly around neck edge and work as for hem edge.
Sew 2 tabs at top of front opening on right side, sew buckles on left side to correspond to tabs.

HOOD Using No 5 circular needle cast on 268 sts and work in double rib for 19¾in. Bind off loosely ribwise.

TO WEAR Pull hood over head, bring all excess to front, twist and insert head through the hole formed.

SKIRT Using No 5 needles cast on 1 st and work as follows:
1st row: p1 k1 into 1st st (right side of work).
2nd row: p2.
3rd row: k1, p1 into 1st st, k1.
4th row: p twice into 1st st, p2.
5th row: p1, k1 into 1st st, p1, k1, p1.
6th row: p to end.
7th row: k1, p1 into 1st st, (k1, p1) × 2
8th row: p twice into 1st st, p to end.
Now cont working in patt as set, and cont increasing at left edge on every foll 4th row, and at right edge on next and every foll alt row, until 38 (42) sts have been increased at right edge in all, and 19 (21) sts have been increased at left edge in all. Leave these 58 (64) sts on st holder. Work 2 more pieces to match.
Place all 174 (192) sts on No 5 circular needle with right side facing, and work in rounds of patt as follows:
1st row: keeping continuity of k and p sts as set, work in k1, p1 rib across round.
2nd row: k to end.
Cont working in patt until work measures 32¾(34¼)in, from lowest point.
Change to No 4 circular needle and cont in st st (every round knit) for 10 rows. Work 1 row purl, then cont in st st for a further 10 rows. Bind off loosely.

SKIRT INSERT Using No 5 needles, cast on 114 (126) sts and work in double rib. Dec 1 st at right hand edge on every alt row, and dec 1 st at left hand edge on every row until 2 sts remain. K2tog. Fasten off.

TO FINISH Using small backstitch sew inserts into shaped edge of hem. Cut a piece of elastic to fit waist, turn waistband to inside and hem down. Insert elastic.

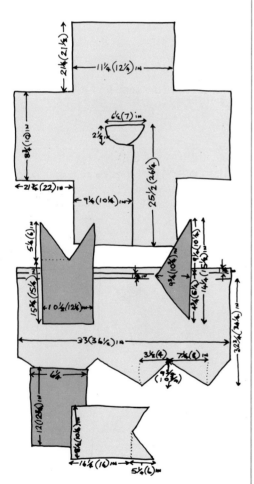

All dimensions are in inches

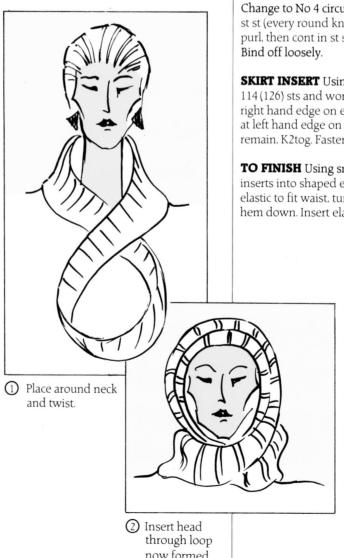

① Place around neck and twist.

② Insert head through loop now formed.

MANHATTAN

Brown and gray jacket with fringed shawl

GAUGE Using No 5 needles, MC over st patt, 22 sts and 30 rows = 4in square.

BACK Using No 5 needles and MC, cast on 119 (125;131) sts and cont patt as follows:
1st row: p5, *k1, p5, rep from * to end.
2nd row: k5, *p1, k5, rep from * to end.
Rep these 2 rows 4 more times.
11th row: p2, *k1, p5, rep from * to last 3 sts, k1, p2.
12th row: k2, *p1, k5, rep from * to last 3 sts, p1, k2.
Rep these last 2 rows 4 more times.
These 20 rows form the patt. Cont in patt until work measures 11 (11½;12)in. Place armhole markers at each end of last row. Cont in patt until work measures 27 (28;29)in. Bind off.

POCKET BAGS (make 2). Using No 5 needles and col A. cast on 31 (32;33) sts and work in st st until work measures 7½in ending with a k row. Leave sts on holder.

GRADE ★ ★			
Sizes to fit	32	34	36	in
Actual size	42	44	46	in
Back length	27	28	29	in
Sleeve seam	16½	17	17½	in
Materials				
Jacket	21	24	28	MC
	7	7	7	A
Shawl	19	19	19	A
oz knitting worsted				

1 pr No 3 needles ● 1 pr No 4 needles ●1 pr No 5 needles ● 2 large buttons
Suggested yarn: Kitten by Reynolds. Alpaca Andéan

Abbreviations alt – alternate ● beg – beginning ● cont – continue ● dec – decrease ● foll – following ● inc – increase ● k – knit ● p – purl ● patt – pattern ● rem – remaining ● rep – repeat ● st(s) – stitch(es) ● st st – stockinette stitch ● tog – together ● MC – main color ● A – 1st color

RIGHT FRONT Using No 5 needles and MC, cast on 65 (68;71) sts and cont patt as follows:
1st row: p2 (0;2), k1 (0;1), *p5, k1, rep from * to last 2 sts, p2.
2nd row: k2, *p1, k5, rep from * to last 3 (0;3) sts, p1 (0;1), k2 (0;2).
Placement of patt is now set. Cont in patt until work measures 7½in ending with a wrong side row.

PLACE POCKET Next row: patt 17 (18;19) sts, bind off next 31 (32;33) sts, patt to end.
Next row: patt 17 (18;19), patt across pocket bag, patt to end.
Cont in patt to the same row as back armhole marker. Place an armhole marker at left side. Cont in patt until work measures 19¼(20¼;21¼)in ending with a wrong side row.

BUTTONHOLE Next row: patt 5 sts, bind off next 3 sts, patt to end.
Next row: patt to last 5 sts, cast on 3 sts, patt to end.**

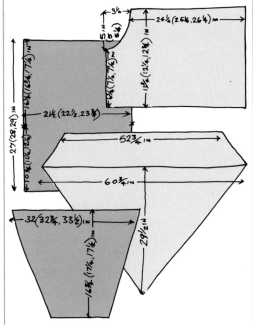

All dimensions are in inches

Patt 28 more rows. Rep from ** to **. Cont in patt until work measures 24¼(25¼; 26¼)in ending with a wrong side row.

SHAPE NECKLINE 1st row: bind off 8 (9;10) sts, patt to end.
2nd row: patt to last 2 sts, patt 2 tog.
3rd row: bind off 5 sts, patt to end.
4th row: as 2nd row.
5th row: bind off 3 sts, patt to end.
Dec 1 st at neck edge of next 5 rows. Dec 1 st at neck edge of foll 4 alt rows. Cont in patt on rem 38 (40;42) sts until work measures 27 (28;29)in. Bind off.

LEFT FRONT Work to match right front reversing patt placement and shapings and omitting buttonholes.

SLEEVES Using No 5 needles and MC, cast on 73 (75;77) sts and commence patt as follows:
1st row: p0 (1;2), *k1, p5, rep from * to last 1 (2;3) sts, k1, p0 (1;2).
2nd row: k0 (1;2), *p1, k5, rep from * to last 1 (2;3) sts, p1, k0 (1;2).
Placement of patt is now set. Cont in patt and inc 1 st at each end of next and every foll alt row until there are 177 (181;185) sts. Cont in patt without shaping until work measures 16¾(17¼;17½)in, ending with a wrong side row. Bind off 36 sts at beg of next 4 rows. Bind off rem 33 (37;41) sts.

SLEEVE HEM & FACING (both the same) Using No 5 needles and A, with right side facing, pick up 69 (71;73) sts across bottom of sleeve. Work 4 rows st st beg with a p row. K1 row. Work 6 rows st st beg with a k row. Cont in st st and inc 1 st at each end of next and every foll alt row until work measures 8½in from beg of hem. Bind off.

NECKBAND Using small backstitch, sew both shoulder seams.
Using No 5 needles and A, with right side facing, pick 35 (37;39) sts along right front neckline, pick up 39 (41;43) sts across back neckline, pick up 35 (37;39) sts along left front neckline. 109 (115;121) sts. P1 row. Change to No 4 needles. K1 row increasing 1 st at each end of row. P1 row. Change to No 3 needles. K1 row increasing 1 st at each end of row. K1 row. K1 row decreasing 1 st at each end of row. Change to No 4 needles. P1 row. K1 row decreasing 1 st at each end of row. Change to No 5 needles. P1 row. Bind off.

RIGHT FRONT HEM & FACING Using No 5 needles and A, with right side facing, pick up 125 (131;137) sts along front edge. Work 4 rows st st beg with a p row and inc 1 st at each end of 2nd and 4th rows. K1 row. Work 10 rows st st beg with a k row and decrease at each end of 1st and 3rd rows. Fold work to the inside and place markers on needle at buttonholes. K to 1st marker, turn work and work 4 more rows st st on these sts. Break yarn and rejoin to rem sts. K to 2nd marker, turn work and work 4 more rows st st on these sts. Break yarn and rejoin to rem sts. Work 5 rows st st on these sts. P across all sts. Work 1 (3;5) more rows st st. Cont in st st for 4 rows and inc 1 st at beg of next and foll 3rd row. Work 3 more rows st st. Bind off.
Work left front hem and facing to match, omitting buttonholes.

POCKET BANDS (both the same) Using No 5 needles and A, with right side facing, pick up 27 (28;29) sts across pocket top. K1 row. Work 1¼in st st beg with a k row. Bind off. Sew pocket flap down to outside of work.

BOTTOM HEM Using small backstitch, sew sleeve tops into armholes between markers and sew underarm seams. Using No 5 needles and Alpaca, with right side facing, pick up 60 (62;64) sts across left front, pick up 111 (115;121) sts across back, pick up 60 (62;64) sts across right front. 231 (239;249) sts. Work 4 rows st st beg with a p row and inc 1 st at each end of 2nd and 4th rows. K1 row. Work 4 rows st st beg with a k row and dec 1 st at each end of 1st and 3rd rows. Bind off.

SHAWL Using No 5 needles and A, cast on 292 sts. Work 2 rows st st beg with a k row. [Work 3 rows st st beg with a k row and inc 1 st at each end of every row. P1 row] × 6. Work 3 rows st st beg with a k row and inc 1 st at each end of every row. 336 sts. K1 row.** Work 3 rows st st beg with a k row and dec 1 st at each end of every row. P1 row. Rep from ** until 2 sts remain. K2 tog. Fasten off. Fold in and stitch down long side facing. Cut strands of each yarn in various lengths between 15½ and 19½in. Fold strands in half and loop through 2 edges of shawl.

TO FINISH Using small backstitch, sew the 4 front miters and sleeve seams. Fold in hems and facings and slip stitch down. Sew down pocket bags. Oversew both layers of buttonholes tog. Sew on 2 front buttons.

CAP D'ANTIBES
Appliqué Cardigan
(see page 45 for instructions)

GAUGE Using No 5 needles over st patt, 21 sts and 35 rows = 4in square.

BACK Using No 3 needles, cast on 77 (83;87;93) sts and work in single rib as follows:
1st row: k2, *p1, k1, rep from * to last st, k1.
2nd row: k1, *p1, k1, rep from * to end.
Rep these 2 rows until work measures 2¼in, ending with a 1st row.
Next row: rib 4 (2;4;2) *rib 3 (3;3;4), inc in next st, rib 3 (4;4;4), rep from * to last 3 (1;3;1) sts, rib to end. 87 (93;97;103) sts.
Change to No 5 needles and cont in patt as follows:
1st row: p3 (6;8;11), *p19, rep from * to last 4 (7;9;12) sts, k1, p to end.
2nd row: p.
These 2 rows form the patt. Cont in patt until work measures 12¼(12¼;12½;12½)in, ending with a wrong side row.

SHAPE ARMHOLES Bind off 4 sts at beg of next 2 rows, then cont in patt until work measures 24 (24½;25;25¼)in, ending with a wrong side row.

SHAPE SHOULDERS Bind off 10 (11;12;13) sts at beg of next 2 rows, and 11 (12;13;14) sts at beg of foll 2 rows. Bind off rem 37 (39;39;41) sts loosely for back neck.

LEFT FRONT Using No 3 needles, cast on 41 (43;45;49) sts and work in single rib as for the back, until work measures 2¼in, ending with a 1st row.
Next row: rib 1 (2;3;1), *rib 4 (4;4;5), inc in next st, rib 5 (5;5;6), rep from * to last 0 (1;2;0) sts, rib to end. 45 (47;49;53) sts.
Change to No 5 needles and cont in patt as follows:
1st row: p3 (6;8;11), [k1, p19] rep from * to last 2 (1;1;2) sts, k1, p1 (0;0;1).
2nd row: p.
These 2 rows form the patt. Cont in patt until work measures 12¼(12¼;12½;12½)in, ending at the armhole edge.

SHAPE ARMHOLES Bind off 4 sts at beg of next row. Cont in patt until work measures 22¼(22¾;23½;23¾)in, ending at neck edge.

GRADE ★					
Sizes to fit	30	32	34	36	in
Actual size	34	36	38	40	in
Back length	23½	24	24½	25	in
Sleeve seam	17½	17¾	18	18¼	in
Materials	14	15	15	17	
	oz bulky yarn				

1 pr No 5 needles ● 1 pr No 3 needles ● 5 buttons
Suggested yarn: Wendy Dolcé

Abbreviations alt – alternate ● beg – beginning ● cont – continue ● dec – decrease ● foll – following ● inc – increase ● k – knit ● p – purl ● patt – pattern ● rem – remaining ● rep – repeat ● st(s) – stitch(es) ● st st – stockinette stitch ● tog – together

SHAPE NECKLINE Next row: cast off 4 sts. Patt to end.
Next row: patt to last 2 sts, p2tog.
Next row: bind off 2 sts. Patt to end.
Next row: patt to last 2 sts, p2tog.
Rep the last 2 rows twice more, then dec 1 st at neck edge only of next 6 (6;6;8) rows. At the same time, when work measures 23 (23½;24;24½)in, ending at armhole edge.
Bind off 10 (11;12;13) sts at beg of next row and 11 (12;13;14) sts at beg of foll alt row.

RIGHT FRONT Work as for the left front, reversing shapings and patt, the patt being:
1st row: p1 (0;0;1), *k1, p19, k1, rep from * to last 4 (7;9;12) sts, p3 (6;8;11).
2nd row: p.

SLEEVES Using No 3 needles, cast on 45 (47;49;53) sts and work in single rib as for the back, until work measures 2¼in, ending with a 1st row.
Next row: rib 3 (4;5;7), *inc in next st, rib 1, rep from * to last 2 (3;4;6) sts, rib to end. 65 (67;69;73) sts.
Change to No 5 needles and cont in patt as follows:
1st row: p2 (3;4;6), *k1, p19, rep from * to last 3 (4;5;7) sts, k1, p2(3;4;6).
2nd row: p.
These 2 rows form the patt. Cont in patt and at the same time, inc 1 st at each end of every foll 4th row, until there are 117 (121;127;131) sts, then cont without shaping until work measures 17¾(18;18¼;18½)in. Place armhole marker at each end of the last row, then work a further 8 rows.

SHAPE SLEEVE TOPS Bind off 18 sts at beg of next 6 rows. Bind off rem 9 (13;19;23) sts. Work 2nd sleeve to match.

BUTTONHOLE BAND Using No 3 needles, cast on 7 sts and work in single rib for 4 rows, *next row, rib 4, turn and work 3 rows on these 4 sts. Rejoin yarn to rem sts and work 4 rows on these 3 sts. Work in rib across all sts for 38 (40;42;42) rows. Rep from * 3 more times. Leave work on safety pin.

BUTTONBAND Work as for buttonhole band, omitting buttonholes.

NECKBAND Using small backstitch, sew both shoulder seams. Working from right side, pick up 7 sts of buttonhole band, 23 (24;25;26) sts from right front, 39 (41;43;45) sts from back, 23 (24;25;26) sts from left front and 7 sts from buttonband. 99 (103;107;111) sts. Work in single rib for 6 rows, placing one more buttonhole over previous buttonholes on 1st to 4th rows. Bind off ribwise when the 6 rows are completed.

TO FINISH Using small backstitch, sew sleeves into armholes, placing last 8 rows of sleeve against the 4 bound-off sts of armhole. Sew underarm seam from wrist to hem. Sew buttonband and buttonhole band into place. Sew buttons onto buttonband.

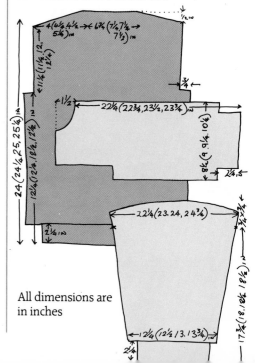

All dimensions are in inches

TOPSY

Girl's lace top with frilled yoke

GAUGE Using No 3 needles over lace pattern. 27 sts and 32 rows = 4in square.

BACK AND FRONT (both the same) Using No 1 needles, cast on 81 (89;95;103) sts and work in single rib as follows:
1st row: k2, *p1, k1, rep from * to last st. k1.
2nd row: k1, *p1, k1, rep from * to end.
Rep these 2 rows until work measures 1½in, ending with a 1st row.
Next row: rib 5 (5;5;6), [inc in next st, rib 9 (10;8;9)] × 7 (7;9;9), inc in next st, rib to end. 89 (97;105;113) sts.
Change to No 3 needles and cont in st patt as follows:
Work 4 rows st st beg with a k row.
5th row: k4, *yo, k2tog, k6, rep from * to last 5 sts, yo, k2tog, k3.
Work 9 rows st st beg with a p row.
15th row: K8, *yo, k2tog, k6, rep from * to last 9 sts, yo, k2tog, k7.
Work 5 rows st st, beg with a p row.
These 20 rows form the patt. Cont in patt until work measures 8½(10;11½;12½)in from beg, ending with a wrong side row.

SHAPE ARMHOLES AND NECKLINE Bind off 5 sts at beg of next 2 rows. Dec 1 st at each end of the next and every foll alt row until 63 (67;71;75) sts remain, ending with a wrong side row. Cont in patt and work neck shapings as follows:
1st row: k2tog, patt 20 (22;24;26) sts, turn.
2nd and every alt row: sl 1, patt to end.
3rd row: k2tog, patt 11 (14;17;20) sts, turn.
5th row: k2tog, patt 4 (7;12;15) sts, turn.
2nd, 3rd & 4th sizes only:
7th row: k2tog, patt 2 (7;11) sts, turn.
3rd & 4th sizes only:
9th row: k2tog, patt 3 (7) sts, turn.
4th size only:
11th row: k2tog, patt 3 sts, turn.
Rep 2nd row once more. Break yarn.
Next row: sl 38 (39;40;41) sts, rejoin yarn to rem sts and work 2nd side to match 1st side. Leave rem 57 (59;61;63) sts on a free needle.

FRONT Work as the back until 67 (71;75;79) sts remain, ending with a wrong side row.

SHAPE ARMHOLES AND TOP OF SLEEVES Bind off 5 sts at beg of next rows. Dec 1 st, at each end of next and every foll alt row, until 35 (37;39;41) sts remain, ending with

GRADE ★ ★ ★					
Sizes to fit	24	26	28	30	in
Actual size	26	28	30	32	in
Back length	14	16	18	20	in
Sleeve seam	2¼	2¼	2¾	2¾	in
Materials	3	4	4	5	
		oz sports yarn			

1 pr No 1 needles ● 1 pr No 3 needles ●1 No 1 circular needle ● 1 No 3 circular needle

Suggested yarn: Rubertin by Nevada

Abbreviations beg – beginning ● cont – continue ● dec – decrease ● foll – following ● inc – increase ● k – knit ● p – purl ● patt – pattern ● rep – repeat ● sl – slip ● st(s) – stitch(es) ● st st – stockinette stitch ● tog – together ● yo – yarn over needle

a wrong side row. Cont in patt and work neckline shapings as follows:
1st row: k2tog, patt 7 (8;9;10) sts, turn.
2nd and all alt rows: sl1, patt to end.
3rd row: k2tog, patt 4 (5;7;8) sts, turn.
5th row: k2tog, patt 1 (3;5;6) sts, turn.
2nd, 3rd & 4th sizes only:
7th row: k2tog, patt 1 (3;4) sts, turn.
3rd & 4th sizes only:
9th row: k2tog, patt 1 (2) sts, turn.
4th size only:
11th row: k2tog, patt 1, turn.
All sizes:
Work 2nd row once more. Break yarn and sl next 17 sts onto free needle, rejoin yarn to rem sts and work 2nd side to match 1st side. Leave rem 29 (31;33;35) sts on free needle.

YOKE Using small backstitch, sew the raglan seams.
With right side facing, sl first 28 (20;30;31) sts of front on to a double-pointed needle. Using No 3 circular needle, k2tog, k25 (26;27;28), k2tog, from right sleeve – k2tog, k25 (27;29;31), k2tog, from the back – k2tog, k53 (55;57;59), k2tog, from the left sleeve – k2tog, k25 (27;29;31), k2tog, from the front – k2tog, k26 (27;28;29), turn. 163 (171;179;187) sts.
Next row: k to end, turn.
Next row: k to end, turn.
Next and every alt row: p to end, turn.
1st row: k6 (10;6;10), [k2tog, k8 (8;9;9)] × 15, k2tog, k to end. 147 (155;163;171) sts.
3rd row: k5 (9;6;10), [k2tog, k7 (7;8;8)] × 15, k2tog, k to end. 131 (139;147;155) sts.
5th row: k to end.
7th row: k5 (9;5;9), [k2tog, k6 (6;7;7)] × 15, k2tog, k to end. 115 (123;131;139) sts.

9th row: as 5th row.
11th row: as 5th row.
13th row: k4 (8;5;9), [k2tog, k5 (5;6;6)] × 15, k2tog, k to end. 99 (107;114;123) sts.
15th row: as 5th row.
16th row: as 5th row.
Change to No 1 circular needle and cont as follows:
1st row: cast on 100 (106;112;118) sts, k2, *p1, k1, rep from * to last st, p1.
2nd row: cast on 100 (106;112;118) sts, k1, *p1, k1, rep from * to end. 299 (319;339;359) sts.
Cont in rib for 1in. Bind off ribwise.

SLEEVES Using No 1 needles, cast on 41 (47;53;59) sts, and work in single rib as given for the back and front until work measures 1in, ending with a 1st row.
Next row: rib 5 (4;3;3), [rib 0 (1;1;4), inc in next st, rib 1 (2;2;4)] × 16 (10;12;16), rib rem 4 (3;2;2) sts. 57 (57;65;65) sts.
Change to No 3 needles and cont in st st, for 8 (6;10;8) rows, then commence st patt at row 5. AND at the same time, inc 1 st at each end every 3rd (2nd;3rd;2nd) row until there are 61 (67;73;79) sts, then cont until work measures 2¼ (2¼;2¾;2¾)in, ending with a wrong side row.

FRILL Using No 3 needles, cast on 13 sts.
1st row: sl1, k1[yo, k2tog] × 2. k1 [yo, sl1, k1, psso] × 2. yo, k2.
2nd and every alt row: p to end.
3rd row: sl1, k1 [yo, k2tog] × 2. k2 [yo, sl1, k1, psso] × 2. yo, k2.

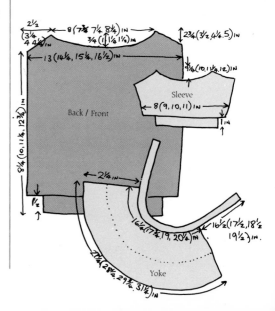

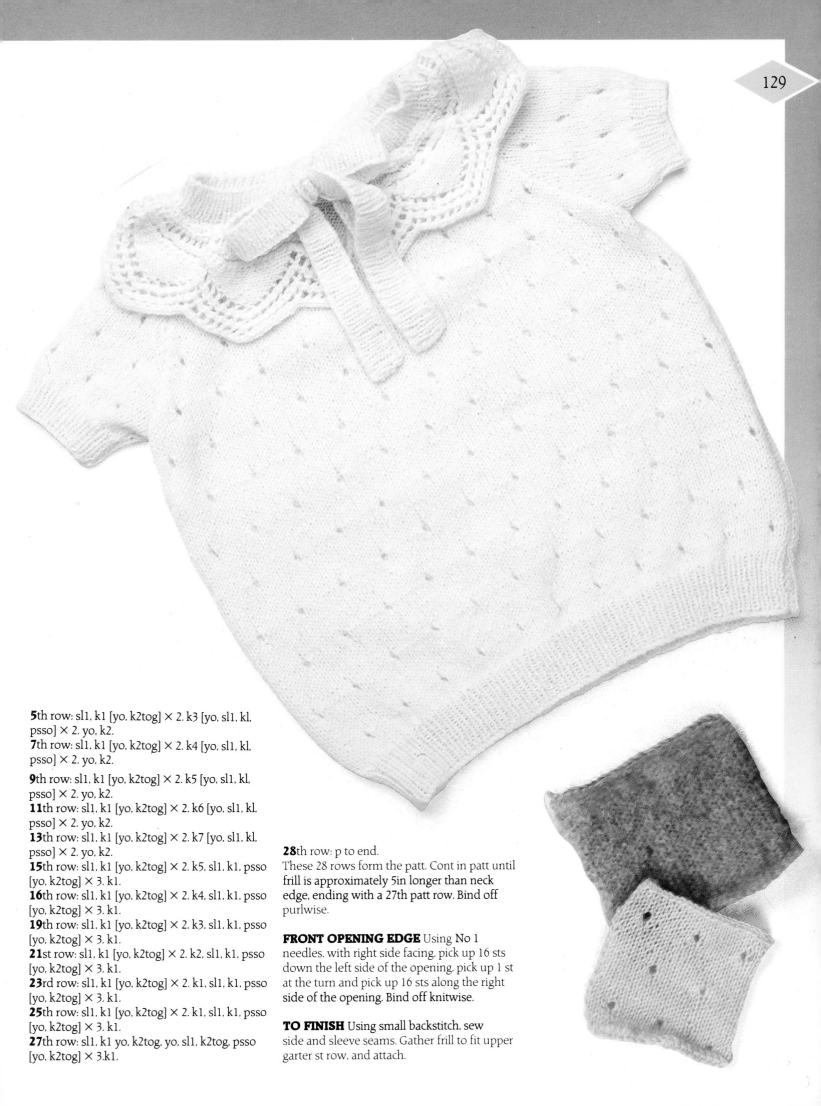

5th row: sl1, k1 [yo, k2tog] × 2. k3 [yo, sl1, k1, psso] × 2. yo, k2.

7th row: sl1, k1 [yo, k2tog] × 2. k4 [yo, sl1, k1, psso] × 2. yo, k2.

9th row: sl1, k1 [yo, k2tog] × 2. k5 [yo, sl1, k1, psso] × 2. yo, k2.

11th row: sl1, k1 [yo, k2tog] × 2. k6 [yo, sl1, k1, psso] × 2. yo, k2.

13th row: sl1, k1 [yo, k2tog] × 2. k7 [yo, sl1, k1, psso] × 2. yo, k2.

15th row: sl1, k1 [yo, k2tog] × 2. k5, sl1, k1, psso [yo, k2tog] × 3. k1.

16th row: sl1, k1 [yo, k2tog] × 2. k4, sl1, k1, psso [yo, k2tog] × 3. k1.

19th row: sl1, k1 [yo, k2tog] × 2. k3, sl1, k1, psso [yo, k2tog] × 3. k1.

21st row: sl1, k1 [yo, k2tog] × 2. k2, sl1, k1, psso [yo, k2tog] × 3. k1.

23rd row: sl1, k1 [yo, k2tog] × 2. k1, sl1, k1, psso [yo, k2tog] × 3. k1.

25th row: sl1, k1 [yo, k2tog] × 2. k1, sl1, k1, psso [yo, k2tog] × 3. k1.

27th row: sl1, k1 yo, k2tog, yo, sl1, k2tog, psso [yo, k2tog] × 3. k1.

28th row: p to end.
These 28 rows form the patt. Cont in patt until frill is approximately 5in longer than neck edge, ending with a 27th patt row. Bind off purlwise.

FRONT OPENING EDGE Using No 1 needles, with right side facing, pick up 16 sts down the left side of the opening, pick up 1 st at the turn and pick up 16 sts along the right side of the opening. Bind off knitwise.

TO FINISH Using small backstitch, sew side and sleeve seams. Gather frill to fit upper garter st row, and attach.

ROMAN Á CLEF
Chunky cardigan with key motif

GAUGE Using No 10 needles over patt st 14 sts and 24 rows = 4in square.

BACK Using No 8 needles and MC, cast on 65 (75;81) sts and work in single rib as follows:
1st row: k1, *k1, p1, rep from * to last 2 sts, k2.
2nd row: *k1, p1, rep from * to last st, k1.
Rep these 2 rows until work measures 3¼in from beg, ending with a 2nd row, and inc 5 sts evenly across last row worked. 74 (80;86) sts.
Change to No 10 needles and work in patt as follows:
1st row: using AB, k.
2nd row: using AB, k.
3rd row: using MC, k6, *sl1, k5, rep from * to last 2 sts, sl1, k1.
4th row (and all alt rows): using MC, k all k sts of previous row, sl1 yf, all sl sts.
5th row: using A, k1, sl1, *k3, sl1, k1, sl1, rep from * to last 6 sts, k3, sl1, k2.
7th row: using MC, k4, *sl1, k1, sl1, k3, rep from * to last 4 sts, sl1, k1, sl1, k1.
9th row: using A, k3, *sl1, k1, sl1, k3, rep from * to last 5 sts, sl1, k1, sl1, k2.
11th row: using MC, k4, *sl1, k5, rep from * to last 4 sts, sl1, k3.
12th row: using MC, as 4th row.
These 12 rows form the patt. Cont in patt until work measures 15½in from beg, ending with a wrong side row. Mark each end of last row worked to indicate start of armholes. Cont in patt until armhole measures 10¼(10½;11¼)in.

SHAPE SHOULDERS Bind off 11 (12;14) sts at beg of next 2 rows. Bind off 12 (14;15) sts at beg of next 2 rows. Bind off rem 28 (28;28) sts.

LEFT FRONT Using No 8 needles and MC, cast on 25 (29;35) sts and work in single rib as given for the back, and inc 3 sts evenly across last row worked. 28 (32;38) sts.
Change to No 10 needles and work in patt as follows:
1st row: using A, k.
2nd row: using A, k.
3rd row: using MC, k6, *sl1, k5, rep from * to last 4 (2;2) sts, sl1, k3 (1;1).
4th row (and all alt rows): using MC, k all k sts of previous row, and sl1 yf, all sl sts.
5th row: using A, k1, sl1, *k3, sl1, k1, sl1, rep from * to last 8 (6;6) sts, k3, sl1, k4 (2;2).
7th row: using MC, k4, *sl1, k1, sl1, k3, rep from * to last 6 (4;4) sts, sl1, k1, sl1, k3 (1;1).

9th row: using A, k3, *sl1, k1, sl1, k3, rep from * to past 7 (5;5) sts, sl1, k1, sl1, k4 (2;2).
11th row: using MC, k4, *sl1, k5, rep from * to last 6 (4;4) sts, sl1, k5 (3;3).
12th row: as 4th row.
These 12 rows form the patt. Cont in patt until work measures 15½in from beg, ending with a wrong side row. Mark the end of last row worked to indicate the start of the armhole. Cont in patt until armhole measures 8½(8¾;9¼)in, ending with a right side row.

SHAPE NECKLINE Bind off 2 (3;4) sts at beg of next row. Work 1 row. Dec 1 st at beg of next, and foll 2 (2;4) alt rows. Cont straight until armhole measures same as back, ending with a wrong side row.

SHAPE SHOULDERS Bind off 11 (12;14) sts at beg of next row. Work 1 row. Bind off rem 12 (14;15) sts.

RIGHT FRONT Work as given for the left front, reversing shapings and reversing the patt, so the 3rd row is:
MC, k3 (1;1), *sl1, k5, rep from * to last 7 sts, sl1, k6.

SLEEVES Using No 8 needles and MC, cast on 37 (43;43) sts and work in single rib as for the back, until work measures 3¼in from beg and inc 1 st in last st worked.
Change to No 10 needles, and work in patt as for the back. Inc 1 st at each end of every foll 4th (5th;5th) row until there are 74 (78;80) sts, working the extra sts into the patt. Cont

straight until work measures 17¾(18¼;18¼)in from beg. Bind off.

BUTTON BANDS *Button border* (left front) Using No 8 needles and MC, cast on 17 sts and work in single rib as for the back until work measures 22¼(23;23½)in. Bind off 38 (44;44) sts.
Buttonhole border rep as for the left side, making 4 buttonholes. The 1st should be ½in from the lower edge, leave 7¼(7½;7¾)in between each one, the last one being ½in from the top.
1st row of buttonhole rib 6 sts, bind off 4 sts, rib to end.
2nd row of buttonhole rib 7 sts, cast on 4 sts, rib to end.

NECKBAND Using No 8 needles and MC, join shoulder seams. With right side of work facing, pick up and knit 16 (18;18) sts from right front, 27 sts from back and 16 (18;18) sts from left front. Work 1¼in in k1, p1 rib as for the back. Bind off in rib; 59 (63;63) sts.

TO FINISH Join side and sleeve seams. Sew on front bands. Sew on buttons to match buttonholes. Set in sleeves.

GRADE ★ ★			
Sizes to fit	32-34	36-38	40-42	in
Actual size	40	44	48	in
Back length	25	25½	26	in
Sleeve seam	17½	18	18	in
Materials	19	22	26	MC
	12	12	14	A
	oz bulky yarn			

1 pr No 8 needles ● 1 pr No 10 needles ● 4 buttons
Suggested yarn: Phildar Vizir

Abbreviations alt – alternate ● beg – beginning ● cont – continue ● dec – decrease ● foll – following ● inc – increase ● k – knit ● p – purl ● patt – pattern ● rem – remaining ● rep – repeat ● sl – slip ● st(s) – stitch(es) ● sll yf – sl 1 with yarn foward ● tog – together ● yb – yarn back ● yf – yarn forward ● MC – main color ● A – 1st color

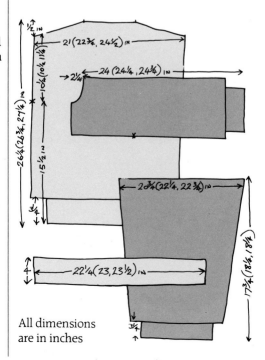

All dimensions are in inches

THE SUZY WONG
Floral Chinese-style top with back buttons

GAUGE Using No 5 needles over st st, 24 sts and 32 rows = 4in square.

NOTE When working the color patt, the yarns must be woven in very loosely across the back of the work so that the tension is not affected and the weaving in should not be noticeable from the right side.

FRONT Using No 3 needles and MC, cast on 116 (122) sts and work ¾in in g st (knit every row), ending with a wrong side row. Change to No 5 needles. Working in st st, follow patt from chart.

1st row: patt 13 (1) sts, work 30 sts of patt, rep 3 (4) times then patt rem 13 (1) sts. When work measures 12in from beg, ending with a wrong side row, mark each end of last row to indicate start of armholes. When work measures 21 (22)in from beg, bind off.

RIGHT HALF BACK Using No 3 needles and MC, cast on 60 (62) sts and work ¾in in g st, ending with a wrong side row. Change to No 5 needles. Follow patt from chart.

1st row: patt 0 (1) sts, work 30 sts of patt, rep twice then patt rem 0 (1) sts. When work measures 12in from beg, mark armholes. When work measures 21 (22)in from beg, bind off.

GRADE ★ ★ ★ ★			
Sizes to fit	32-34	36-38	in
Actual size	38	40	in
Back length	21	22	in
Sleeve seam	17½	18	in
Materials	12	12	MC
	5	5	A
	1	1	B
	1	1	C
	1	1	D
	3	3	E
	oz knitting worsted		

1 pr No 3 needles ● 1 pr No 5 needles ● 6 buttons
Suggested yarn: Pomfret Mark II by Brunswick

Abbreviations alt – alternate ● beg – beginning ● cont – continue ● dec – decrease ● foll – following ● g st – garter stitch ● inc – increase ● k – knit ● p – purl ● patt – pattern ● rem – remaining ● rep – repeat ● st(s) – stitch(es) ● st st – stockinette stitch ● tog – together ● MC – main color ● A – 1st color ● B – 2nd color ● C – 3rd color ● D – 4th color ● E – 5th color

LEFT HALF BACK Work as given for right half back until the 1st 2 (4) rows of chart have been worked. Make buttonhole.

1st row: patt 2 sts, bind off 3 sts, patt 55 (57) sts to end.

2nd row: patt 55 (57) sts, bind on 3 sts, patt to end.

Cont as given for left half back, making 5 more buttonholes, over the previous buttonhole, working 24 rows between each buttonhole. Work to end. Bind off.

SLEEVES Using No 3 needles and MC, cast on 60 (62) sts and work ¾in in g st, ending with a wrong side row.

Change to No 5 needles. Work in patt from chart as given for 1st patt row of back. And inc 1 st at each end of every 4th row, incorporating the sts into the patt until there are 116 (126) sts. Cont straight until work measures 17½ (18)in from beg. Bind off.

COLLAR Using small backstitch, join 4½ (5)in of both shoulder seams. Using No 3 needles and MC, with right side of work facing, pick up and knit 36 (34) sts from left half back, 64 (62) sts from front, and 36 (34) sts from right half back. 136 (130) sts. Work 5in in g st. Bind off loosely. Fold neckband in half to outside.

BACK EDGINGS Using No 3 needles and MC, pick up and knit 130 (134) sts, along center back edges. Bind off knitwise.

TO FINISH Using small backstitch, set in sleeves matching sleeve side seam with start of armholes. Join side and sleeve seams. Sew on buttons.

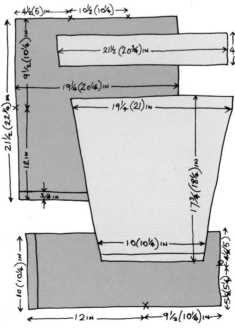

All dimensions are in inches

☐ main col ▨ col C ⎤ Use oddments of
■ col A ▨ col D ⎦ different colors
▨ col B ☐ col E

MOHAIR MAGIC
Mohair fan lace with a large collar

GAUGE Using No 8 needles over patt st, 15 sts and 22 rows = 4in square.

BACK Using No 5 needles, cast on 73 (81;87) sts and work in k1p1 rib.
1st row: k1, *k1, p1, rep from * to last 2 sts, k2.
2nd row: *k1, p1, rep from * to last st, k1.
Rep these 2 rows as set until work measures 2³⁄₄in from beg, ending with a 2nd row and increasing 1 st at each end of the last row (75;83;89) sts.
Change to No 8 needles and cont in st patt as follows:
1st row: k3 (2;5), yo, *k3, k3tog, k3, yo, k1, yo, rep from * to last 12 (11;14) sts, k3, k3tog, k3 yo, k3 (2;5).
2nd row: p7 (6;9), *sl1, p9, rep from * to last 8 (7;10) sts, sl1, p7 (6;9).
3rd row: k4 (3;6), *yo, k2, k3tog, k2, yo, k3, rep from * to last 11 (10;13) sts, yo, k2, k3tog, k2, yo, k4 (3;6).
4th row: as 2nd row.
5th row: k4 (3;6), *k1, yo, k1, k3tog, k1, yo, k4, rep from * to last 11 (10;13) sts, k1, yo, k1, k3tog, k1, yo, k5 (4;7).
6th row: p6 (5;8), *cluster 3 sts, p7, rep from * to last 9 (8;11) sts, cluster 3 sts, p6 (5;8).
7th row: k2 (1;4), k2tog, k1, *k2, yo, k1, yo, k3, k3tog, k1, rep from * to last 10 (9;12) sts, k2, yo, k1, yo, k3, k2tog, k2 (1;4).
8th row: p12 (11;14), *sl1, p9, rep from * to last 13 (12;15) sts, sl1, p12 (11;14).
9th row: k2 (1;4), k2tog, k1, *k1, yo, k3, yo, k2, k3tog, k1, rep from * to last 10 (9;12) sts, k1, yo, k3, yo, k2, k2tog, k2 (1;4).
10th row: as 8th row.
11th row: k2 (1;4), k2tog, k1, *yo, k5, yo, k1, k3tog, k1, rep from * to last 10 (9;12) sts, yo, k5, yo, k1, k2tog, k2 (1;4).
12th row: p11 (10;13) sts, *cluster 3 sts, p7, rep from * to last 14 (13;16) sts, cluster, p11 (10;13).
These 12 rows form the patt. Cont in patt until work measures 15½in from beg, ending with a wrong side row. Place a marker at each end of the last row to indicate the start of the armhole. Cont in patt until armhole measures 4½(4³⁄₄;5)in from the marker. Change to single rib, still using No 8 needles. When armhole measures 9½(10;10½)in from marker, bind off loosely ribwise.

1 pr No 5 needles ● 1 pr No 8 needles
Suggested yarn: Anny Blatt Mohair

Abbreviations alt – alternate ● beg – beginning ● cluster 3 sts – yarn back, slip 3, yarn forward, return sts to left needle and purl ● cont – continue ● dec – decrease ● foll – following ● inc – increase ● k – knit ● p – purl ● patt – pattern ● rem – remaining ● rep – repeat ● sl – slip ● st(s) – stitch(es) ● sl1 yfwd – slip 1 with yarn forward ● st st – stockinette stitch ● tog – together ● yo – yarn over needle ● A – 1st color ● B – 2nd color ● C – 3rd color ● D – 4th color

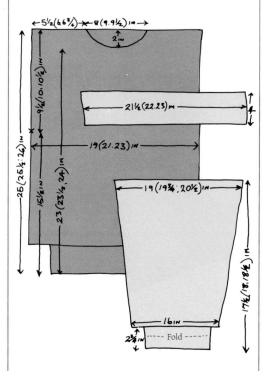

All dimensions are in inches

FRONT Work as given for the back until the armhole measures 7½(7³⁄₄;8)in from the marker.

SHAPE NECKLINE Next row: work 26 (28;30) sts. Turn. Cont working on these sts. Dec 1 st at neck edge on the next and foll every alt row until 21 (23;25) sts remain. Cont working straight until the armhole measures same as back. Bind off ribwise. Rejoin yarn to rem sts at neck edge. Bind off center 23 (27;29) sts. Work onto rem 26 (28;30) sts and work to match 1st side of neck, reversing shaping.

SLEEVES Using No 5 needles, cast on 41 sts and work in single rib as given for the back until work measures 2³⁄₄in from beg, ending with a 1st row. Work one more row in rib and inc 20 sts evenly across row (61 sts).
Change to No 8 needles and work in patt as given for the 2nd size until work measures 17½(18;18½)in from beg. AND at the same time inc 1 st at each end of the 9th (13th;13th) rows and then every foll 14th (10th;10th) rows until there are 71 (75;77) sts, working the extra sts into the patt. When work measures the required length, bind off.

COLLAR Using No 8 needles and some waste yarn of equal thickness, cast on 17 sts and work in single rib as given for the back until the 6th row. Then change to main yarn and cont until work measures 21½(22;23)in from beg of main yarn. Work 6 more rows in waste yarn. Bind off.

TO FINISH Using a small backstitch, join both shoulder seams. Remove waste yarn and graft ends of collar together. Sew collar in position along neck edge, placing the grafted seams against the center back. Set in sleeves, matching the side seam with the markers indicating the start of the armhole. Sew side seams and sleeve seams.

IN THE BLEACHERS

Boy's ribbed jacket

GAUGE Using No 6 needles over brioche rib pattern 20 sts and 20 rows = 4in square.

BACK Using No 4 needles, cast on 71 (75;81;85) sts and work in single rib as follows:
1st row: k2, *p1, k1, rep from * to last st, k1.
2nd row: k1, *p1, k1, rep from * to end.
Rep these 2 rows until work measures 2in, ending with a 1st row.
Next row: rib 3 (2;2;1) sts, *rib 5 (5;6;6) sts, inc in next st, rib 5 (6;6;7) sts, rep from * to last 2 (1;1;0) sts, rib to end. 77 (81;87;91) sts.
Change to No 6 needles and cont in patt as follows:
1st row: (right side) k1, p1, *k1b, p1, rep from * to last 3 sts, k1b, p1, k1.
2nd row: k to end.
Rep these 2 rows 8 (6;8;6) times in all, then work 1st row once more.
Change to No 4 needles and work 2 rows in st st, starting with a p row. Change to No 6 needles and work 2nd row of patt. These 20 (18;20;18) rows form the patt. Cont in patt until work measures 12 (13½;15;16½)in, ending with a wrong side row. Place armhole marker at each end of the last row, then cont in patt without shaping until work measures approximately 18 (20;22;24)in, ending with a 16th (14th;16th;14th) patt row. Then continuing to rep the 1st 2 rows of patt until the measurement has been reached. Bind off. Place neckline markers each side of center 25 (27;29;31) sts.

LEFT FRONT Using No 4 needles, cast on 35 (37;39;41) sts and work in single rib as given for the back, until work measures 2in, ending with a 1st row.
Next row: rib 2 (1;2;1) sts, *rib 3 (4;4;4) sts, inc in next st, rib 4 (4;4;5) sts, rep from * to last 1 (0;1;0) sts, rib to end. 39 (41;43;45) sts.
Change to No 6 needles and cont in patt until work measures 3½in, ending with a wrong side row.

PLACE POCKET Patt across 1st 13 sts, turn and work on these sts as follows:
Cast on 24 sts, patt to end of row. Now cont working in patt on the 13 sts, and working in st st on the cast-on group of 24 sts, until 21 rows have been worked in all on this group of sts. Bind off the 24 sts at beg of next row, then patt to end. Rejoin yarn to rem sts and work 22

GRADE ★					
Sizes to fit	26	28	30	32	in
Actual size	29	31	33	35	in
Back length	18	20	22	24	in
Sleeve seam	12	13	14	15	in
Materials	22	24	26	28	
	oz Aran thick yarn				

1 pr No 6 needles ● 1 pr No 4 needles ● 6 buttons
Suggested yarn: Phildar Pegase

Abbreviations alt – alternate ● beg – beginning ● cont – continue ● dec – decrease ● foll – following ● inc – increase ● k – knit ● klb – knit into stitch on row below (dropping stitch on needle) ● p – purl ● patt – pattern ● rem – remaining ● rep – repeat ● st(s) – stitch(es) ● st st – stockinette stitch ● tog – together

rows in patt. Rejoin yarn to all sts and cont in patt until work measures 17¼ (18¾;20¾;22)in, ending at neck edge. Place armhole marker to correspond with back armhole marker.

SHAPE NECKLINE Next row: bind off 3 sts. patt to end.
Now dec 1 st at neck edge of next 10 (11;11;12) rows, then cont without shaping until work measures 18 (20;22;24)in, working last few rows to match back. Bind off rem 26 (27;29;30) sts.

RIGHT FRONT Work as given for left front, reversing shaping and position of pockets.

SLEEVES Using No 4 needles, cast on 31 (33;35;37) sts and work in single rib as for the back, until work measures 2in, ending with a 1st row.
Next row: rib 1 (2;3;4) sts, *rib 2, inc in next st, rib 2, rep from * to last 0 (1;2;3) sts, rib to end. 37 (39;41;43) sts.
Change to No 6 needles and work the 2 rows of brioche rib patt for a total of 14 (8;8;0) rows, then commence the 20 (18;20;18) rows of patt as given for the back. At the same time, inc 1 st at each end of every 3rd row (from end of ribbing for cuff) until there are 65 (69;73;77) sts, then cont without shaping until work measures 12 (13;14;15)in, ending with a 16th (14th;16th;14th) patt row. Then continue to rep the 1st 2 rows of patt, until measurement has been reached. Bind off. Work 2nd sleeve to match.

BUTTONHOLE BAND Using No 4 needles, cast on 7 sts and work in single rib for 3 rows.
*Rib 3 sts, turn and work 1 row, break yarn and rejoin to rem 4 sts. Work 2 rows on these sts. break yarn and rejoin to all sts, work 18 (20;22;24) rows. Rep from * 4 more times. Leave sts on stitch holder.

BUTTONBAND Work as for buttonhole band. omitting buttonholes.

NECKBAND Using small backstitch join shoulder seams. Work from the right side and using No 4 needles, pick up 7 sts from buttonband, 61 (65;69;73) sts evenly around neckline, and 7 sts from buttonhole band. 75 (79;83;87) sts. Work in single rib for 5 rows. Bind off ribwise on next row.

POCKET BANDS (make 2) Using No 4 needles and working from the right side, pick up 27 sts along pocket edge and work in single rib as for the back for 5 rows, starting with a 2nd row. And work a further buttonhole over the previous buttonhole, on rows 2 and 3. Bind off ribwise on next row.

TO FINISH Using small backstitch. sew sleeves into armhole between markers. Sew underarm seam from wrist to hem. Sew pockets to inside. Sew buttons into place.

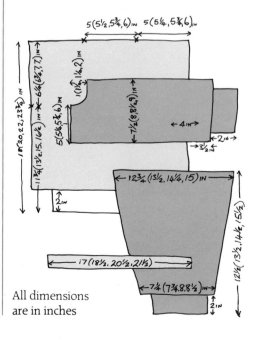

All dimensions are in inches

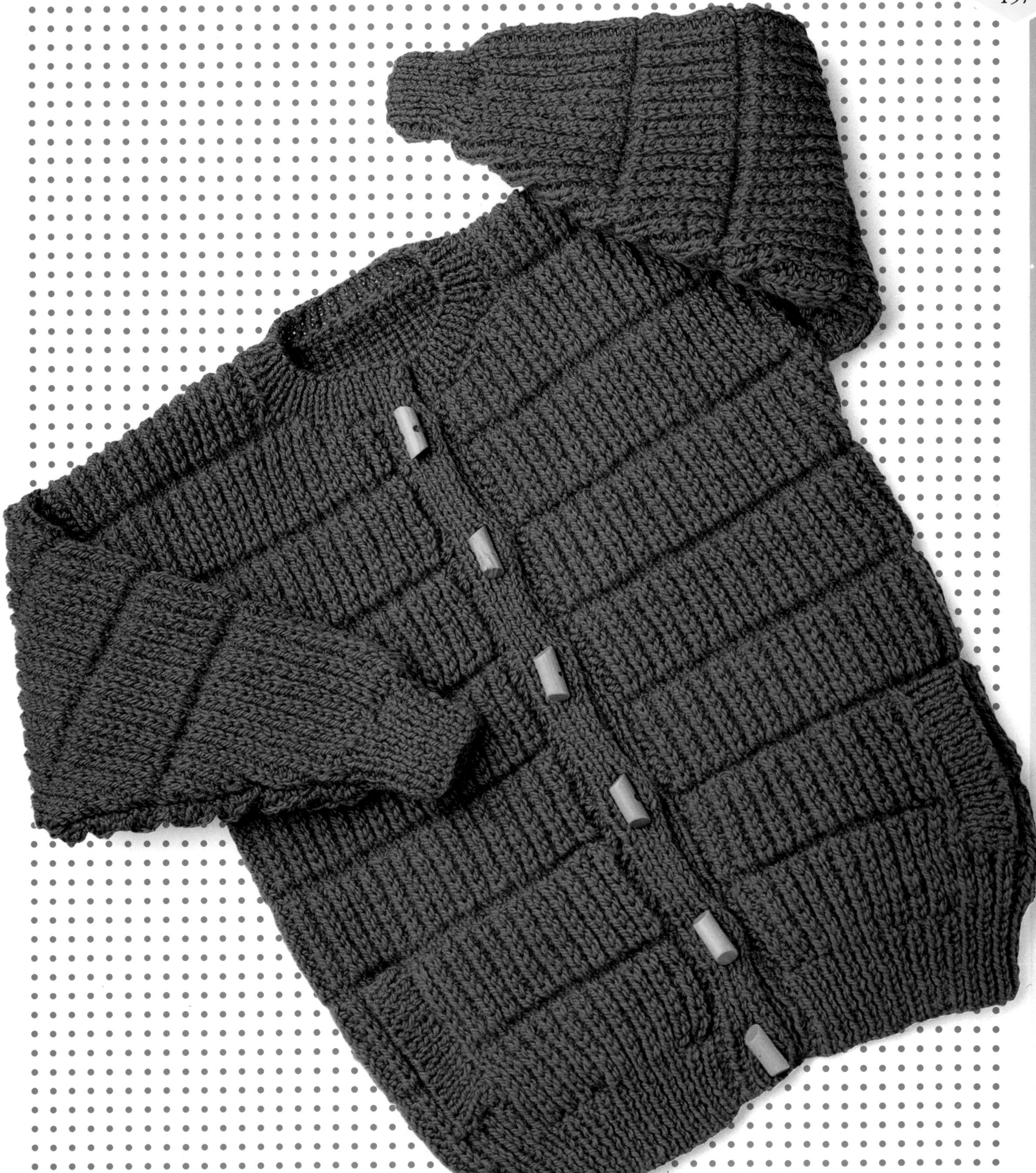

GLENGARRY

Plaid sweater with scarf collar

GAUGE Using No 5 needles over st st, 24 sts and 32 rows = 4in square.

NOTE Use separate balls of yarn for each color area; do not strand.

BACK Using No 3 needles and MC, cast on 103 (111;117;123;129) sts and work in single rib as follows:
1st row: k2, *p1, k1, rep from * to last st, k1.
2nd row: k1, *p1, k1, rep from * to end.
Rep these 2 rows until work measures 2¼in, ending with a 1st row.
Next row: rib 3 (7;4;7;4), [inc in next st, rib 7 (7;8;8;9)] × 12, inc in next st, rib to end. 116 (124;130;136;142) sts.
Change to No 5 needles and cont foll the chart as follows:
1st & 5th sizes only:
1st row: k6MC, k1B, *k5MC, [(k1A, k1MC) × 2, k2MC] × 3, k3MC, rep from * to last 6 sts, k5MC, k1A.
2nd size only:
1st row: (k1MC, k1A) × 2, k6MC, *k5MC [(k1A, k1MC) × 2, k2MC] × 3, k3MC, rep from * to last 10 sts, k5MC [k1A, k1MC) × 2, k1MC.
3rd size only:
1st row: *k5MC [(k1A, k1MC) × 2, k2MC] × 3, k3MC, rep from * to end.
4th size only:
1st row: k3MC, *k5MC [(k1A, k1MC) × 2, k2MC] × 3, k3MC, rep from * to last 3 sts, k2MC.
Working in st st cont to follow chart until work measures 16½(16¾;17¼;17½;17¾)in from beg. Place armhole markers at each end of the last row and cont in patt until work measures 24 (24½;25;25½;26)in from beg, ending with a p row. Bind off, placing each neckline marker in sts 43 (46;48;50;52) and 74 (79;83;86;91).

FRONT Work to match the back until work measures 22 (22½;23;23½;24)in from beg, ending with a p row.

SHAPE NECKLINE Next row: patt 53 (56;59;61;64) sts, bind off next 10 (12;12;14;14) sts, patt to end. Cont on last group of sts as follows:
1st row: patt to last 2 sts, p2tog.
***2**nd row: bind off 4 sts, patt to end.
3rd row: as 1st row.
4th row: bind off 2 sts, patt to end.
Dec 1 st at neck edge of every row until

GRADE ★ ★ ★ ★					
Sizes to fit	32	34	36	38	40	in
Actual size	38	40	42	44	46	in
Back length	24	24½	25	25½	26	in
Sleeve seam	17½	18	18	18½	18½	in
Materials	14	14	17	17	21	MC
	25	25	28	28	32	A
	3	3	3	3	3	B
	oz knitting worsted					

1 pr No 3 needles ● 1 pr No 5 needles
Suggested yarn: Berella Sportspun by Bernat

Abbreviations alt – alternate ● beg – beginning ● cont – continue ● dec – decrease ● foll – following ● inc – increase ● k – knit ● p – purl ● patt – pattern ● rep – repeat ● st(s) – stitch(es) ● st st – stockinette stitch ● tog – together ● MC – main color ● A – 1st color ● B – 2nd color

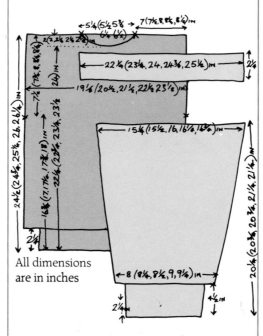

All dimensions are in inches

44 (47;49;51;53) sts remain. Dec 1 st at neck edge of foll 2 alt rows. Cont in patt without shaping until work measures 24 (24½;25;25;26)in from beg, ending with a p row. Bind off.*
Rejoin yarn at neck edge and rep from * to *

SLEEVES Using No 5 needles and MC, cast on 43 (47;47;49;51) sts and work in single rib as given for the back, beg with a 2nd row until work measures 2¼in. Change to No 3 needles and cont in rib until work measures 5in from beg, ending with a 2nd row.
Next row: rib 5 (5;5;6;5) [inc in next st, rib 7 (8;8;8;9)] × 4, inc in next st, rib to end. 48 (52;52;54;56) sts.
Change to No 5 needles and cont in st patt as follows:
1st size only:
1st row: k2MC (k1A, k1MC) × 2, k10MC, [(k1A, k1MC) × 2, k2MC] × 3, k8MC, (k1A, k1MC) × 2, k2MC.
2nd & 3rd sizes only:
1st row: *k3MC, (k1A, k1MC) × 2, k10MC, (k1A, k1MC) × 2, k2MC, k1A, k1MC, k1A, rep from * to end.
4th size only:
1st row: k1A, *k3MC, (k1A, k1MC) × 2, k10MC, (k1A, k1MC) × 2, k2MC, k1A, k1MC, k1A, rep from * to last st, k1MC.
5th size only:
1st row: k1MC, k1A, *k3MC, (k1A, k1MC) × 2, k10MC, (k1A, k1MC) × 2, k2MC, k1A, k1MC, k1A, rep from * to last 2 sts, k2MC.
Cont in patt and inc 1 st at each end of the 5th and every foll 4th row until there are 92 (94;96;98;100) sts. Cont in patt without shaping until work measures 20 (20½;20½;21;21)in from beg, ending with a p row. Bind off.

COLLAR Using No 3 needles and MC, cast on 17 sts and work in single rib as given for the back until work measures 22 (23;23½;24;25)in. Bind off ribwise.

TO FINISH Using small backstitch, sew shoulder seams, sew sleeve tops into armholes, sew side and sleeve seams. Pin collar around neckline to center front neck and sew in place. Tie the ends of the collar.

DON'T FENCE ME IN

Man's color cable sweater

GAUGE Using No 5 needles over st st, 20 sts and 26 rows = 4in square.

NOTE Use separate balls of yarn for each color panel. Do not strand. Always twist yarns together before changing colors.

BACK Using No 3 needles and MC, cast on 105 (111;115;121;125) sts and work in single rib as follows:
1st row: k2, *p1, k1, rep from * to last sk, k1.
2nd row: k1, *p1, k1, rep from * to end.
Rep these 2 rows until work measures 3in, ending with a 1st row. Inc 1 (0;1;0;1) st in last st worked. 106 (111;116;121;126) sts.
Next row: rib 3 (6;8;2;4) sts, *rib 5 (5;5;6;6) sts, inc in next st, rib 5 (5;5;6;6) sts, rep from * to last 4 (6;9;2;5) sts, rib to end. 115 (120;125;130;135) sts.
Change to No 5 needles and cont in patt as follows:
1st row: *using MC, k15 (16;17;18;19) sts, using col A, p2, k6, p2, rep from * to last 15 (16;17;18;19) sts. Using MC, k to end.
2nd row: p all the k sts and k all the p sts, using colors as set in previous row.
Rep the 1st 2 rows once more.
5th row: *using MC, k15 (16;17;18;19) sts. Using col A, p2, C6, p2, rep from * to last 15 (16;17;18;19) sts. Using col A, k to end.
6th row: as 2nd row.
Rep rows 1 & 2 once more.
9th row: *using col A, k15 (16;17;18;19) sts, p2, k6, p2, rep from * to last 15 (16;17;18;19) sts, k to end.
10th row: *using col A, k15 (16;17;18;19) sts, k2, p6, k2, rep from * to last 15 (16;17;18;19) sts, k to end.
Rep the last 4 rows two more times, then rep 1st 2 rows once more.
Rows 5-20 form the patt. Cont in patt until work measures 19 (19;19½;19½;20)in. Place armhole markers at each end of last row, then cont in patt without shaping until work measures 26 (26½;27;27½;28)in, ending with a wrong side row.

SHAPE SHOULDERS Bind off 18 (19;20;21;21) sts at beg of next 2 rows. Bind off 19 (20;20;21;22) sts at beg of foll 2 rows. Bind off rem 41 (42;45;46;49) sts loosely for back neck.

GRADE ★ ★						
Sizes to fit	36	38	40	42	44	in
Actual size	40	42	44	46	48	in
Back length	27	27½	28	28½	29	in
Sleeve seam	17½	18	18	18½	18½	in
Materials	14	14	15	17	17	
	12	14	14	15	15	
	oz knitting worsted					

1 pr No 3 needles ● 1 pr No 5 needles
Suggested yarn: Candide

Abbreviations alt – alternate ● beg – beginning ● CN – cable needle ● C3B – sl 3 sts onto CN and hold at back ● C6 – cable 6, C3B, k3, k3CN ● k3CN – k3 sts from CN ● cont – continue ● dec – decrease ● foll – following ● inc – increase ● k – knit ● p – purl ● patt – pattern ● rem – remaining ● rep – repeat ● st(s) – stitch(es) ● st st – stockinette stitch ● tog – together ● MC – main color ● A – 1st color

FRONT Work as for the back until work measures 24½ (25;25½;25¾;26¼)in, ending with a wrong side row.

SHAPE NECKLINE Patt across 49 (51;53;55;57) sts, bind off center 17 (18;19;20;21) sts, patt rem 49 (51;53;55;57) sts. Turn and work on this last group of sts only as follows:
Next row: patt to last 2 sts, p2tog.
Next row: bind off 3 sts, patt to end.
**Rep the last 2 rows once more. Then dec at neck edge only of next 4 (4;5;5;6) rows. Cont without shaping to 26 (26½;27;27½;28)in, ending at armhole edge.

SHAPE SHOULDERS Bind off 18 (19;20;21;21) sts at beg of next row and 19 (20;20;21;22) sts at beg of foll alt row**.
Rejoin yarn to rem sts at neck edge and work as follows:
Next row: bind off 3 sts, patt to end.
Next row: patt to last 2 sts, k2tog.
Now complete neck as given for 1st side, from ** to **

SLEEVES Using No 3 needles and MC, cast on 53 (55;57;59;61) sts and work in single rib as for the back until work measures 3in ending with a 1st row.
Next row: rib 2 (3;1;2;3) sts, *rib 4 (4;5;5;5) sts, inc in next st, rib 5, rep from * to last 1 (2;1;2;3) sts, rib to end. 58 (60;62;64;66) sts.

Change to No 5 needles and cont in patt as follows:
1st row: using MC, k24 (25;26;27;28) sts. Using col A, p2, k6, p2. Using MC, k24 (25;26;27;28) sts.
2nd row: p all the k sts, and k all the p sts using colors as set of previous row.
The position of the cable panel is now set. Cont working in this manner as for the patt of the back. At the same time, inc 1 st at each end of every foll 8th row until there are 82 (86;86;90;90) sts, then cont in patt without shaping until work measures 17½ (18;18;18½;18½)in, ending with a wrong side row.

SHAPE SLEEVE TOPS Bind off 12 (12;13;13;14) sts at beg of next 2 rows., bind off 12 (13;13;14;14) sts at beg of next 2 rows. Cont in cable patt on the rem 10 sts of center cable until work measures 6 (6½;6¾;7;7;7¼)in. Bind off. Work 2nd sleeve to match.

NECKBAND Using No 3 needles and MC, cast on 99 (103;107;107;111) sts and work in single rib and inc 1 st at each end of every row for 8 rows. Work next row as a p row, then cont in single rib, and dec 1 st at each end of every row for 8 rows. Bind off ribwise.

TO FINISH Using small backstitch, sew shoulders to each side of cable panel at end of sleeve. Sew top of sleeves to armholes between markers. Sew underarm seam from wrist to cuff. With right sides together, sew neckband to neck so that it overlaps to right of garment. Turn neckband to inside and hem down.

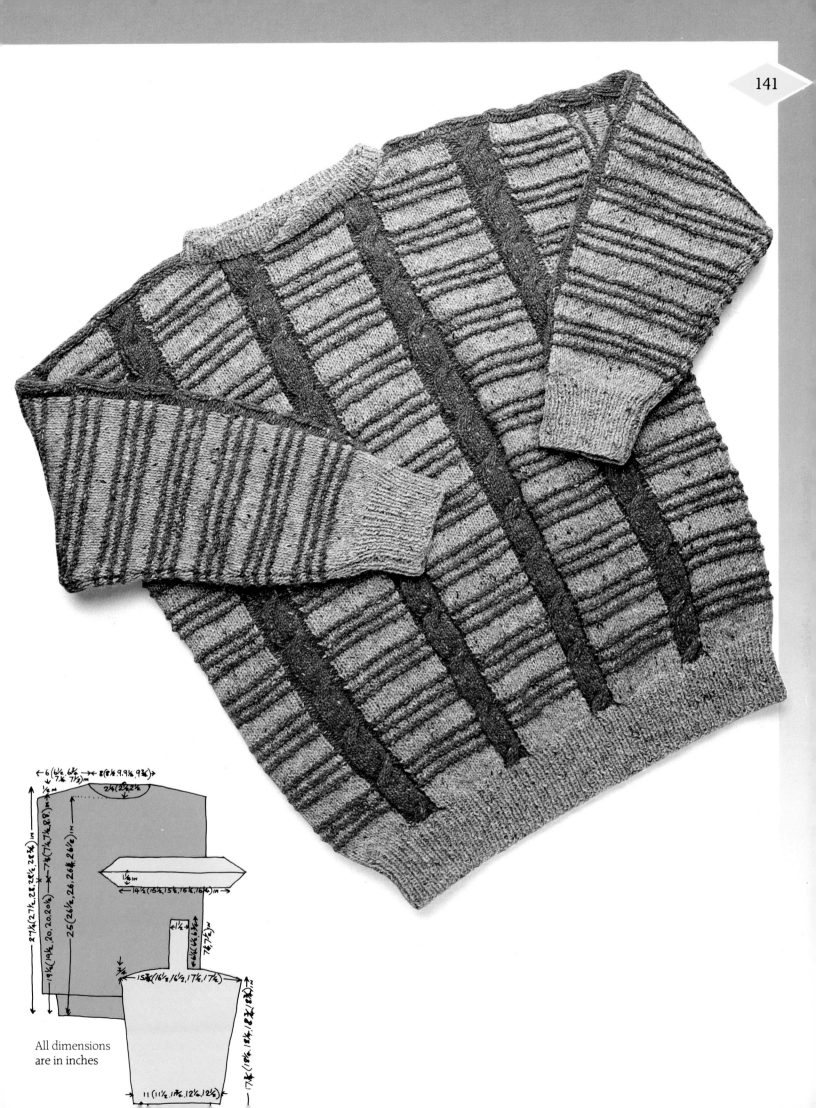

All dimensions
are in inches

CHRISTMAS CRACKER
Child's multi-colored sweater

GAUGE Using No 4 needles over st st, 23 sts and 30 rows = 4in square.

BACK Using No 2 needles and A, cast on 62 (70;78;90) sts.
1st row: *k2, p2, rep from * to last 2 sts, k2.
2nd row: *p2, k2, rep from * to last 2 sts, p2.
Rep these 2 rows until work measures 2¼in ending with a 1st row.
Next row: rib 3 (4;6;4), [inc in next st, rib 4 (4;4;7)] × 11 (12;13;10), inc in next st, rib to end. 74 (83;92;101) sts.
Change to No 4 needles and cont in st patt as follows:
1st row: k1B, *k8B, k1C, rep from * to last st, k1C.
2nd row: p1C, *p2C, p7B, rep from * to last st, p1B.
3rd row: k1B, *k6B, k3C, rep from * to last st, k1C.
4th row: p1C, *p4C, p5B, rep from * to last st, p1B.
5th row: k1B, *k4B, k5C, rep from * to last st, k1C.
6th row: p1C, *p6C, p3B, rep from * to last st, p1C.
7th row: k1B, *k2B, k7C, rep from * to last st, k1C.
8th row: p1C, *p8C, p1B, rep from * to last st, p1B.
9th row: k1A, *k8A, k1D, rep from * to last st, k1D.
10th row: p1D, *p2D, p7A, rep from * to last st, p1A.
11th row: k1A, *k6A, k3D, rep from * to last st, k1D.
12th row: p1D, *p4D, p5A, rep from * to last st, p1A.
13th row: k1A, *k4A, k5D, rep from * to last st, k1D.
14th row: p1D, *p6D, p3A, rep from * to last st, p1A.
15th row: k1A, *k2A, k7D, rep from * to last st, k1D.
16th row: p1D, *p8D, p1A, rep from * to last st, p1A.
These 16 rows form the patt. Cont in patt until work measures 9¾(10½;11¾;13¼)in from beg. Place armhole markers at each end of the last row and cont in patt until work measures 15½(16½;18;20) in from beg. Bind off, placing each neckline marker in sts 25 (28;31;34) and sts 50 (56;62;68).

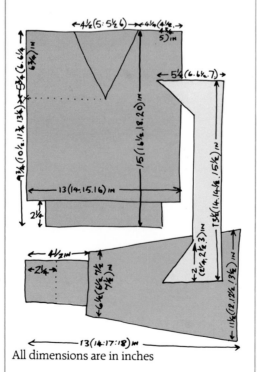

All dimensions are in inches

FRONT Work as given for the back until work measures 9¾(10½;11¾;13¼)in from beg, ending with a right side row.

SHAPE NECKLINE Next row: *1st & 3rd sizes only* patt 37 (46) sts, turn. *2nd & 4th sizes only* patt 40 (49) sts, patt 2 tog, turn.
Cont on these 37 (41;46;50) sts in patt and dec 1 st at neck edge of the next and every foll 3rd row until 24 (27;30;33) sts remain. Cont in patt without shaping to same patt row as the back at binding off. Bind off.
Rejoin the yarn to rem sts and rep from * to *

SLEEVES Using No 2 needles and A, cast on 30 (30;34;34) sts and work in double rib as given for the back beg with a 2nd row until work measures 4½in ending with a 1st row.
Next row: rib 0 (0;3;3), [inc in next st, rib 3 (3;2;2)] × 7 (7;9;9), inc in next st, rib to end. 38 (38;44;44) sts.
Change to No 4 needles and commence st patt as follows:
1st row: k1 (1;4;4)B, *k8C, k1B, rep from * to last 1 (1;4;4) sts, k1 (1;4;4) C. The position of the st patt is now set. Cont in patt and inc 1 st at each end of every foll 4th (4th;5th;5th) row until there are 66 (70;74;78) sts. Cont in patt without shaping until work measures 13 (14;17;18)in from beg Bind off.

COLLAR Using No 2 needles and A, cast on 94 (98;102;110) sts and work in double rib as given for the back and dec 1 st at each end of the 2nd and every foll alt row until 72 (74;78;86) sts remain.
Cont in rib without shaping until work measures 4in.
Next row: rib 23 (23;23;26) sts, bind off 26 (28;32;34) sts, rib to end. Cont in rib on last group of 23 (23;23;26) sts only, as follows:
Next row: rib to last 2 sts, rib 2tog.
Cont in rib and dec 1 st at the same edge as the 1st dec on every foll 2nd (2nd;2nd;3rd) row until 1 st remains. Fasten off. Rejoin yarn to rem 23 (23;23;26) sts and work to match the 1st side, reversing shaping.

TO FINISH Using small backstitch, sew shoulder seams, sew sleeve tops into armholes, sew side and sleeve seams. Pin the collar neatly around the neckline and stitch in place. Sew zipper into front opening of collar.

RITZY KNIT
Ribbed evening suit

GAUGE Using No 2 needles over single rib 37 sts and 34 rows = 4in.

SKIRT Using circular No 2 needle, cast on 321 (339;359) sts and work in single rib, in rounds, until work measures 28½(29½;30½)in. Work next round in purl, then work a further 1in in single rib. Bind off loosely.

TOP Using No 2 needles, cast on 141 (151;161) sts and work in single rib until work measures 18 (19;19½)in, ending on a wrong side row.

SHAPE ARMHOLES Cont in rib and bind off 2 sts at beg of next 2 rows, then dec 1 st at each end of next 4 rows. Now dec 1 st at each end of next 4 alt rows. 121 (131;141) sts.

SHAPE NECKLINE Next row: rib 48 (52;56) sts. turn and work on this group of sts only as follows:
*Dec 1 st at armhole edge on every foll 4th row and, at the same time, bind off 7 sts at beg of next and every alt row at neck edge, until 6 sts have been decreased at the armhole edge in this manner and 42 sts have been bound off at the neck edge.
Now bind off 3 sts at neck edge on every alt row until 0 (3;3) sts remain. Bind off rem sts. Rejoin yarn to rem sts at neck edge and work 2nd side to match 1st side as given from *

COLLAR Using No 2 needles, cast on 69 sts and work in single rib as follows:
1st-**8**th rows: work in rib across all sts.
9th row: rib 51 sts, yf, sl1, yb, return sl st to LN, turn.
10th row: rib to end.
11th-**18**th row: work in rib across all sts.
19th row: rib 33 sts, yf, sl1, yb, return sl st to LN, turn.
20th row: rib to end.
21st-**28**th rows: work in rib across all sts.
29th row: rib 15 sts, yf, sl1, yb, return sl st to LN, turn.
30th row: rib to end.
Rep rows 1-30 until work measures 42½(46;48)in measured along the longer edge. Bind off.

GRADE ★ ★				
Sizes to fit	32	34	36	in
Side seam length	18	19	19½	in
Hips	34	36	38	in
Skirt length	27½	28½	29½	in
Materials				
Top	12	12	14	
Skirt	12	12	14	
	oz knitting worsted			

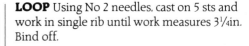

1 pr No 2 needles ● 1 No 2 circular needle ● Elastic (1 in wide) to fit waist ● diamanté
Suggested yarn: Granat Bouclé in double strand

Abbreviations alt – alternate ● beg – beginning ● cont – continue ● dec – decrease ● foll – following ● inc – increase ● k – knit ● LN – left needle ● p – purl ● patt – pattern ● rem – remaining ● rep – repeat ● sl – slip ● st(s) – stitch(es) ● st st – stockinette stitch ● tog – together ● yb – yarn back ● yf – yarn forward

LOOP Using No 2 needles, cast on 5 sts and work in single rib until work measures 3¼in. Bind off.

TO FINISH *Skirt:* fold waist of skirt to inside along purl row and hem down. Insert elastic into hem and sew ends together.
Top: oversew cast-on and bound-off edges of collar together. Using small backstitch, sew side seams. Sew collar to front and back of body, with collar seam at center front, and middle of collar at center back. Sandwich the loop between body and collar at center front. Fold loop to inside of garment, thereby gathering the collar and sew down. Sew diamanté to the loop.

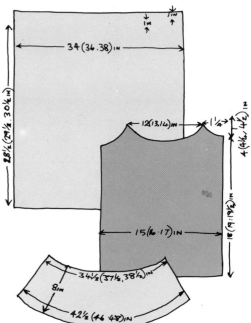

All dimensions are in inches

BYE, BYE BABY BLUE

Boat-necked sweater with triangles

GAUGE Using No 6 needles over patt, 19 sts and 28 rows = 4in

BACK & FRONT (both the same) Using No 2 needles, cast on 75 (85;95) sts and work in single rib as follows:
1st row: k2, *p1, k1, rep from * to end, k1.
2nd row: k1, *p1, k1, rep from * to end.
Rep these 2 rows until work measures 2¼in, ending with a 1st row and inc 1 st in the last st worked. 76 (86;96) sts.
Next row: rib 6, *inc in next st, rib 6 (7;8) sts, rep from * to end. 86 (96;106) sts.
Change to No 6 needles and work in patt, as follows:
1st row: k1, yo, *k3, sl1, k2tog, psso, k3, yo, k1, yo, rep from * ending k3, sl1, k1, psso.
2nd and all alt rows: p to end.
3rd row: k2, yo, *k2, sl1, k2tog, psso, k2, yo, k3, yo, rep from * ending k2, sl1, k1, psso.
5th row: k3, * yo, k1, sl1, k2tog, psso, k1, yo, k5, rep from * ending yo, k1, sl1, k1, psso.
7th row: k4, yo, *sl1, k2tog, psso, yo, k7, rep from * ending sl1, k1, psso.
9th row: sl1, k1, psso, k3, yo, *k1, yo, k3, sl1, k2tog, psso, k3, yo, rep from * ending k1.
11th row: sl1, k1, psso, k2, yo, k1, *k2, yo, k2, sl1, k2tog, psso, k2, yo, k1, rep from * ending k1.
13th row: sl1, k1, psso, k1, yo, k2, *k3, yo, k1, sl1, k2tog, psso, k1; yo, k2, rep from * ending k1.
15th row: sl1, k1, psso, yo, k3, *k4, yo, sl1, k2tog, psso, yo, k3, rep from * ending k1.
16th row: p to end.
These 16 rows form the patt. Cont in patt until work measures 14¾(15½;16¼)in from beg, ending with a p row.

SHAPE RAGLAN SEAMS Next row: k2tog, patt to last 2 sts, k2tog.
Work 2 more rows without shaping.
Cont to dec 1 st at each end of every foll 3rd row 14 (15;16) times in all. 58 (66;74) sts.
Next row: k1 (0;2) sts. *k1, k2tog, rep from * across row.
Bind off rem 39 (44;50) sts loosely.

SLEEVES Using No 2 needles, cast on 37 sts and work in single rib as given for the back, until work measures 2¼in, ending with a 1st row, and inc 1 st in the last st worked (38 sts).
Next row: *inc in next st, ribwise, rep from * across row (76 sts).

GRADE ★ ★ ★ ★			
Sizes to fit	32-34	36-38	40-42	in
Actual size	38	40½	44	in
Center back	20¾	21¾	23½	in
Sleeve seam	18¾	19½	20¼	in
Materials	15	17	19	
	oz knitting worsted			

1 pr No 2 needles ● 1 set 4 No 2 needles ●1 pr No 6 needles ● 10 (12; 14) glass beads
Suggested yarn: Phildar Kid Mohairr

Abbreviations alt – alternate ● beg – beginning ● cont – continue ● dec – decrease ● foll – following ● inc – increase ● k – knit ● p – purl ● patt – pattern ● psso – pass sl st over ● rem – remaining ● rep – repeat ● sl – slip ● st(s) – stitch(es) ● st st – stockinette stitch ● tog – together ● yo – yarn over needle

Change to No 6 needles and work in patt as for the back, and inc 1 st at each end of every foll 13th (10th;8th) row until there are 90 (96;102) sts, then cont without shaping, until work measures 10¾(19½;20¼)in from beg, ending with a p row.

SHAPE RAGLAN SEAMS Dec 1 st at each end of next and every foll 3rd row 14 (15;16) times in all 62 (66;70) sts.
Next row: k2 (0;1) sts, *k1, k2tog, rep from * across row.
Bind off rem 40 (44;47) sts loosely.

'PETALS' Note: When working the increases, make sure that the edges of the 'petals' remain loose.
Cast on 1 st.
2nd row: inc 3 times knitwise.
3rd row: inc in 1st st, p to last st, inc in last st and all alt rows.
4th row: inc in 1st st, yo, sl1, k2tog, psso, yo, inc in last st.
6th row: inc in 1st st, yo, k2, sl1, k2tog, psso, k2, yo, inc in last st.
8th row: inc in 1st st, yo, k4, sl1, k2tog, psso, k4, yo, inc in last st.
10th row: inc in 1st st, yo, k6, sl1, k2tog, psso, k6, yo, inc in last st.
12th row: inc in 1st st, yo, k8, sl1, k2tog, psso, k8, yo, inc in last st.
14th row: inc in 1st st, yo, k10, sl1, k2tog, psso, k10, yo, inc in last st.
16th row: inc in 1st st, yo, k12, sl1, k2tog, psso, k12, yo, inc in last st.
Bind off loosely.
Work 10 (12;14) of these shapes.

NECKBAND Working from right side with set 4 No 2 needles, pick up 134 (164;184) sts and work in st st for 2 rows.
Next row: *yo, k2tog, rep from * across row. Cont in st st for a further 3 rows. Bind off. Fold over and hem down loosely. Sew bead to end of each petal.

TO FINISH Using small backstitch, sew side seams and sleeve seams, sew raglan seams. Place petals as follows: Using half the quantity, place them equally around neckline (ie, around back, front, and 2 sleeves). Pleat each of them in the center by approximately ¼in. Pin them into position. Place the rem petals centrally between each of these first petals, pleating them in the centers as before (they should overlap by no more than 1in; gather the petals a little more if necessary). Sew the petals into place, close to top of neckline, with small backstitch.

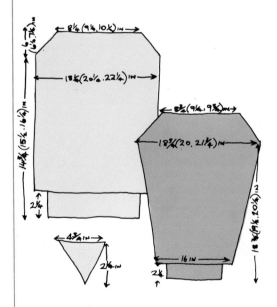

All dimensions are in inches

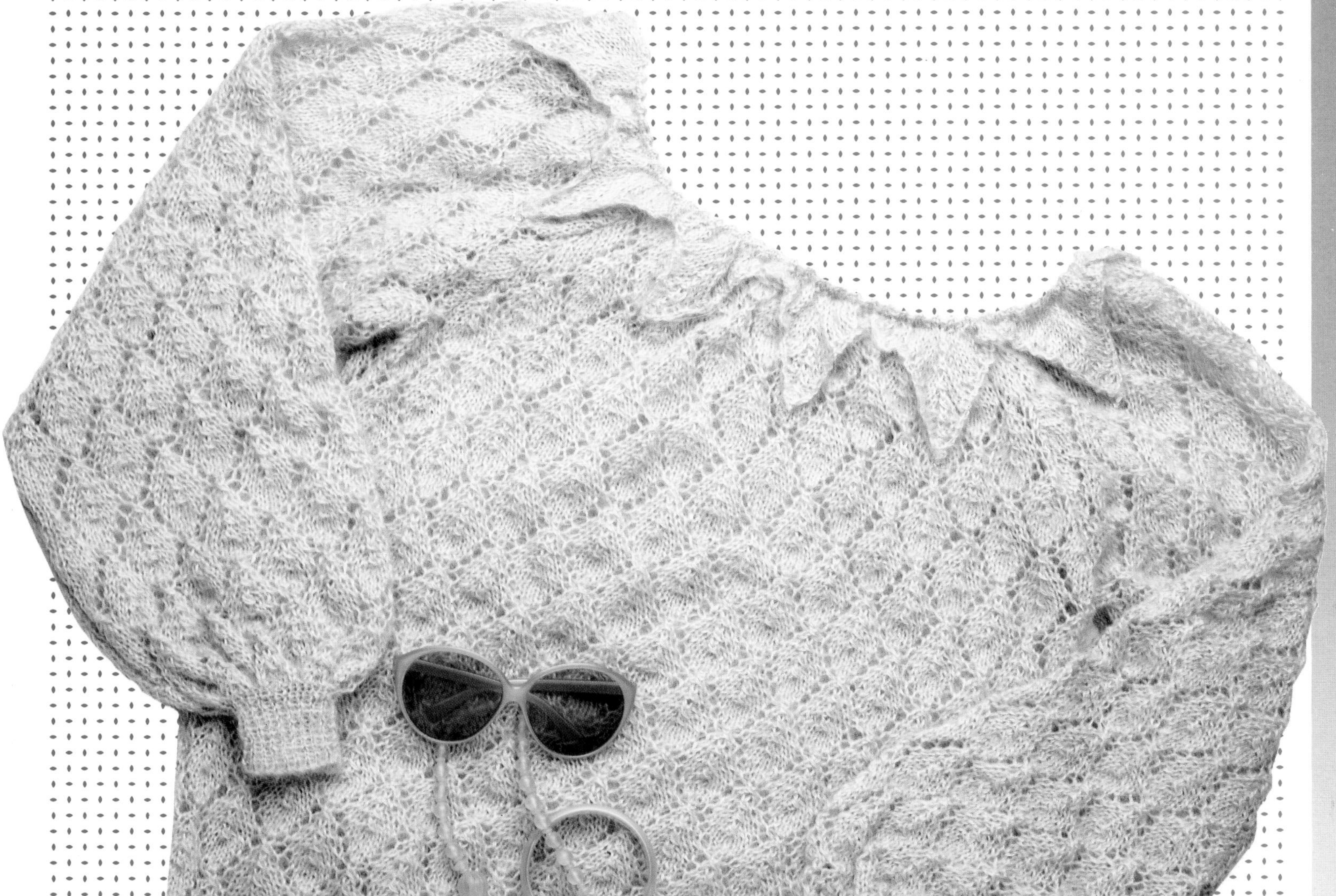

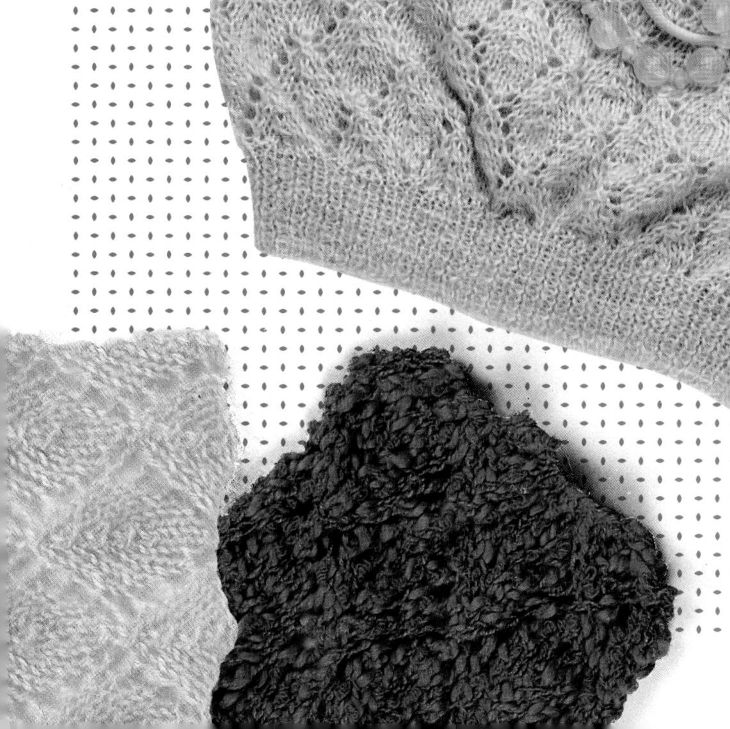

PATCH AND MATCH
Child's patchwork jacket

GAUGE Using No 5 needles over st st, 24 sts and 32 rows = 4in square.

PATCH A In color A make 23
Cast on 30 (32;34) sts.
1st row: *k2, p2, rep from * to last 2 (0;2) sts, k2 (0;2).
2nd row and every alt row: k the p sts and p the k sts of the previous row.
3rd row: C1RP, *p1, C2RP, rep from * to last 0 (2;0) sts, p0 (1;0). k0 (1;0).
5th row: p2, *C2RP, p1, rep from * to last 0 (2;0) sts, C2RK.
7th row: *1st & 3rd sizes only* p1, *C2RP, p1, rep from * to last st, k1.
2nd size only: p1, *C2RP, p1, rep from * to last 3 sts, C2RP.
9th row: *C2RP, p1, rep from * to last 2 (0;2) sts, C1RK (0;C1RK).
Rep rows 3-10 2 more times.
2nd & 3rd size only:
Rep rows 3 and 4 once more.
3rd size only:
Rep rows 5 and 6 once more.
All sizes:
Bind off.

PATCH B In color A make 19
Cast on 26 (28;30) sts.
1st row: p1 (2;1), k to last 1 (2;1) sts, p1 (2;1).
2nd row and every alt row: k1 (2;1), p to last 1 (2;1) sts, k1 (2;1).
3rd row: *1st & 2nd sizes only* p1 (2), *C2RK, C2LK, rep from * to last 1 (2) sts, p1 (2).
3rd size only:
p1, C2RK, *C2LK, C2RK, rep from * to last st, p1.
5th row: as 1st row.
7th row: *1st & 2nd sizes only* p1 (2), *C2LK, C2RK, rep from * to last 1 (2) sts, p1 (2).
3rd size only:
p1, C2LK, *C2RK, C2LK, rep from * to last st, p1.
Rep rows 1-8 2 more times. Rep rows 1 and 2 once more.
2nd & 3rd size only:
Rep rows 3 and 4 once more.
3rd size only:
Rep rows 5 and 6 once more.
All sizes:
Bind off.

PATCH C In color B make 23
Cast on 26 (28;31) sts.
1st row: p0 (0;1), k0 (1;4), *p2, T2RK, p2, k4, rep from * to last 6 (7;6) sts, p2, T2RK, p2, k0 (1;0).

GRADE ★ ★ ★			
Sizes to fit	26	28	30	in
Actual size	31½	33½	35½	in
Back length	17½	18½	19½	in
Sleeve seam	10	10¾	11½	in
Materials	19	21	22	A
	7	7	8	B
	oz knitting worsted			

1 pr No 5 needles ● cable needle
Suggested yarn: Suizy Détente by Vizir

Abbreviations alt – alternate ● beg – beginning ● CN – cable needle ● cont – continue ● ClRP – sl next st onto CN and hold at back, k1, pl from CN ● C2RP – sl next st onto CN and hold at back, k2, pl from CN ● ClRK – sl next st onto CN and hold at back, k1, k1 from CN ● C2LK – sl next 2 sts onto CN and hol at front k2, k2 from CN ● C2RK – sl next 2 sts onto CN and hold at front k2, k2 from CN ● dec – decrease ● foll – following ● inc – increase ● k – knit ● p – purl ● sl – slip ● st(s) – stitch(es) ● st st – stockinette stitch ● tbl – through back of loop ● tog – together ● T2RK – k into the back of the 2nd st on left-hand needle then into the front of the 1st st. sl both sts from left-hand needle ● T2RP – p into the front of the 2nd st on the left-hand needle then into the front of the 1st st. sl both the sts from left-hand needle ● T4R – sl next 3 sts onto CN and hold at back, k1, return lst 2 sts on CN to left-hand needle, p2 k1 from CN ● yb – yarn back ● yf – yarn forward ● A – 1st color ● B – 2nd color

2nd row: p0 (1;0), *k2, T2RP, k2, p4, rep from * to last 6 (7;1) sts, k2 (2;1).
Rep these 2 rows 2 more times.
1st and 2nd sizes only:
TR2P, k2 (2), p0 (1).
7th row: *1st & 2nd sizes only* p1 (2), *k4, p2, T2RK, rep from * to last 5 (6) sts, k4, p1 (2).
3rd size only:
p1, *T2RK, p2, k4, p2, rep from * to end.
8th row: *1st & 2nd sizes only* k1 (2), *p4, k2, T2RP, k2, rep from * to last 5 (6) sts, p4, k1 (2.
3rd size only:
*k2, p4, k2, T2RP, rep from * to lst st, k1.
All sizes:
Rep these last 2 rows 2 times more. Rep rows 1-10 once again.
2nd & 3rd sizes only:
Rep rows 11 and 12 once again.
3rd size only:
Rep rows 1 and 2 once more.
All sizes:
Bind off.

PATCH D In color B make 19
Cast on 22 (24;26) sts.
1st row: p2(3;4), [k1, p2] × 2, k1, p4, [kl, p2] × 2, k1, p2(3;4).
2nd row and every alt row: k2(3;4), [yf, sl1, yb, k2] × 2, yf, sl 1p, yb, k4, [yfd, sl1, yb, k2] × 2, yf, sl1, yb, k2(3;4).
Rep these 2 rows once more.
5th row: p2 (3;4), T4R, p2, k1, p4, T4R, p2, k1, p2 (3;4).
7th row: as 1st row.
9th row: as 1st row.
11th row: p2 (3;4), k1, p2, T4R, p4, k1, p2, T4R, p2 (3;4).
Rep rows 1-12 once again.
2nd & 3rd sizes only:
Rep rows 1 and 2 once more.
3rd size only:
Rep rows 3 and 4 once more.
All sizes:
Bind off.

TO FINISH Sew patches tog as shown in the diagram. Fold fronts tog inside out and sew back of shoulder patches.

FRONT BANDS (make 2) Using col A, right side facing, pick up 95 (100;105) sts along center front edge. *Work 6 rows in st st beg with a p row and inc 1 st at each end of 1st and foll 2 alt rows. K1 row. Work 6 rows in st st beg with a k row and dec 1 st at each end of 1st and foll 2 alt rows. Bind off.*

2nd row: k to end.
Rep these 2 rows 2 more times. K1 row.
Next row: k2tog (k to 1 st from next marker, inc in next 2 sts) × 4, k to last 2 sts, k2tog tbl.
Next row: p to end.
Rep these last 2 rows 2 more times. Bind off.

BOTTOM EDGING Using color A, right side facing, pick up 190 (200;210) sts along bottom edge.
Rep from * to * as given for the front bands.

CUFFS Using color A, right side facing, pick up 100 (106;112) sts along wrist edge of sleeve. Work 6 rows in st st, beg with a p row. K1 row. Work 32 (34;36) rows in st st beg with a k row. Bind off.
Sew sleeve tops into armholes matching shoulder patches as indicated on the diagram. Sew sleeve seam. Sew miters of edgings, fold edgings to inside and stitch down. Fold cuffs and sleeve facing to inside and stitch down.

NECKBAND Using col A, right side facing, beg at right center front, pick up 19 (20;21) sts across patch C, put a marker on the right-hand needle, pick up 19 (20;21) sts along patch D, put another marker on right-hand needle, pick up 38 (40;42) sts across back neck, put a 3rd marker on right-hand needle, pick up 19 (20;21) sts along patch B, put on a 4th marker, pick up 19 (20;21) sts across patch A. 114 (120;126) sts.
1st row: Inc in 1st st [p to 2 sts before the next marker, p2tog, p2tog tbl] × 4, p to last st, inc in last st.

SCARF Using col A, cast on 71 sts and work in single rib as follows:
1st row: k2, *p1, k1, rep from * to last st, k1.
2nd row: k1, *p1, k1, rep from * to end.
Rep these 2 rows until work measures 60in. Bind off ribwise.
Cut lengths of yarn 9in long, fold in half and loop through ends of the scarf for fringing.

SEEN ABOUT TOWN
Woman's suit and hooded sweater

GAUGE Using No 5 needles over st st 24 sts and 32 rows = 4in square.

JACKET BACK Using No 5 needles and MC, cast on 123(135;147) sts and cont in st patt as follows:
1st row: in MC, k to end.
2nd row: in MC, p to end.
Rep these 2 rows once more.
5th row: k1MC, *k3MC, rep from * to last 2 sts, k1A, k1MC.
6th row: as 2nd row.
Rep rows 1 and 2 once more. Rep 1st row once more.
10th row: *p3MC, p1A, rep from * to last 3 sts, p3MC.
These 10 rows form the patt. Cont in patt until work measures 14(14;14½)in from beg, Place armhole markers at each end of the last row and cont in patt until work measures 24(24½;25)in from beg. Bind off placing each neckline marker in sts 41(46;51) and sts 83(90;97).

LEFT FRONT Using No 5 needles and MC, cast on 55(61;67) sts and work 1st 4 rows of st patt, as for the back.
5th row: k1MC, *k1A, k3MC, rep from * to last 2(0;2) sts, k1A, k1MC.
Work 6th-9th rows as for the back.
10th row: p3(1;3)MC, *p1A, p3MC, rep from * to end.
Cont in patt to same patt row as back of armhole marker. Place a marker at side edge of last row and cont in patt until work measures 21(21½;22)in from beg, ending with a right side row.

SHAPE NECKLINE Keeping patt correct, bind off 6(7;8) sts at beg of next row. Dec 1 st at neck edge of foll 5 rows. Dec 1 sts at neck edge of foll 4 alt rows. Cont in patt without shaping to the same row as the back at casting off. Bind off.

RIGHT FRONT Work to match left front, reversing patt placement and shapings.

SLEEVES Using No 5 needles and MC, cast on 119(123;127) sts and work 5in in st st, ending with a p row.
**1st row: in MC, k to end.
2nd row: in A, p to end.
3rd row: as 1st row.

GRADE ★ ★ ★			
Sizes to fit	32-34	36-38	40-42	in
Jacket			
Actual size	40	44	48	in
Back length	24	24½	25	in
Sleeve seam	22½	23	23½	in
Skirt			
Waist	28	32	34	in
Hips	34	38	42	in
Length	29	29½	30	in
Sweater			
Actual size	37	41	45	in
Back length	25	25½	26	in
Sleeve seam	17½	18	18½	in
Materials			
Jacket	15	17	19	MC
	8	8	10	A
Skirt	12	15	17	MC
	1	3	3	A
Sweater	28	31	35	MC
Belt & purse	3	3	3	MC
	oz knitting worsted			

1 pr No 3 needles ● 1 pr No 5 needles ●1 No 5 circular needle ● elastic to fit waist
Suggested yarn: Wendy Shetland

Abbreviations alt – alternate ● beg – beginning ● cont – continue ● dec – decrease ● foll – following ● inc – increase ● k – knit ● p – purl ● patt – pattern ● rem – remaining ● rep – repeat ● st(s) – stitch(es) ● st st – stockinette stitch ● tog – together ● MC – main color ● A – 1st color

4th row: *p1MC, p1A, rep from * to last st, p1MC.
5th row: in A, k to end.
6th row: *p1A, p1MC, rep from * to last st, p1A.
Rep rows 1-3 once more.**
Next row: in MC, k to end.
Rep from ** to ** once again.
Cont in st patt as given for the 1st size of the back, beg with a 2nd row until work measures 22½(23;23½)in from beg, ending with a wrong side row.
Rep from ** to ** once more. Bind off in MC.

FRONT BANDS (both the same) Using No 5 needles and MC, pick up 127(129;131) sts along center front edge. **Rep from * to * as given for the sleeve border working k rows as p rows and p rows as k rows and inc 1 st at each end of first and every alt row. 137(139;141) sts.
Next row: in MC, p to end.
Work 9 rows in st st in MC beg with a p row and dec 1 st at each end of 1st and every alt row. Bind off.***

NECKBAND Using small backstitch, sew both shoulder seams.
Using No 5 needles and MC, right side facing, pick up 39(41;43) sts along right front neckline, pick up 42(43;45) sts across back neck, pick up 39(41;43) sts along left front neckline. 119(125;131) sts.
Rep from *** to *** as for the front bands.

BOTTOM EDGE Using small backstitch, sew sleeve tops into armholes, sew side and sleeve seams.
Using No 5 needles and MC, right side facing pick up 50(56;62) sts along bottom edge of left front, pick up 117(127;139) sts across bottom edge of back, pick up 50(56;62) sts along bottom edge of right front. 217(239;263) sts.
Rep from *** to *** as for the front bands.

TO FINISH Fold edgings to the inside and sl st down. Fold sleeve facings to the inside between the 2 border patts and sl st down.

SKIRT PANELS (make 4) Using No 5 needles and MC, cast on 55(61;67) sts.
1st row: in MC, k33(39;43) sts, turn.
2nd row: in MC, p11(17;19), turn.
3rd row: k3(2;3)MC, [k1A, k3MC] × 4(6;6), k1A, k1(0;2)MC, turn.
4th row: in MC, p31(37;41), turn.
5th row: in MC, k to end.
6th row: in MC, p to end.
7th row: as 5th row.
8th row: p3(2;1)MC, *p1A, p3MC, rep from * to l;ast 0(3;2) sts, p1A, p0(2;1) MC.
9th row: as 5th row.
10th row: as 6th row.
Cont in spot patt and dec 1 st at each end of the next and every foll 6th row until 45(51;57) sts remain. Cont in patt without shaping until work measures 20½(21;21½)in from beg. Cont in patt and dec 1 st at each end of the next and every foll 10th(8th;6th) row until 41(45;49) sts remain. Cont in patt without shaping until work measures 29½(30;30¾)in from beg. Bind off.

SKIRT SEAM BANDS (make 4) Using No 5 needles and MC, cast on 177 (179;181) sts. Rep from * to * as given for the sleeve border patt. Bind off.

WAISTBAND Using small backstitch, join the 4 panels and 4 seam bands together, leaving 1 seam open.
Using No 5 needles and MC, right side facing, pick up 40 (44;48) sts across the top edge of each skirt panel and 3 sts across each seam band. 172 (188;204) sts.
1st row: in MC, k to end.
2nd row: in A, p to end.
3rd row: as 1st row.
4th row: *p1MC, p1A, rep from * to end.
5th row: in A, k to end.
6th row: *p1A, p1MC, rep from * to end.
Rep rows 1-3 once more.
Next row: in MC, k to end.
In MC, work 9 rows in st st beg with a k row. Bind off.

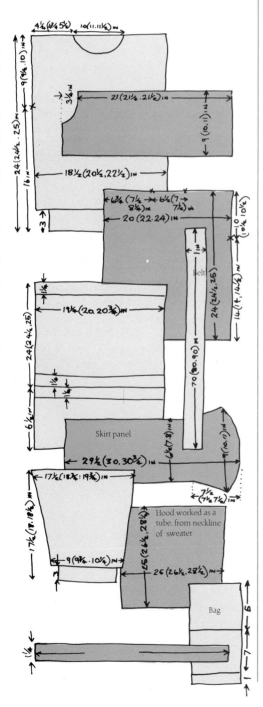

SKIRT HEM Using No 5 needles and MC, right side facing, pick up 55 (61;67) sts across the bottom edge of each skirt panel and 5 sts across each seam band. 240 (264;288) sts.
In MC, work 9 rows in st st beg with a p row. P1 row. Work a further 9 rows in st st, beg with a p row. Bind off.

TO FINISH Using small backstitch, sew rem seam. Fold up hem to inside and sl st down. Make a ring of elastic to fit the waist. Fold the waistband over the elastic and sl st down.

SWEATER BACK Using No 3 needles and MC, cast on 147 (159;177) sts and work in single rib as follows:
1st row: k2, *p1, k1, rep from * to last st, k1.
2nd row: k1, *p1, k1, rep from * to end.
Rep these 2 rows until work measures 3in, ending with a 1st row.
Next row: rib 7 (7;5), [inc in next st, rib 11 (12;14)] × 11, inc in next st, rib to end. 159 (171;189) sts.
Change to No 5 needles and cont as follows:
1st row: *k3, p3, rep from * to last 3 sts, k3.
2nd row: *p3, k3, rep from * to last 3 sts, p3.
These 2 rows form the patt. Cont in patt until work measures 16in from beg. Place armhole marker at each end of the last row and cont in, patt until work measures 25 (25½;26)in from beg.
Next row: bind off 37 (41;48) sts, patt the next 85 (89;93) sts, bind off rem sts. Leave the 85 (89;93) sts on a free needle for back neck.

SWEATER FRONT Work as given for the sweater back until the front measures 22½(23;23½)in from beg, ending with a 2nd patt row.

SHAPE NECKLINE Next row: patt 63 (68;76) sts, turn and cont on this group of sts only as follows:
***1**st row: bind off 8 (9;9) sts, patt to end.
2nd row: patt to last 2 sts, patt 2 tog.
3rd row: bind off 5 sts, patt to end.
4th row: as 2nd row.
5th row: bind off 2 sts, patt to end.
Dec 1 st at neck edge of every row until 40 (44;51) sts remain. Dec 1 st at neck edge of every foll alt row until 37 (41;48) sts remain. Cont in patt without shaping until work measures 25 (25½;26)in from beg. Bind off.*
Slip 33 (35;37) sts onto a st holder and rejoin yarn to rem 63 (68;76) sts.
Rep from * to *.

SWEATER SLEEVES Using No 3 needles and MC, cast on 63 (69;75) sts and work in single rib as given for the sweater back until rib measures 3in, ending with a 1st row.
Next row: rib 3 (1;4), [inc in next st, rib 4 (5;5)] × 11, inc in next st, rib to end. 75 (81;87) sts.
Change to No 5 needles and cont in main rib patt as given for the sweater back and inc 1 st at each end of every 3rd row until there are 147 (157;165) sts. Cont in patt without shaping until work measures 17½(18;18½)in from beg. Bind off in patt.

SWEATER HOOD Using small backstitch, sew both shoulder seams.
Using No 5 circular needle, right side facing, beg at left shoulder seam, pick up 46 (49;55) sts along left side of front neck, patt across the 33 (35;37) sts on st holder for center front neck, pick up 46 (49;55) sts along right side of front neck to shoulder seam, patt across the 85 (89;93) sts of back neck. 210 (222;240) sts.
Work in rounds as follows:
Next round: p0 (2;3), k1 (3;3), *p3, k3, rep from * to last 5 (1;0) sts, p3 (1;0), k2 (0;0).
Rep this round until hood measures 18in from beg. Bind off purlwise.

TO FINISH Using small backstitch, sew sleeve tops into armholes, sew side and sleeve seams.

BELT Using No 3 needles and MC, cast on 11 sts and work in single rib as given for the sweater back until belt measures 70 (80;90)in. Bind off ribwise.

PURSE Using No 3 needles and MC, cast on 59 sts and work in single rib as given for the sweater back until work measures 5in from beg, ending with a 1st row. K1 row. Work a further 8in in single rib, beg with a 1st row. Bind off ribwise.
Using small backstitch, sew sides of purse together folding along the k row. Fold back of purse at top to form a 1in hem on the wrong side. Hem down. Then thread onto the belt.

All dimensions are in inches

THE COUNTRY GENTLEMAN

Man's dogtooth waistcoat and bow tie

GAUGE Using No 2 needles over st patt, 30 sts and 40 rows = 4in square.

BACK Using No 2 needles and MC, cast on 145 (153;161;169;177) sts.
1st row: k0 (2;0;2;0)MC, *k1A, k3MC, rep from * to last 1 (3;1;3;1) sts, k1A, k0 (2;0;2;0)MC.
2nd row: p1 (3;1;3;1)MC, *p1A, p3MC, rep from * to lst 0 (2;0;2;0) sts, p0 (1;0;1;0)A, p0 (1;0;1;0)MC.
3rd row: k2 (0;2;0;2)A, *k1MC, k3A, rep from * to last 3 (1;3;1;3) sts, k1MC, k2 (0;2;0;2)A.
4th row: p3 (1;3;1;3)A, *p1MC, p3A, rep from * to last 2 (0;2;0;2) sts, p1 (0;1;0;1)MC, p1 (0;1;0;1)A.
These 4 rows form the patt. Cont in patt until work measures 8¾(8¾;9¼;9¼;9½)in, ending with a wrong side row.

SHAPE ARMHOLES Bind off 6 sts at beg of next 2 rows. Bind off 4 sts at beg of foll 2 rows. Dec 1 st at each end of next 5 (5;6;6;7) rows. Dec 1 st at each end of foll 3 (4;4;5;5) alt rows. 109 (115;121;127;133) sts. Cont in patt without shaping until work measures 18¾(19¼;20;20½;21¼)in from beg, ending with a wrong side row.

SHAPE SHOULDERS Bind off 11 (11;12;13;13) sts at beg of next 2 rows. Bind off 10 (11;12;12;13) sts at beg of foll 2 rows. Bind off 10 (11;11;12;13) sts at beg of foll 2 rows. Bind off rem 47 (49;51;53;55) sts for back neck.

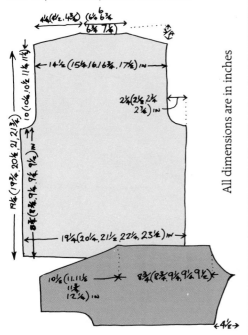

GRADE ★ ★					
Sizes to fit	36	38	40	42	44	in
Actual size	38	40	42	44	46	in
Back length	19½	19¾	20½	21	21¾	in
Materials	4	4	6	6	8	MC
	4	4	6	6	8	A
	2	2	2	2	2	B
			oz sports yarn			

1 pr No 2 needles ● 1 circular No 1 needle ● 3 buttons ● elastic
Suggested yarn: Phildar Luxe

Abbreviations alt – alternate ● beg – beginning ● cont – continue ● dec – decrease ● foll – following ● inc – increase ● k – knit ● p – purl ● patt – pattern ● rem – remaining ● rep – repeat ● st(s) – stitch(es) ● MC – main color ● A – 1st color ● B – 2nd color

LEFT FRONT Using No 2 needles and MC, make a loop. P2 into the loop. Commence foll the chart at the 3rd row until there are 78 (82;86;90;94) sts ending with a right side row. Work 3 rows in patt without shaping.
Next row: patt 71 (75;79;83;87) sts, bind off next 4 sts, patt 3 sts.
TO MAKE BUTTONHOLE Next row: patt 3 sts, cast on 4 sts, patt to end.
Cont in patt until work measures 4¼(4½;4¾;5;5¼)in along center front edge. Make a 2nd buttonhole in the same position as the 1st over the next 2 rows. Cont in patt until work measures 8½(8½;8¾;8¾;9¼)in along center front edge. Make a 3rd buttonhole in the same position as previous holes over the next 2 rows. Cont in patt to same patt row as back at armhole shaping.

SHAPE ARMHOLE & NECKLINE Bind off 6 sts at beg of next row. Bind off 4 sts at beg of foll alt row. Patt 1 row. Dec 1 st at armhole edge of next 5 (5;6;6;7) rows. Dec 1 st at armhole edge of foll 3 (4;4;5;5) alt rows. At the same time,

SHAPE NECKLINE Dec 1 st at neck edge of 1st and every foll 3rd row until 31 (33;35;37;39) sts remain. Cont in patt without shaping until work measures 18½(19;19½;20;20½)in from the end of the front point shaping ending at armhole edge.

SHAPE SHOULDER Bind off 11 (11;12;13;13) sts at beg of next row. Bind off 10 (11;12;12;13) sts at beg of foll alt row. Bind off 10 (11;11;12;13) sts at beg of foll alt row.

RIGHT FRONT Work to match left front reversing shapings and omitting buttonholes. The 4th row should be worked as follows:
1st, 2nd, 4th & 5th sizes only:
Inc in 1st st, p2A, p1MC in 4th row of st patt.
3rd size only:
Inc in 1st st, p1A, p2MC in 2nd row of st patt.

TO FINISH Using small backstitch, sew both shoulder seams. Using No 1 circular needle and B with right side facing, pick up 169 (175;181;187;193) sts evenly around armhole. Turn and bind off knitwise. Work other armhole to match.
Using small backstitch, sew side seams. Using No 1 circular needle and B with right side facing, beg at tip of right front point, pick up 36 (36;38;40;40) sts to bottom of center front edge, pick up 70 (70;73;73;76) sts to beg of neckline shaping, pick up 86 (89;92;95;98) sts to right shoulder, pick up 45 (47;49;51;53) sts across back neck, pick up same sts down left side as for right. 429 (437;455;467;481) sts. Turn and bind off knitwise.
Using No 1 circular needle and B with right side facing, beg at tip of left front point, pick up 50 (52;54;56;58) sts to left side seam, pick up 133 (141;149;157;165) sts across back, pick up 50 (52;54;56;58) sts to tip of right front point. Turn and bind off knitwise. Join end of edges and sew on buttons.

BOW TIE Using No 2 needles and B, cast on 13 sts.
1st row: *k1, p1, rep from * to last st, k1.
Rep this row until work measures 19¼in. Bind off.
Using No 2 needles and B, cast on 9 sts.
Rep patt as for main strip until work measures 2½in. Bind off.

TO FINISH Mark center of main strip, fold strip 2¼in either side of this mark back to center, fold both ends out again and stitch down along center. Wrap short strip around center of bow and stitch ends together on the wrong side. Join ends of the elastic to each end of the tie to fit neatly around neck.

All dimensions are in inches

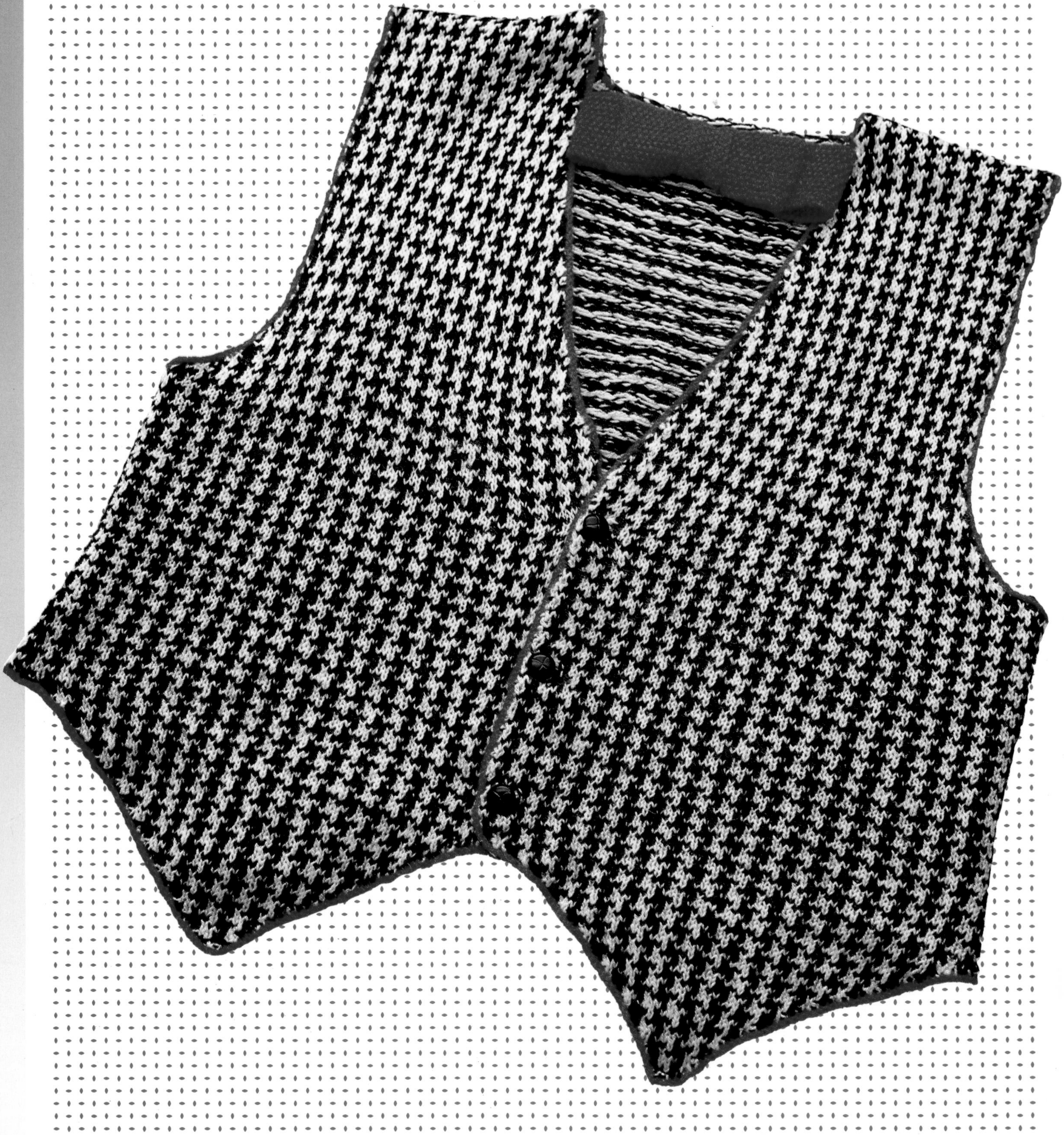

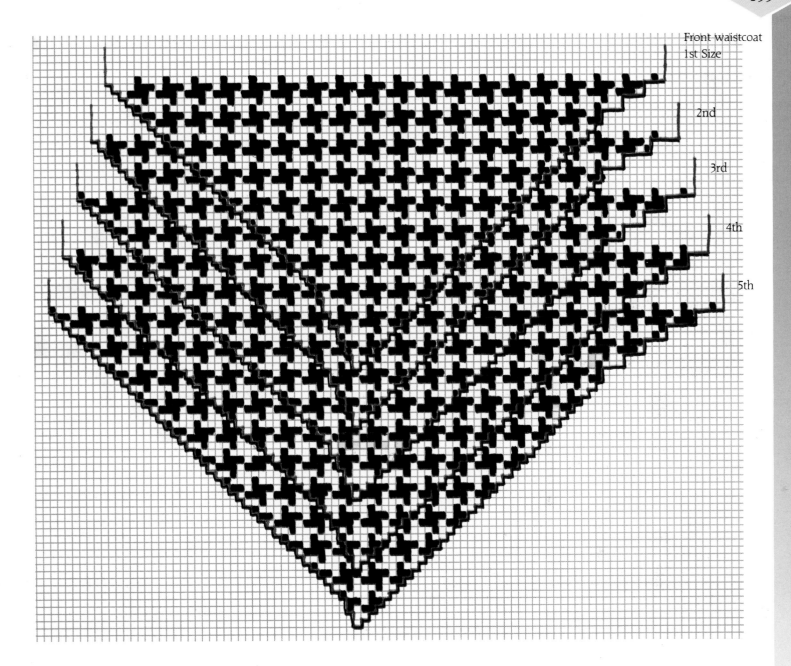

Above: Use this chart to keep the dogtooth
pattern correct on the front of the waistcoat for
your chosen size.

Front waistcoat
1st Size

2nd

3rd

4th

5th

GUIDE TO SUPPLIERS

Most of the mail order companies listed below have catalogs or sample cards that can be obtained for a small fee.

Art/Needlecraft
P.O. Box 394, Uxbridge, MA 01569

B & M Yarn Company
151 Essex, New York, New York 10002

Black Sheep Weaving and Craft Supply
530 SW Fourth Street, Corvallis, OR 97333

Broadway Yarns—Cascade Fiber Company
P.O. Box 1350, Sanford, NC 27330

Brunswick
P.O. Box 276, Pickens, SC 29671

J.H. Clasgens
Plant # 1, 2383 State Route 132, New Richmond, OH 45151

Colonial Woolen Mills
5611 Hough Avenue, Cleveland, OH 44103

Contessa Yarns
Box 37, Lebanon, CT 06249

Coulter Studios
118 East 59th Street, New York, New York 10022

Davidson's Old Mill Yarns
109 East Elizabeth Street, Box 8, Eaton Rapids, MI 48827

Eager Weaver's Stitchery Studio
182 Jefferson Road, Rochester, NY 14623

Earth Guilde, Inc.
1 Tingle Alley, Asheville, NC 28801

The Fiber Studio
Foster Hill Road, Henniker, NH 03242

Greenmont Yarns and Looms
RR 1, Box 2312, Bennington, VT 05201

The Handweaver
1643 San Pablo Avenue, Berkeley, CA 94702

Henry's Attic
5 Mercury Avenue, Monroe, NY 10950

Intertwine
130 East 900 South, Salt Lake City, UT 84111

New York Yarn Center
61 West 37th Street, New York, New York 10018

Sax Arts and Crafts
Box 2002, Milwaukee, WI 53201

School Products, Inc.
1201 Broadway, New York, New York 10001

Straw Into Gold
3006 San Pablo Avenue, Berkeley, CA 94702

West Side Yarn Company
2350 Broadway, New York, New York 10024

Wonoco Yarn Company
35 Clay Street, Brooklyn, NY 11222

ABBREVIATIONS

alt – alternate
col – color
dec – decrease
g st – garter stitch (every row knit)
in – inch
inc – increase
k – knit
klb – knit into st on row below
(dropping loop on needle)
LB – left needle
m1 – make 1 st. by lifting running
thread between sts, then k or p
into it tbl
no – number
p – purl
pr – pair
psso – pass sl st over
rem – remaining
rep – repeat
RN – right needle
sl – slip 1 st, always inserting
needle purlwise (from right to
left) through st. Leave yarn where
it is unless otherwise stated.
sl 1 yf – slip 1 with yarn forward
st(s) – stitch(es)
st st – stockinette stitch (1 row knit,
1 row purl)
tog – together
tbl – through back of loop
yb – yarn back

yf – yarn forward
yo – yarn over needle to make 1 st

CABLE ABBREVIATIONS
CN – cable needle
C1B (also C2B, C3B etc) – sl next 1
(or more) sts onto CN and hold
at back
C1F (also C2F, C3F etc) – sl next 1
(or more) sts onto CN and hold
at front
C4 (C6-C8 etc) – cable 4 (or more)
sts in the manner shown in the
instructions
K1CN (also K2CN, K3CN etc) – k1
(or more) sts from CN
LTK – left twist knitwise; knit into
front of 2nd st on LN, from
behind the 1st st, do not
remove from LN, knit into front
of 1st st, and remove both sts
from LN tog
MB – make bobble in the manner
shown in the instructions
P1CN (also P2CN, P3CN etc) - p1
(or more) sts from CN
RTK – right twist knitwise; k2 tog,
do not remove from LN. Knit
into the 1st of the 2 sts, then
remove both from LN tog

COLOR ABBREVIATIONS
MC – main color
A – 1st color
B – 2nd color
C – 3rd color, etc

	2 ply	3 ply	4 ply	Worsted weight	Aran
APPROXIMATE GAUGE OF YARNS WHEN THEY ARE KNITTED TOGETHER					
2 ply	Gauge over st st, 4 sts and 9 rows to 1in on No 3 needles				
3 ply	Gauge over st st, 6 sts and 8 rows to 1in on No 4 needles	Gauge over st st, 6 sts and 7½ rows to 1in on No 5 needles			
4 ply	Gauge over st st, 5½ sts and 7½ rows to 1in on No 5 needles	Gauge over st st, 5 sts and 7 rows to 1in on No 6 needles	Gauge over st st, 4½ sts and 5½ rows to 1in on No 7 needles		
Worsted weight	Gauge over st st, 5 sts and 6½ rows to 1in on No 6 needles	Gauge over st st, 4½ sts and 6 rows to 1in on No 7 needles	Gauge over st st, 4 sts and 5 rows to 1in on No 8 needles	Gauge over st st, 4 sts and 5 rows to 1in on No 9 needles	
Aran	Gauge over st st, 4 sts and 5½ rows to 1in on No 7 needles	Gauge over st st, 4 sts and 5 rows to 1in on No 8 needles	Gauge over st st, 4 sts and 5 rows to 1in on No 9 needles	Gauge over st st, 3½ sts and 4½ rows to 1in on No 10 needles	Gauge over st st, 3 sts and 4 rows to 1in on No 10½ needles

INDEX

ACKNOWLEDGEMENTS

So many people have helped me write this book that it would be impossible to mention them all. However, I would like to thank all my knitters for their patient and painstaking work, in particular Jean Trehane and Doris Carl, and also Coral Stewart for writing many of the patterns. Thanks are also due to the press officers of the various yarn spinners with whom I have dealt, as they have all been most helpful. Finally, I would like to thank my friends, who encouraged me with cups of tea and were still there when I eventually emerged from the office. *Ruth Maria Swepson*

The publishers wish to thank *Creativity Yarns* for supplying wool, yarns and knitting equipment, for photography.